Happy Dancing

2008

Love,
Bobbie, Dick

My Appalachia

My Appalachia

A Memoir

Sidney Saylor Farr

THE UNIVERSITY PRESS OF KENTUCKY

Publication of this volume was made possible in part by a grant from the
National Endowment for the Humanities.

Editorial and Sales Offices: The University Press of Kentucky
663 South Limestone Street, Lexington, Kentucky 40508-4008
www.kentuckypress.com

11 10 09 08 07   5 4 3 2 1

Library of Congress Cataloging-in-Publication Data

Farr, Sidney Saylor, 1932–
    My Appalachia : a memoir / Sidney Saylor Farr.
        p.   cm.
    ISBN 978-0-8131-2450-6 (hardcover : alk. paper)
    1. Farr, Sidney Saylor, 1932– 2. Farr, Sidney Saylor, 1932– Childhood and
youth. 3. Farr, Sidney Saylor, 1932– Family. 4. Farr, Sidney Saylor, 1932–
Philosophy. 5. Appalachian Region, Southern—Social life and customs.
6. Mountain life—Appalachian Region, Southern. 7. Stoney Fork (Ky.)—Social
life and customs. 8. Stoney Fork (Ky.)—Biography. 9. Librarians—Kentucky—
Berea—Biography. 10. Women authors, American—Biography. I. Title.
    F217.A65F37 2007
    976.9'53—dc22
    [B]   2007013815

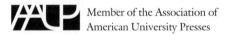

To my brother and sisters still living:
Della, Clara, Lee Roy, Minnie, Lola, *and* Sharon Rose—

and to those gone on before us:
Hazel, James, and Fred

Contents

Acknowledgments

For every book written there are people who help in so many different ways.

I want to acknowledge first those but for whom there would have been no book. Susan Kaney spent countless hours transcribing cassette tapes and sending the documents to my computer. Bruce Lawson edited the whole manuscript at least three times and certain chapters several times. Grant Farr read and offered valuable suggestions and corrections. Tom Sawyer advised on the whole concept of this book, and approved chapter 22. Special thanks to Trish Ayers, who gave advice and edited the final manuscript.

Others I wish to thank are my sisters, Della Whitehead, Minnie Brown, and Sharon Rose Clark; and Sally Thompson, a family friend. Dr. Gerald F. Roberts, mentor and friend, urged me to write this book. Thanks to all of you for your love and faith in me.

I

Beginning

*There is no place in the world where I would
rather spend a year than in the mountains of
southeast Kentucky.*

I believe that each of us is a link between the past and the future, and that it is our duty to pass along family history; otherwise, legends, stories, songs, and traditions will be lost. I want my story to reveal past events that affected the lives of my people and me.

By the time my father was a young man most of the cleared fields on Stoney Fork, Kentucky, where he and his family lived, were worn out, and new ground constantly had to be cleared for corn. Dad courted and married Mama in 1930. She was from Laurel Fork in Leslie County, Kentucky. He built a log cabin on Coon Branch at the head of Stoney Fork, just over the hill from Grandpa. Two years later, on October 30, 1932, I was born in that cabin.

I have since learned that 1930 was known as the year of the drought. People were starving because of the scarcity of crops and wild game. The first charity my family ever took was when the Red Cross came in with food to help during the drought. Wild game—groundhog, possum, and coon—was very scarce, but Dad loved to hunt and managed to keep meat on the table. Mama baked possum when there was no other fresh meat, though I never learned to like it.

The men of Stoney Fork loved to go hunting in the autumn—especially for coon. Right about the time the leaves started falling the men hit the hills after dark with a pack of dogs two or three nights a week on school days and stay out till maybe 11:00 P.M. On Friday and Saturday nights they might not get home before daybreak. They scoured the hills for good places to hunt. They went out in small groups of four or five hunters at most and usually came home with just an unlucky opossum or two.

They carried carbide lights to light their way through the woods. But they also had at least one serious flashlight, which never got turned on unless they needed to see if a coon was up the tree. That flashlight, with two batteries, would usually last all season. On the rare occasions when they did take a coon, the owner of the treeing dog got to keep the hide. He would display it on the side of a smokehouse or anyplace else it could be seen, much the way you see deer heads mounted in sporting goods stores.

The man whose dog treed a coon would be locally famous for a while, and he would be offered a higher price for his coon dog. A raccoon tasted better than no meat at all, but it was stringy and tough. Coons were so scarce that eating one was a novelty.

A lean groundhog, on the other hand, taken early in spring, before it started fattening up on weeds and tasting like whatever it was eating, could weigh up to twenty or twenty-five pounds and cooked up sweet and tender. I loved groundhog the way my mother fixed it. She first parboiled the pieces of meat with the broken limbs of a spice bush, then placed the meat in a baking pan. Around the meat she wedged quartered sweet potatoes, then spooned bacon fat over the meat and potatoes, poured in a cup of water, and baked it in the oven. Served with cornbread, it made a delicious meal.

Groundhogs were good for more than just their meat. If you scraped and tanned the hide properly, you could sell it to be used as a resonator head for a five-string banjo. It would stretch tighter than anything made of synthetic material.

My family lived as far back in the "hollers" as it was possible to go in Bell County, Kentucky. Dad worked in the timber woods and at a sawmill when there was employment to be found. We ate what we grew on our land or could glean from the hillsides. Just about everything was made by hand. We had little contact with people outside our region; there were no newspapers and no radio in our house.

Every two years a new baby was born in our family. I helped with the cooking, washing, cleaning, and milking, and I took care of the younger children when Mama went to dig roots in the hills or hoe corn in the fields with Dad. I remember a time when I was three years old and Mama went to the field to help Dad hoe corn. She spread a quilt in a shady place and left me to care for Della, who was not yet a year old. My little sister was crawling by this time, and I had a hard time keeping her on the quilt.

By the time Della, Hazel, and Clara had followed me, Dad had just about given up hope that he would ever have a son, but then three boys came along, one every two years. The firstborn became Dad's pride and joy. Mama wanted to name him after her only living brother, Dewey. Dad wanted to name this first son for his favorite uncle, James. I never understood why they didn't compromise by giving him both names. However, the birth certificate recorded his legal name as Dewey Saylor. But from day one, Dad called him Jeems, and soon the rest of us, except Mama, took up the name. For mountain people, who softened their words, "James" was pronounced "Jeems," and "Clara" became "Clary"—it was easier to say "Clary" than it was to say "Clara" and "Jeems" than "James."

Dad took Jeems with him everywhere he went—even to his moonshine still. This worried Mama, but she didn't try to stop him. Two years after Jeems was born another boy came along; he was named Fred. Two years after that the third and last son, Lee Roy, was born.

Then Mama gave birth to three other girls, Minnie, Lola, and Sharon Rose.

The day brother Fred was born, Dad took the midwife, whom we called Aunt Mary, home just after dinner. He was not back by suppertime, and Mama began to worry. "Surely to goodness he won't get drunk today," she said. "Surely to goodness he won't stop at Kale Brock's store and start drinking."

I washed the supper dishes, milked the cow, and fed the chickens and hogs before dark. I put the children to bed in the next room and then lay down on a pallet near Mama's bed. Sometime in the night she called me. "I hear your dad, Sidney. It sounds like he's down near the barn. You'll have to take a lantern and go get him."

"I don't want to go down that road by myself, Mama."

"If you don't go than I'll have to get up from this bed and go myself," she said. "We can't leave him down there all night."

I got up, fixed the lantern, and went down the road. Dad had fallen off his horse, which was standing patiently by. I looped the reins over the horse's head, slapped his rump, and told him to go home.

"Dad, let me help you up," I said. He staggered up and walked a few feet, then stopped. "Why did you let her go away?" he demanded. "I'll never see her again. And she had the prettiest yellow hair." He began to cry. Eventually, with Dad staggering, falling, and crying, we got to the front porch, where he puked, splattering his shoes. Then he fell down and passed out. I brought out a quilt to spread over him, then went to unsaddle and feed the horse. Early the next morning Dad awoke and went to bed. I scrubbed the porch before the children got up.

EVERYONE IN OUR COMMUNITY was poor. If it had not been for the small farms and gardens, domestic animals, and wild game brought in from the hills, our people would have starved. But they planted corn and raised gardens, chicken, and livestock. They picked fruit and berries, canned and preserved as much food as they could for winter, and made do with what they had.

Dad and Mama dug ginseng and other roots, which they dried and sold by the pound in the late fall. For a number of years Dad made and sold moonshine whiskey. He was skilled at castrating domestic animals, and the neighbors hired him to perform this service for their hogs, horses, bull calves, and so forth. With money coming in small payments for the castrations, the roots and herbs, the dozen or so eggs sold each week, the occasional gallon of milk or blackberries sold or exchanged for groceries, we managed.

I often think of how close we lived to pioneer days in the 1940s and 1950s. We lagged behind the times in southern Appalachia, at least fifty to seventy-five years in some regions and a hundred years in others. Still, despite my growing up in the mountains of southeastern Kentucky, I had several role models, some in my extended family, others among my neighbors. No one ever told us we were Appalachians, a poor, benighted people, so we did not have that in our consciousness.

We shared with our neighbors and kin. When Dad planned to butcher a hog, he would send word to neighbors up and down the creek that they should come by the next day for a mess of meat. They did come, and Dad would take meat to the older people, and there would be feasting everywhere as families cooked the fresh pork. When our neighbors butchered, they did the same. Mountain people shared everything. They were my teachers, especially the women. I didn't know it at the time, but what they gave me was exactly what I would need one day to write.

Some were storytellers. We lived near Granny Brock, my dad's grandmother, from the time I was five until I was twelve years old. It was said in the family that Granny Brock had seven husbands, some still living, others long gone. But no one knew any personal information about any of them. Her last husband, Andrew Brock, was the only one we knew. Her first child was Dad's mother. It was said of both Granny Brock and Grandma Saylor (my paternal grandmother) that they were two of the most beautiful women in Bell County. I remember Grandma's black hair and her classic cheekbones and sculptured face. Granny Brock was tiny, less than five feet tall, and her beauty was a dark radiance of hair and eyes.

Granny Brock was an independent woman who knew her own mind. She didn't seem to care what other people thought of her; she just did what had to be done to survive. Something about her influenced my love for words. Her language was descriptive, with vivid words and symbols. All of my people talked that way. I always thought it came from our Scots-Irish ancestry.

Granny had weathered incredible storms during her lifetime, but she laughed a lot. She told me stories of pioneer days, how, when she was young, a bad blizzard hit. Another time, a bear tried to get into their log house. It circled the house again and again, snuffling and growling, trying to get in. She told how her mother sat up all night to protect the children.

She spoke of husbands who came and went, and about her children, who stayed and had to be fed—"especially Little Mike," she said. "I did the best that I could for all of them."

"Mike was my little crippled boy," Granny said. She spoke of the night he was born, a night when it snowed so long and hard that even the fence posts were buried in the snow. The midwife had a hard time getting to her, and Mike had a hard time getting born. When he did come, his little feet and legs were all twisted. Granny Brock said she cried that whole night through, and many other times, too.

Since Mike couldn't run and play, he invented games and made up little songs to amuse himself. One that Granny shared with me was about planting corn in the springtime. "When the whip-poor-wills call, it's corn planting time; when the whip-poor-wills call, it's corn planting time." I asked Granny many times to talk about Little Mike and other things in her life, as I sat next to her, loving the story and loving her.

"Little Mike lived to be eight year old, then the Good Lord just took him home. It was a night almost as bad as the night he was born. It snowed and the wind kept blowing and the cold creeped in. I tried to keep him warm as I could. But I reckon an angel came down on that snowfall and carried him away."

When Granny would tell me sad stories like this, we would sit and not say another word for a long time. Then she would brighten up and tell me something funny or risqué, stories about some of the older folks who lived up and down the creeks, stories that horrified my mother and taught me to hold my tongue.

Some of my happiest memories are when Dad and Granny Brock went fishing in the evenings and Mama allowed me to go with them. I loved to listen to the stories they told. Granny did most of the talking.

"Now, Wilburn," she would say to my father, "do you remember Old Willie Simpson? Now there was a slick, sharp man. They weren't nothing he wouldn't connive at doing."

"Yeah," Dad would agree. "Remember the time he stole corn from Old Man Asher's corncrib?"

"Willie Simpson spotted Old Man Asher stealing corn from a corncrib down the creek," Granny said. "Willie followed the man back to his corncrib and watched him dump in the corn. Willie waited until Asher went back for a second load, then filled his own sack and took the corn home. I reckon Old Man Asher carried stolen corn and dumped it into his own corncrib all night long."

"But come daylight and he couldn't see any of it in his crib!" Dad laughed.

"No," Granny joined his laughter, "because it was all in Willie Simpson's corncrib."

Then Dad and Granny would fish awhile in silence until one of them remembered another story. I'd sit and listen to them until the moon was high in the sky.

I had the good fortune to spend hours with Granny Brock, especially nights and weekends. Her house was on my way home from the one-room school I attended, and I usually stopped for a visit. Often she would tell me to look in the warming closet of her wood-burning stove and I would find something to eat. Usually it was baked sweet potatoes.

How I wish I could have tape-recorded Granny's stories. Here are some snippets, as close to being in her own words as I can remember.

"BEFORE I WAS EVER MARRIED, I fell in love with an Asher man. He promised to marry me, but then took up with another girl and married her. I was pregnant by that time, but I did not tell him. I had a girl child, named her Susie—she's your grandma."

"They's a place called Dark Holler. Who can say why it's called that? I reckon they was dark deeds done there in days gone by. But that's where they buried my Joe and Little Mike."

"My first husband died young. He got lung fever and seemed like no time a-tall then Joe was gone. That left me with no one to help me. My kinfolk had all died out—not meaning, of course, them in the old country."

"Some folks said what I done was wrong, and maybe it was. But I reckon the Good Lord will take everything and add it up and judge me a fair judgment. I'm a-counting on that."

"I never slept with a neighbor woman's husband. It was mostly traveling men passing through Cumberland Gap. And them in the community with no women of their own. They give me food and clothes for Little Mike and me."

"Little Mike. Lordy, he had the prettiest yellow hair and sky blue eyes. I can see him plain as day sometimes, though it's been sixty years now since he died."

"Sometime after that—I don't know how long it was, but I recall the cornstalks were goldy-colored—I married Jake Howard and we moved to

Renfro Valley. But we'd just got settled when a train killed Jake and I had to come back home."

"I don't deny a thing I've done. I never was one to prettify up a picture to make out I was better than I am. It was lonesome, and Susie and I still had to eat."

"The next man I married was Jim Farmer. Jim was plumb foolish about Susie. But she was a wild one, I'm here to tell you. Guess she took after her mother. But I didn't worry about her too much. I always say, give a wild girl a good man—why, it's like honeybees. Take wild bees out of a bee tree and put 'em in a good hive and they'll tame down right quick."

"Susie married Sol Saylor when she's just fifteen. He built her a house up on Peach Orchard. He squared the logs and rived the boards himself. He was a good man, and Susie tamed down quick. They had a passel of boys—Wilburn [my father], Squire, Otis, Andrew, Willie B—and two girls, Betty and Laura. And Susie was still the prettiest woman in all of Bell County. Why, people from near and far, strangers passing through Cumberland Gap, talked about how beautiful she was. I am proud to say your grandma was a virgin when she married Solomon Saylor."

"Jim said he'd druther Sol would build his house near us. I told him life's not druthers. . . . If'n you get to thinking it is, I told him, just you study the acorns under that oak tree out there, all raring to be giant oak trees. See how many do, I told him."

"If'n I could've had my druthers! If'n I had, my Joe'd sleep beside me ever night. Little Mike'd have grandchildren now. If'n life was all druthers there'd be no graves up in Dark Holler. Dark Holler—I don't rightly know how it got its name. But come every spring and the wild honeysuckle lights up the place real pretty."

I STARTED WRITING STORIES AND POEMS a decade later, and it seemed only natural when Granny's voice appeared in my poems.

Aunt Dellie, who was married to Dad's brother Otis, was a reader, and she introduced me to stories in books. A young woman with black hair, brown eyes, and the whitest teeth I ever saw, Aunt Dellie was probably part Cherokee, as were many of the folks around our part of the land. Her adopted father and mother lived near Pineville, and sometimes they got discarded books from the town library for Aunt Dellie. She read every one of them and then gave each book to me. One book I will never forget was the Book of Mormon. It confused and frightened me. When I asked Aunt Dellie what it meant, she confessed that she did not understand it either. It did not seem a bit odd to either of us that we had read every word of that book in spite of our confusion, for we both loved the printed word. It was through Aunt Dellie that I got to read *Little Women, Heidi, Pilgrim's Progress, Lorna Doone, Gone with the Wind,* and other classics.

Aunt Betty and Aunt Laura, my dad's sisters, taught me about nature and the imagination, two lessons that I'm not sure you can ever really learn inside the walls of a classroom. Aunt Betty was thirteen years older than I, but we were friends. She was a big, strong woman who cut down trees and sawed them into logs for firewood, repaired fences and roofs, and performed other kinds of outdoor work.

Aunt Betty was a loner; she never much wanted to go out where there were crowds of people. She taught me to recognize varieties of trees and what kind of mast they produced. She taught me to know ginseng. Together, we dug roots and gathered wild herbs, which she dried to sell in late autumn for cash. We gathered wild greens in early spring, bringing home tiny spears of poke. Whenever Aunt Betty talked about something, she always related it to nature. She would say, "That was when a fire burned on Black Mountain," or, "That was just after the corn was laid by last summer . . ." In a way, Aunt Betty taught me about metaphors.

Aunt Laura, Dad's youngest sister, was reckless and wildly imaginative. I remember when I was four and she was just eight years old. One weekend we were in Grandpa's barn playing in the hay. She rolled down the side of a pile of hay and fell through an open place in the floor. I started to cry for fear she was killed. The lower part of the barn was open on either end, and one of Grandpa's big hogs had wandered in to sleep in the shade. Aunt Laura landed on the pig's back. "Well, shoot pig," she said, "I have done killed you!" I laughed so hard I nearly fell after her.

Aunt Laura's imagination was as wild as her physical recklessness. We romped in the woods and would go to Gum Spring around the hillside, where we got our drinking water. Gum Spring was made into a hospital in our imagination. Two tall trees grew near the spring; these were the doctor and the nurse in our fantasy. The smaller bushes were patients. Aunt Laura was the voice for all. As the doctor, she diagnosed dreadful diseases for all of us. For me, the doctor prescribed a gallon a day of Grandma Saylor's bitters (which Grandma brewed every winter and insisted that we all drink every time we got near her kitchen). I cried when I had to drink the bitter brew.

From Aunt Laura I learned to be adventurous and reckless about my physical safety, climbing trees, rooftops, and high rocks. I learned to be creative by listening to the imaginary people and situations she introduced to me in the woods and in playhouses.

My mother was another creative force in my life, but her brand of creativity was somehow a little different than Aunt Laura's. I always saw it coupled with frugality and hard work, and I came to understand that imagination lived side by side with both these things.

My mother had a big family to care for and no time or energy to create pretty and frivolous things. But she found a way to satisfy her creative yearnings by the patterns she chose to use, the colors of her materials, and the tiny stitches in her quilting. She planted flowers in cans and boxes and filled our yard and front porch with colorful blooms. Certainly my mother had a green thumb. She could make anything flourish and grow. After I married and left home, many times she would visit, taking home with her slips and cuttings of my plants. Months or years later I would go to her house to get new cuttings and start over while hers seemed to live on and on. Nothing ever died under her care.

I don't remember my mother ever having idle time. Besides keeping the house and children as clean as possible she worked in the garden and picked berries from the hillsides during the summer; in winter, when the weather was right, she made hominy and lye soap. I hated soap-making. I especially hated the smell of the cakes of lye soap. I used to dream of having a whole washtubful of pretty, nice-smelling soap.

"When I grow up and have my own home, I will never make lye soap," I declared. "I will buy pretty soap that smells good."

My mother smiled and with a twinkle in her eye said, "If you have enough money to buy things like that, why then I reckon you won't ever have to make your own soap." But Mama always knew more than she ever said. I would make poems instead of soap much of my adult life, but the lessons of my mother I took with me.

2

A Way of Life

Early in my life while still only feeling,
before thinking, before writing, I heard the
mountains' call.

The earliest memory I have is the day I turned three years old. Mama was holding my hand as we came through the gate and climbed the steps to the front porch of Grandpa's house. "Today's your birthday," she said. "You are three years old and a big girl now." I felt proud to be three, but it was cold and wet and I was tired and hungry. The door opened and we were in the kitchen where Grandma was cooking supper. I don't remember anything else about being there—just that brief experience of being wet and cold, knowing I was three years old, and Grandma's warm kitchen with the smell of food being cooked. And Grandma's words: "Come in, chil'ren, come in here and eat some supper!"

Time passed. It was my fifth birthday. I remember it was a brisk fall day, and I came out of the house to watch Mama sweep the front porch. She asked if I felt like a big girl now that I was five years old. Piled against the porch wall were several orange pumpkins and two or three green-striped cushaws. Looking at them made me feel happy.

Sometime after my fifth birthday, Dad bought a boundary of land down on Straight Creek at the foot of Pine Mountain. (A "boundary" was a piece of land owned by one person; it could be as small as a single acre or as large as several hundred.) He built a log house and moved us there from Coon Branch so I could be near a school. Our new land had been the site of a home in earlier times, perhaps dating back to the pioneer days. The house and outbuildings were long gone, but apple trees, pussy willows, flowering quince, and a tall pear tree still grew there.

Most of the apple trees were very old and sinewy from neglect. They were all around us, edging the yard, down by the sulfur spring where we got our drinking water, near the barn, and over in a narrow strip of meadow. The pear tree grew beside a big rock with a hollow depression in the top. People said the Indians had used that rock to pound their corn into meal. It was an ideal place for little girls to play. My sisters and I spent many hours on and around that rock, which was located in front of the smokehouse.

The sulfur spring had lovely red mud, perfect for mud pies. Mama constantly complained about how the mud stained everything it touched. Two big pussy willows grew at the front gate near the spring. Mama loved them, but Dad threatened to cut them down. His bees made honey from the blossoms of the pussy willows that was thick and mealy-tasting, not good like that made from clover and other flowering plants. As we grew up our seasons were filled with fruit-tree blossoms in the spring and fruit in the summer and fall.

Sulfured Apples and Northern Lights

Mama canned and dried the apples from our trees, and Dad used them to make sulfured apples. I shall always remember the first year he made them. It began with a hot, sticky day in August. The clouds looked like half-melted marshmallows. Dad brought in barrels for the apples and boxes of sulfur from the store. Mama, Della, and I peeled and cut the apples. Dad put the barrels in the smokehouse, which was empty at that time of year. First he put a flat rock in the bottom of the barrel; then he placed a pie pan on top of the rock. He did this so the heat would not catch the bottom of the barrel on fire. He put two tablespoons of sulfur in the pie plate and set it on fire. It smoked for hours.

Next, he placed a stout stick across the top of the barrel. Mama brought him one of her big willow baskets that had a handle. They filled it with cut apples and hung it on the stick across the center of the barrel. Mama brought out an old quilt and helped arrange it over top of the barrel to keep the fumes and smoke from escaping. The fruit shrank to a third of its size. Later, Dad would store the apples in another barrel. Then, during the winter, when Mama wanted to make fried apple pies or just a baked pie, she would pull out handfuls of the apples. They would be as pretty and white as ever. But she would have to wash the sulfur off before we could eat them. The fumes from the sulfuring process (sulfur dioxide) killed the bacteria and kept the apples from spoiling.

Along about dusky dark the evening Mama and Dad sulfured the apples, a bad storm came up, with lightning and rolling thunder bouncing from the mountaintops. Some of our apple trees were uprooted, others had limbs torn off, and green apples covered the ground under the remaining trees. We went to bed that night with the smell of the rain-wet earth and the sulfur still around us.

Sometime during the night Dad awoke us, saying, "Hurry! Come out on the porch." We tumbled out onto the front porch. I thought that daylight had come until I saw how strange it looked outside. Lights—first yellow, then blue and red—were moving over the hills. Dad said it might be the end of the world, and Mama leaned against the porch railing, praying out loud. We lined up along the railing and stared at the spectacular lights. After a while the lights died down and it was dark again.

I later learned that the strange phenomenon was called the aurora borealis. That was the only time I ever saw them in our part of the country. People on Stoney Fork spoke of the "Northern Lights" for years afterward. I shall never forget the thunder and lightning, the smell of the sulfured apples, and the astounding colored lights. The next morning we had the sad work of picking up and disposing of all the green apples. Mama saved those that she could by canning them.

Superstitions

As I was growing up in the 1940s, my life and the lives of my family and neighbors were hemmed in by all kinds of superstitions. There was a "saying" for almost anything that happened in the natural world. If a blossom bloomed out of season, it was said there would be a death in the family. When tree leaves turned underside over it would soon rain. Never have a tooth pulled if the signs of the zodiac are in the head, but if you plan to castrate an animal, you want the signs to be in the head or upper part of the body. There are preferred times to plant root crops, and different times for crops that will mature above ground. We lived by the *Farmer's Almanac.*

"The first three days in May are flower days," Mama would say. "If you plant anything like cucumbers and squash during flower days, you will get thousands of blossoms but no cucumber or squash will set."

By the time I was a young woman I did not believe in superstitions; I deliberately planted cucumber seeds in my garden during flower days. Sure enough, thousands of blossoms came, but when the cucumbers started to emerge they rotted and fell off before they were half an inch long. When Mama saw my garden her only comment was "I've always heard it's best not to plant cucumbers during the first three days in May."

One superstition told how you could discover the name of the man you would marry. On the first day of May, get up early in the morning, just at the edge of daylight. Take a plate of cornmeal and go out into the garden or field. Find a snail, put it in the meal, and wait. As the snail crawls around, it will write the name of the man you will marry someday. For this to work, however, you must keep it a secret. Tell no one, and speak to no one while the snail is at work. If you speak a word the spell will be broken.

Mama got up at five o'clock every morning to start breakfast. She always spotted me whenever I was in the yard and demanded to know what I was doing out there. "Whatever it is, leave it and come help with breakfast," she demanded. The spell was always broken, and I did not learn the name of the man I would marry until years later.

I learned other things, too. Some people in the mountains had the power to draw fire out of a burn on the body. If the seventh son of a seventh son blew his breath into the mouth of a baby suffering from thrush, it would be cured. I never witnessed any of these events, but my parents firmly believed in them.

Grandma believed that she could stop anyone's bleeding. When someone had an accident and was bleeding pretty badly, she would stand behind the victim and say a Bible verse to herself. People said that once she had done this you could often see the flowing blood slow down to a drop. "She would not tell me what she said for a long time," Uncle Andrew said of my grandmother. Eventually, though, she did tell him, and he told me. It was a verse from Ezekiel 16:6: "When I passed by thee, and saw thee polluted in thine own blood, I said unto thee . . . Live."

Dad believed in witches and the magic they perpetrated. Aunt Ollie, an old woman who lived on Ben's Branch, was said to be a witch. She asked Dad to sell her our cow. Dad refused, and in a short time Daisy started drying up, even though she had had a new calf a couple of months before. Her milk yield became less every day.

"Rachel, something has to be done," Dad said to Mama. "I will try to break the spell." He poured milk in a pan and heated one of his plow points, and then, carrying the red-hot metal with a pair of big pliers, he plunged it into the pan of milk.

The hiss and splutter made me feel sick. I "saw" flames leaping up around the legs of Aunt Ollie and heard her screaming. "Daddy, you're burning Aunt Ollie!" I cried. Mama led me from the room, saying, "You read too many of Aunt Dellie's old books, Sidney. Now you hush up." Two or three days later Daisy started giving more milk, and in a week she was back to her regular yield.

Other superstitions governed our lives. For instance, Mama would never let any of her children look in a mirror before they were a year old. She believed that if a baby saw itself, it would die. She also believed that if we told our bad dreams before breakfast they would come true.

Dad was always careful when clearing new ground, tilling the garden or field, or doing general work outdoors. He did not want to accidentally kill a toad frog. He said if you killed a toad, your cow would give bloody milk.

We trusted in the right phase of the moon for planting potatoes.

Dad and Mama warned us to be especially careful during the dog days of August because at that time dogs were likely to have fits and go mad. In addition, snakes went blind during dog days and would strike out wildly at anything that moved.

In addition to these superstitions, my family practiced all kinds of folk remedies. We lived far away from any medical facilities and had no money for doctors to cure minor ailments. My people did as they had done down through generations, which was to make do with what they had. They used roots, herbs, bark, and leaves from trees to treat a variety of ailments; and they followed hundreds of superstitions to avoid such ailments. For example:

To cure the shingles, cut off the head of a black hen and let the blood drip on the affected part. Grandma and Mama would talk about this anytime shingles were mentioned.

To prevent whooping cough, hang an adder stone—a precious stone that was reputed to draw out poison—around your neck.

To cure a child of whooping cough, pass the child under the belly of a donkey, three times three.

To prevent a cold, smell your socks when you go to bed, the right one first.

A dirty sock or stocking worn around the throat will cure a sore throat.

Tying an onion to a bedpost will keep away colds.

Pass a child with rickets through a split in an ash tree for a sure cure.

Put an ax under the bed to cut the pain of childbirth.

To stop foot cramp, turn your shoe upside down before going to bed.

To cure a sty, rub the tail of a black cat over the eye.

If you carry a buckeye in your pocket or purse, you will not have head-aches; it will also keep you from being bothered by hemorrhoids.

When you cut your hair do not let a bird use any of it to build a nest; if it does, you will have headaches.

Club moss gathered on the third day of the new moon is good against all diseases of the eye.

Sap from a grapevine will grow hair on a bald head.

A white tablecloth left on the table overnight means the household will soon be in need of a shroud (that is, someone will soon die).

If you carry a shovel through the house, a grave will soon need to be dug.

If you sweep your house at night, it will bring bad luck; but if you sweep it in the morning, evil spirits will be swept out.

If a pregnant woman drinks from a cracked cup, her baby will be
harelipped.

If a crow flies over your house and caws thrice, someone in the family will die.

If a rooster stands on the front porch, looks outward, and crows,
it means someone will be carried out the door sick or dead. (My
mama took a broom to any rooster that dared come up on our
porch.)

Living by such superstitions as these came very natural to those of us
who lived in the mountains. There, the shadowy world of dimly glimpsed
magic appeared so true it was hard to distinguish it from the real world.
Also, because the inscrutable world of nature was always close at hand,
the capricious world of spirits, spells, witches, and charms was inevitably
as close.

This acceptance of the abnormal in our everyday life probably helped
me in my later years to accept new ideas about God and spirituality.

3
Oral History

At night our world closed down; the woods were
lonely and mysterious. It was inevitable that
some of the dark tales and superstitions brought
here by the early immigrants from Scotland and
Ireland should flourish in Appalachia.

A treasured "patchwork" folder reposes in my files. In this folder are transcripts of taped talks with my dad, grandpa, and others. It holds accounts of memories handed down from generations back; ghost tales, hunting trips, and strange occurrences during other treks through the woods. It is a record of the good and bad times in this century in the hills of southeastern Kentucky.

One morning early in the spring, after I was married and living in my own house, Grandpa and Dad came by on their way down to the mouth of Stoney Fork to the post office. I invited them in to have some coffee. I had just built a fire in the heater and put on some coffee to boil. They sat near the stove as they drank the hot coffee, and they talked about hunting dogs and exciting fox chases and coon hunts.

I had borrowed a reel-to-reel tape recorder some days earlier to tape some songs, and I asked Dad and his father, my grandpa, if I could record their talk about the old times. They agreed, and we spent the rest of the morning together. Much of this chapter is a literal transcript from that morning years ago.

Haints and Other Mysteries

Grandpa talked a lot about "haints" (ghosts) he had heard of around the old home place at the head of Stoney Fork.

"When I's a year old, why my old man moved to the head of Stoney Fork. I's born in Rockcastle County at Brodhead, Kentucky. But Pap was born and raised at the head of Stoney Fork, and he moved us back thar when I's about a year old. Pap said his old man and my great-uncle Samp were the first ones ever to come into this territory. Somebody told them about how they was good farming land at the head of Stoney Fork and around in Peach Orchard. There was a natural spring, Pap said, in that little meadow thar betwixt Indian Rock and Peach Orchard. Pap or Uncle Samp—one, I forget which—hollered out a piece of a log, like a bee gum you know, and put it down over the spring. It was named Gum Spring."

I listened to Grandpa with fascination, glad that I had the tape recorder on.

"Well sir, Pap allus said they's a haint [he pronounced it "hant"] around that spring. He said it was jist like a blue light about two feet off the ground. Hit's been seed thar and it's follered people partway home. Jist a little blue light a-moving clost to the ground.

"Pap said they's other things to be heard around in thar, too. Especially around the old home place. In those days they built double houses—two log houses jined under one roof. There's a space, called a dogtrot, betwixt each log house. You could walk through from one side to the other. Well, Pap said ever night due as the night would come, it was just like two big bulldogs a-fighting betwixt them houses. He said his dogs would run out, run all around the house, but never could find nary thing. They'd come back up on the porch with their tails betwixt their legs. Pap said it sounded jist plimeblank like two big bulldogs fighting.

"Pap said ever since he was a little boy they'd heard things around in thar. He said none of them never knowed what it was. Figgered it might have been an Indian or white hunter who died dissatisfied. But it was shore different noises.

"Well sir, Susie and me got married and built us a house right near the place where the old house stood. One time we's a-milking the cows and it was gettin' dark, you know. The children was all small-like then, and when we got back they's a-scared to death. Said they seed something jist like a big calf, or a big dog, walk right in the door with its eyes all blared out. They's skeered jist about to death.

"Then after that, why my boy Squire he climbed up in the loft—well, the fact of it was we had a bed up in the loft for some of the children to sleep up thar, you know. He climbed up thar and there laid what looked like a big shepherd dog quiled up on the floor.

"Then one night we's a-laying there, and if you'd got up in the loft and dropped a big sackful of dry shuckbeans—it went jist plimeblank like you'd just dropped a big sackful of dry shuckbeans down in the loft.

"And the purtiest music I ever heard in my life I heard it in that loft one night. It went like a talking-machine a-playing. Why, that was the purtiest music I ever heard.

"Your Aunt Betty was in the house one day by herself. Thar's a wornet tree stood right outside the house—you remember that wornet tree? Well, she said they's something just like a sewing machine sewing up in that tree—you know how a sewing machine goes. But she couldn't see nary thing. She said it kept on a right smart spell of time.

"I've been outside times on top of times and it would go like someone throwed a big soggy chunk of wood right behind me. Sometimes it'd go like a big flat rock—if you'd throw a flat rock in a pile of rocks. I'd turn around and look and not see nary thing. I never did see a haint, but I shore have heard some strange things in my lifetime."

"Mama has also seen strange things from time to time around the old home place," Dad said.

"Yeah," Grandpa agreed. "One day me and the boys was a-working in the field late and Susie had to go after the cows." Grandpa turned toward Dad. "She was a-driving them back up the road fernist Indian Cliff. She looked ahead and thar stood a little girl right in the middle of the road. She said she studied on it a few minutes, puzzled about what was a little girl doing thar by herself. She kept walking toward her, a-watching her. She said the girl had on a pretty checked dress and her hair hung down her back in long curls. She said she guessed she turned her eyes away for a split second and when she looked back the girl was gone.

"Another time it was getting late at night. Susie'd been canning peaches most of the day. She stepped outside for just a minute before go-ing to bed. She was standing there, cooling off in the fresh air, when she seed a light down by the creek. Then it sort of gathered like a big ball of fire and started rolling up the hill. It was smooth and easy, she said, just a-rolling up the hill. It went over the mountain and out of sight. We studied on it a whole lot but never could figure out what it meant."

Grandpa cut a chew of tobacco to put in his mouth. Then he got up and stretched and walked out into the yard to chew his tobacco. I refilled Dad's coffee mug.

"Pap talks about the strange things they've seed and heard up at the old home place at the head of Stoney Fork," Dad said. "I've heard things up there, too. But I think the most haints I've ever heard or heard about was up around the water gap—near what is now the Ritter Lumber Camp. The water gap was a barrier across the creek to keep stock from going into the fields and eating up the corn. They put two logs across, one of them up high and the othern down here low. Then they nailed planks up and down and the water jist went on through, you know.

"Brother Otis was working on the WPA [Works Progress Administration] and was a-coming home one night. He walked awhile with a bunch of men who worked with him. But he had to cross the Stoney Fork Bridge and go up through the bottom to get home. The other men went on up the Pine Mountain side. Otis had to cross the bridge there above Water Gap to get home.

"You couldn't cross the creek ferniest his house. They were an old traveling path at that time right up through the edge of the field. Otis had some home brew with him but knowed it wouldn't go far in the whole crowd. After he crossed the bridge he walked along, taking a nip ever now and then. Right below the old graveyard there was corn planted in the bottom. I believe Morgan Helton was farming it that year.

"Suddenly he heard something big come right up near him and start eating them big years of corn, just scrushing them all to pieces. He said he could hear it, just scrushing the corn all to pieces. He was shure it was a horse got in the field. The next morning on his way to work he looked and couldn't see nary thing bothered in that field. No horse had walked in thar, and no corn had been eat that he could see.

"I remember how Edgar Elliott, who used to live out thar with Aunt Mandy Hoskins, and he would go down through that bottom before daylight to his work at Sonnie LeFever's sawmill. He said he heard the same thing Otis did. Something big scrushing years of corn—even in winter-time when they's no corn in the field. Other times he'd hear a sound right behind him, he said jist like a windstorm. Like it was going to blow every-thing in the world away. It would be as clear a time as ever was and as still a time as ever was. But through that field it sounded like ever bit of the corn was blowing away in a big storm, he said.

"One time me and Sonnie Nunn was up in that bottom walking along the path through the edge of the field. It was getting long towards dark—well, you could say it's good dusky-dark. Up ahead we suddenly seed a big white horse looking at us. Then it started running right straight at us. I jist knowed it's going to run smack-dab over us afore we got out of the way. Well sir, it got right up near us and jumped in the air and went right over our heads, jist like a horse a-jumping a fence. And it never did come back down to the ground. We don't know to this day what it was.

"Brother Squire and me and a bunch of men used to hang out at the schoolhouse and drink. One time a bunch of us was thar. And Bass Hoskins was thar. His wife would foller him sometimes if he was gone too long. We looked up and seed a woman a-crossing the swinging bridge. Bass made shore it was his wife and got up and went to meet her, just like a man would, you know. He got out thar and never could get ahold of her. He'd reach for her and she'd just disappear. Then she'd be standing thar again. After the second time he reached for her and she wasn't thar, he got skeered. You never heard such a kerbangen in your life as him trying to run back acrost that swinging bridge.

"The woman was dressed in white. We all seed it with our own eyes. It had to be a haint. No real woman could disappear that a-way."

Dad's Early Days

At this point Grandpa came back inside. I offered him more coffee and he settled down in his chair. Dad remained seated, and I asked him to de-scribe life when he was a young boy.

"When I was a boy, I'd say maybe once a month we'd go to the store. We'd buy coffee, salt, sody, sugar. Ever once in a while we'd buy a sack of flour for Sunday biscuits—rest of the time we ate cornbread. We didn't have fancy foods like nowadays, like light bread. We's a lot healthier too. We used a lot of fresh milk, fresh butter, beans, and vegetables from the garden, all fresh. Wouldn't no cold storage in them days. In the wintertime we had dried beans, potatoes, milk and butter, eggs, chickens, pork. Lived better then than we do now.

"Back them days we let our hogs run wild in the mountains; they ate chestnuts. Besides chestnuts they also ate hickory nuts and a few acorns. 'Boys, we will kill us a hog when they come in after eating chestnuts,' Pap would say. Before too long they would come in just a-wobbling like a big fat goose.

"Lots of the hogs went wild that way. To identify our own hogs we marked them. Pap and us boys used the same mark: smooth crap the left ear and split the right and top bit the right, was our mark.

"When we wanted to kill a hog we went to the woods and hunted one down—unless we wanted to kill one in the summer, then we caught a hog and pen-fed it on corn to harden the meat. Mast fed hogs had soft fat, and it would drip out of the meat in summertime."

I realized with a thrill of pride that Dad was as good a storyteller as Grandpa. I was so glad I had the reel-to-reel recorder. Dad continued to tell his stories while Grandpa finished his coffee and went back outside.

"When I was a young man I went hunting a wild male that had tushes exactly six inches long. I shot him in the head with a savage twenty-two rifle six times (and you could have covered the bullet holes with a quarter; I was an expert shot in them days) before I got him down. He snapped off bushes big as your arm. The dogs hemmed him near the roots of a fallen tree. I climbed up through the branches of the top part of the tree where I could shoot him. He knocked one dog way up in the air, and she hit the ground a-running. Next time I saw her was at the house. The skin of that hog was so tough a knife wouldn't cut it. He's pretty old, but would have killed you in a minute.

"One time Granny Brock and one of her stepsons was a-fishin' just a little below the gap, and long after dark, why they's two men come a-walking down through the field, walked right down beside them, walked right into the water—they could hear them go right into the water still a-talking. Granny said she and Roy stood right still, not a-knowing what was a-going on. They waited for them men to come back out of the water, but they never did. She said they walked right into that hole of water—it was maybe three times over a man's head there in that hole of water. No doubt it worried Granny. She said they left—they'd caught enough fish by that time anyway.

"One time along after that me and Squire and Ed Brock and Otis had been out on a trip and we's hungry. We took a notion to lay out in the schoolhouse. Ed and Squire went to Carter Helton's store to buy us food. Otis and me went on and broke into the schoolhouse and built us a fire in the heating stove. We didn't have no light. Well, they was gone ages of time. We laid down on the floor around the stove waiting for them to bring the grub. We's laying there listening for them to come ever minute—they's riding a horse.

"Finally we heard a horse a-coming and made shore it was them. The horse hit the ford of the creek and come right on and it come right up the steps right through the door and walked up between him and me. And us a-laying there with no light. When it come in the door that's when I knowed it wasn't a natural horse. By that time I didn't try to figger out what it was—my hair was a-crawling on my head! Otis never said nary a word to me and I didn't say nary a word to him. The horse was there between us one minute and the next it was gone. We couldn't see it for we didn't have no light. But we knowed when he's gone.

"A little while later we heard another horse a-coming, and it was Ed and Squire. They laughed when we told them about the horse a-coming in the schoolhouse. That schoolhouse was about a quarter of a mile below the water gap.

"One time I left the house about the edge of dark to go to Squire's house up on Ben's Branch. He'd run off some moonshine and I wanted some to sell at the mill next day. When I got there he'd already taken it to Pap's on the head of Stoney Fork. I turned around and headed for Pap's.

"By the time I's on my way back home it was getting towards daylight. As I come through the ford there above the water gap, I had a little rise to go over. I went up over the rise about half-asleep. There come a noise like a big pole broke, you know, like you'd stepped on it. There was several other different kinds of noises as I rode along. Next, over in the bottom of corn—I believe Levi Saylor was tending it that summer—come a noise like somebody hoeing corn of a wet time with a gooseneck hoe. They'd hit the hoe over a rock to knock the mud off. This was about three in the morning—the birds was a-whistling for daylight. I kinda roused up.

"Reckon Uncle Levi's hoeing corn at this time of morning," I thought. Then something come into the creek just as I passed the water gap and turned up the hill. It sounded like the water went thirty feet high. It skeered my mule and he run a piece with me, until I got him stopped and wheeled back into the road. I throwed my light into the road and no doubt I jerked out my gun. I watched for something to come up out of the water but I never did see nothing. My mule just stood there and trembled with me.

"One time I'd been to Dewey Brock's store, which used to set up the hill half a mile from the gap. I'd been out a-fooling around, you know. Anyway, it come up a quick storm late in the evening and it got dark real quick. It was so dark I couldn't see a stymie.

"Dewey fixed me a new carbide light—took it right out of the box and filled it up with carbide. As I got down to this schoolhouse where that swinging bridge is—well, fact is I guess I'd passed it about a dozen yards—and if you'd a-throwed a thousand feet of dry lumber on the bridge it wouldn't a-made no more racket. I walked back and throwed my light from one end of the bridge to the othern, but that bridge was just like it had always been, just like it is today. Wasn't nothing bothered. It made me kinda study, like anybody would I guess, about what could the racket have been.

"Sonny Nunn and Tom Trosper night-watched at the Ritter Lumber Mill when it was first set up there in that bottom. Tom told me it'd go like ever piece of that lumber in the yard would fall. He'd grab his light and go see, and when he got out there, why not a piece of it was bothered.

"Sonny said he's watching one night and laying beside a boiler to keep warm and he said right on the other side of that boiler was the purtiest music he ever heard in all of his days. He said it played for something like ten or fifteen minutes before it stopped. He said it shore was purty music.

"Tom stepped out one night from the mill just a little way. The fact is he stepped out in the bushes to squat and do his business. He pulled down his pants and squatted down. He said he'd swear it to his dying day that something blowed its breath right against his butt—and there he was squatted with his pants down."

At this point Grandpa came back into the house and chuckled as Dad finished his story about Tom Trosper.

"One time I's out on a trip; come in and unsaddled my mule," Dad said. "The moon was shining bright, and I didn't need no light a-tall. I had a little crib with a door about halfway up the side of it. I had to stoop over to get corn out to feed the mule. I heard a racket, and as I raised my head up I saw a big cat go down the hill a-playing with a bind of fodder. It made enough racket that I raised up and looked. It went right through a house wall I'd started to build. It looked like a cat about the size of a small dog. A big cat. It was big enough to handle a bind of fodder and make enough racket that I paid notice to it. It was walking on its hind feet and playing with the fodder with its forefeet, tossing it up and catching it as it come back down. It never paid no attention to me. The bind of fodder looked like gold—except it rattled, like dry fodder will. The cat was black and it had big, bright eyes, almost as bright as lights. But it never did pay no more attention to me than anything. I shore was glad of that!

"Nowadays, you don't hear nobody talking about seeing or hearing things, and it's hard to understand why. There's nothing like they was in them days. It could be there's people so thick-settled now and they don't pay no attention to it."

That morning I spent with Grandpa and Dad became a treasured memory. Later on I transcribed the tapes and later still had the reel-to-reel transferred to cassette tapes.

Grandpa had mentioned that when his father was just a boy, he and another boy slipped off from home and walked to London, Kentucky, to see the first trains. I wanted to hear about that.

"Grandpa, will you come back tomorrow and talk some more about haints and things like that?" I asked. "I also want to hear about Uncle Milt Simpson. Will you come with him, Dad?" They promised to come the next morning. The sun was high overhead when they left for the post office.

The next morning I had coffee and doughnuts ready for them, and the tape recorder set to go. They again sat near the heating stove.

"Grandpa," I said, "I also want to record the story about a trip your pap took into Virginia." Dad chuckled and settled down to listen.

The First Trains of London

"When Pap was a boy," began Grandpa, "the first train that ever come to London, why him and one of them Bingham boys slipped off and went to London to see the train.

"They lived right here on the head of Left Fork, and they slipped off and walked plumb to London to see the train. Well, he said they got there—I don't remember how many days he said it took them to walk thar—but anyhow he said they got down there and watched the trains going and coming till it's dark, you know, and neither one of them no money and didn't know where to go to spend the night.

"Well, he said, they started out walking, said they looked out in a bottom, seen a light and said they took a notion to go and see if they could stay all night there, you know, it's gettin' dark. Said the man told them, 'Yeah,' when they told him what come them there, and he said, 'Yeah, come in and stay just as long as you want to.' I reckon they stayed three days and nights with him to watch them trains, and their parents not a-knowin' where in the world they's at; just slipped off like two crazy boys will. Now what about crazy boys now drawing up that idea to go that fur to git to see a train!"

Dad chuckled, and both men were quiet for a minute. "Pap, remember the time when Uncle Eli lived in Virginia and Grandpa went to visit him?" Dad asked.

"Yeah, I remember Pap talking about that," Grandpa said.

"Tell me about it," I said.

Going to Virginia

"Uncle Eli lived in Virginia," Grandpa began. "He come out here, and then Pap went back with him. It was election time and they just fared best in the world ever where they asked to stay all night, they would say, 'Yeah, come in.' And jist soon as they got in the house Uncle Eli'd find out how they was—you know—Democrats or Republicans, and ever how they was, why that's how he was. So Pap said they made the trip plumb through and it never cost them one penny.

"Well, Pap said he got out there and hired out to a man and stayed the next summer. Then Uncle Mike, he come out to Virginnie and begged Pap to come back to this country with him.

"Well, he said, they hit out, and he said not a place could they git to stay all night. Election time was over. He said he remembered them places him and Uncle Eli had stayed; but when they would call, the answer was, 'No, full up; can't keep you.' Finally one man told them he was crowded in the house but they could sleep in the barn loft. The man had a bulldog that he turned loose at night. Well, he said, long about midnight that dog found them out in the barnloft. He said right thar they had to stand. Every time the dog jumped, he hung his forefeet on the edge, and they would kick him off. About eight o'clock in the morning the man happened to hear the dog, and come out and called him off.

"Yeah, man! He said they couldn't git nothing to eat; people wouldn't sell them a thing. They starved three days and nights. Finally they looked out and seed a little old log cabin. Pap said he told Uncle Mike, 'Right thar we're goin' to git somethin' to eat.' He seed an old-like woman settin' on the porch. Said he walked up and asked her, said, 'Aunt, how about gittin' somethin' to eat here?' She said, 'Yes, honey, come in, I'll fix ye somethin' to eat.'

"Well, he said, they went in, said she flew right in, wasn't jist a few minutes till she had a good dinner fixed. He said when they sot down he happened to cast his eye up and seed some middlings of meat hanging from the rafter. Said he told her, 'Aunt, how about bakin' us a pone of bread and cuttin' us a piece of that meat to take with us?' She said, 'Yeah, honey, that's what I've got hit fer, to sell.' She baked them a big pone of bread, then went to that meat and sot her knife right middleway and she jist split it open and wrapped it up and give it to them. They asked her, 'How much do we owe you?' and she said, 'Oh, I reckon about fifty cents.'

"He said they had plenty to eat from thar on home. Brought some of the meat home with them. They walked all the way from West Virginia to Foresters Creek, Kentucky, up on the Cumberland River."

"Grandpa," I said, "I've heard Dad and Granny Brock tell tales about a man they called Uncle Milt Simpson. Did you know him?"

"He was my age," Grandpa said. "I didn't know him as a friend. But I knew some of the tricks he pulled on people."

Uncle Milt Simpson

"He was sure a slick, sharp man. One time he boasted to Uncle Larkin Howard that he could steal a sheep from him and tell him about it. He said Larkin would never know it.

"One night, it'd been drizzling rain and was a dark foggy time. He went down and knocked one of Larkin's big black wethers in the head and laid it across his shoulders and walked right through Larkin's yard. Called out to Uncle Larkin, 'Go home with me, Uncle Larkin.'

"'No, come in, Uncle Milt,' said Larkin.

"'No, I've got to go home, the wether's dark and heavy.'

"Uncle Milt picked out dark, foggy weather to steal Uncle Larkin's wether. Later he told Uncle Larkin about it.

"He's the awfullest man ever was. Ever word told is true too. He'd get to wanting to buy a certain milk cow off one of his neighbors, and if the neighbor said no, he would slip to the pasture and milk her, at first a little bit, then each day a little more, until pretty soon it looked to the neighbor like his cow was going dry. He'd pass by and say, 'You ever took a notion to sell me that cow?'

"'Yeah, believe I will,' the man would usually say, thinking he was going to pull one over on Uncle Milt. So Milt would git his cow.

"One time he went to another old man's house, passed by his pigpen, and drove a nail through their foreheads—there's three of them–while they's sleeping. He went early next morning to the old man's house and said, 'Say, Uncle, all three of your hogs is lying dead.' The old man thought cholera had killed them.

"'Well, guess I'll have to haul them off.'

"'Tell you what. I'll haul 'em away for you, take them home, and let the old women make them up in soap.' The old man was glad to get rid of them, and Uncle Milt took them home, cleaned 'em, and salted them down in his smokehouse."

"He was a likable fellow, you know," Dad interjected. "He'd steal from people, then go tell 'em how he did it. They admired his way of being so slick and usually told him he could keep whatever he stole."

"One time," Grandpa continued, "why they's a young married man come to him and said, 'Uncle Milt, I have a problem. I have only one hog to kill this year. Several neighbors have give me messes of fresh meat, and when I kill mine they'll expect a mess of meat back. I won't have much left.'

"'Well, son, this is what you do. Kill your hog late in the evening and hang it up outside and let the night air-cool it off while it drains out good. Next day tell the neighbors somebody stole it.'

"The young man did as advised, and that night Uncle Milt stole it. Next day the man rushed to him and said, 'Uncle Milt, somebody stole my hog last night.' Uncle Milt grinned and replied, 'You said that like it was the real truth. Just stick to that.'

"'But Uncle Milt, somebody did steal it. I swear they did.'

"'That's the way, son, say it just that way, your neighbors will really believe you,' Uncle Milt said."

THIS TIME THAT DAD AND GRANDPA spent with me is precious to remember. Both are now long dead, but I have their recorded voices talking to me in the mountain dialect we all used.

4

Satisfy Hunger, Tickle the Funny Bone

*Midsummer to me is wildflowers—the blue of
chicory, the black-eyed Susan, butterfly weed
flaunting bright orange colors, and lovely white
Queen Anne's lace.*

The kitchen has been the center of most of my family life, just as it
was for the first pioneer settlers who built log cabins in the wilderness.
The red- or blue-checked tablecloth and curtains, a fireplace, the warmth
and smell of good food cooking—these linger in the memories of generations of country people. Thanksgiving and Christmas, fried chicken
and homemade ice cream, and birthday celebrations—it all originates in
the kitchen. As I look back, I realize how that big, warm kitchen knitted the family together. To my way of thinking, family rooms have never
quite succeeded in replacing the kitchen in the hearts and memories of the
family.

When mountain people leave home to go "up north" to find work,
they take along a very real sense of place. Ask any displaced Appalachian
what he or she misses most about being away from the mountains and you
will probably hear about soup beans, cornbread, sallet greens, fresh milk
and butter, eggs, country ham, and hot biscuits every morning.

Reunions

I think of August as the month that ends summer. And I think of summer
as the time of family reunions, although I am sure that reunions are held
during other parts of the year.

Almost everyone born in southern Appalachia feels the pull to return to the place of his or her birth. There seem to be ties with the hills that cannot be broken but must be renewed at intervals. Having lived in the mountains, we almost become a part of them, or they become a part of us. Kinship is a strong bond for families from the mountains, even for those that have scattered, and the bonds are nurtured and strengthened when they return.

There is something about my roots in the mountains that never lets me stray from memories of home. Even though I left years ago, my memories of the old houses, one-room schools, decaying barns, and overgrown fields where I spent my childhood linger on.

To me, there is something mystical about warm rain, early morning dew, the sound of tree frogs and tadpoles. And there is something about the smell of wild honeysuckle floating on air so warm and moist it sticks to our faces and hands. Generation after generation of hill-bred parents know that, no matter where their children may move in the world, their children will come to know "home" as they do. These parents strongly believe, even if they could never articulate it in words, that if they cannot impart this sense of place, then they will have failed their children.

Still, it seems to me that there are not as many family reunions as there used to be, even in the mountains. Should we mourn the passing of family, community spirit, and cooperation? Or are these things being expressed in other ways?

In an unsettled world, with families often scattered north, east, south, and west, coming home always gave me a sense of stability and family unity. And where I came from, most family reunions, barn raisings, and cabin buildings revolved around food, especially for the women. The reunions I remember had no overall plan; nobody told anybody what specifically to bring. When the food was laid out, on plank tables, it was a smorgasbord, country-style. And as the old mountain phrase goes, "They must have put the big pot in the little one," meaning that everybody brought an overabundance of food.

There was sure to be chicken and dumplings, green beans, corn (both fried and on the cob), and platters of sliced tomatoes. There would be fried chicken, baked ham, cornbread, and biscuits. And you could count on fruit salad, potato salad, gelatin salad, and cole slaw, deviled eggs, and fried apples. For dessert, there would be blackberry cobblers, pans of gingerbread, apple pies, cherry pies, black walnut cake, fresh coconut and chocolate cakes, dried apple stack cakes, lemon pies, and banana puddings. Sometimes there would even be cold watermelon and gallons of home-made ice cream, depending on how far along in the season it was.

Generous as they were, the mountain women I knew were hard put to supply recipes, belonging as they did to the "pinch of this and dab of that" school of cooking. By perseverance, however, and by writing down everything they said about their methods and later carefully measuring just how much a "dab" was or how big is a lump of butter the size of a walnut, I managed to record some recipes for the foods I remember.

The United Methodist Church of Stoney Fork, of which I am a charter member, hosts an annual homecoming the first Sunday in July. Families and friends come from Indiana, Ohio, Michigan, Kansas, Iowa, North Carolina, and other places to renew acquaintances and reestablish old ties. Although we cannot all attend every year, I am happy to know that old friends will be there and that perhaps next July we will see each other again.

Having Fun Together

When I was young, we laughed together whenever there was any kind of gathering. There would be preacher jokes, mule jokes, mother-in-law jokes, and gossip jokes. An anecdote about somebody not present would always end with the phrase "bless her [or his] heart."

We laughed in spite of living in what most people would consider harsh circumstances. At home we sat around the fireplace in the winter-time or on the front porch in the summertime and told each other funny stories, riddles, and sayings. There always seemed to be things to laugh about, and we eagerly sought them. Everyone wanted to be the first with an amusing anecdote, joke, or riddle. Dad and the other men loved to tell about escapades they'd had while hunting, dealing with livestock, or eluding the revenuers.

Later, when I grew up, I learned that when an unsettling undercurrent of today's reality sneaks in, humor can help. In addition, humor is almost always the best way to battle Appalachian stereotypes.

The Power of Riddles

Telling riddles is both an intellectual exercise and form of entertainment that goes back as far in history as we have any knowledge of man's intellectual doings. Even the Bible contains riddles. The Anglo-Saxons evidently loved riddles because they preserved many elaborate ones. Down through the years, poets have written riddles in verse. Riddles have been used for various kinds of tests. But the fun of riddles comes from the riddles themselves, not from the discourses about them.

"Riddling" has been a traditional form of social activity in Appalachia; sad to say, though, young people these days know fewer and fewer of the old riddles.

Perhaps the most famous riddle still to be found in Appalachia is the Riddle of the Sphinx, which Oedipus answered in order to become King of Thebes. *What goes on four legs in the morning, two at noon, and three in the afternoon?* Answer: *A human being.*

In the mountains the most suggestive riddles— "bad" riddles with innocent answers—always seemed to be the most popular. The shock of the innocent answer added to the overall impact.

A number of years ago, riddles were gathered from schoolchildren in southeastern Kentucky. One collector suggested that the children ask their parents and grandparents for riddles they might remember. One child came back saying, "My mommy said she knows other old riddles that are kinda bad. She said she would tell them to you if you come and see her."

Here are some of my favorite "good" and "bad" riddles, heard in my childhood.

Crooked as a rainbow,
Teeth like a cat,
Guess all night and

You can't guess that.
(Answer: a briar)   ·

Back to the ground,
Belly to the sun,
Tails begin to wiggle,
And the good begins to come!
(Answer: sow and pigs)

Up she jumped and out she run,
Down she squatted,
And the good began to come.
(Answer: milking a cow)

Green as grass but grass it ain't.
Black as ink but ink it ain't.
What is it?
(Answer: a blackberry)

As I went across London Bridge
I met a London scholar.   ·
He tipped his hat and drew his cane,
And in this riddle I told his name.
(Answer: Andrew)

In yonders lot there is a cup,
And in that cup there is a drop,
And of that drop we all must taste.
(Answer: death)

Round as a biscuit, busy as a bee,
Prettiest little thing you ever did see.
(Answer: a pocket watch)

A hill full, a hole full,
But you can't get a bowlful.
(Answer: fog or mist)

Four stiff standers,
Two lookers, two hookers,
One dirty switch-about
Lags along behind.
(Answer: a cow)

Belly to belly,
Hand on the back.
A little piece of flesh
To stop up the crack.
(Answer: a baby nursing)

On Stoney Fork we moved with the rhythm of nature and life itself. There was meter in our work and cadence in our laughter.

5

Decoration Day

One thing we all need is more light during the
dark days. We must shine brighter ourselves, to
take up the slack when there is need.

In my home in the mountains, we observed Decoration Day on May 30 every spring. Weeks before, people would take up shovels, rakes, hoes, scythes, and other tools and would clear off the graveyards and spruce up the area. Then, on Decoration Day, they would travel to various cemeteries, carrying both fresh and artificial flowers, plants, picnic baskets, and jugs of water and Kool-Aid. They would spend hours on the various hilltops, socializing with other families, sometimes listening to an impromptu sermon or homily if a preacher happened to be on the premises. Then they would return home for another year.

We had an old-fashioned rosebush in our front yard, and there usually were early blooms by the end of May. Mama would take bunches of them to decorate graves on May 30.

Decoration Day had its origins as a day to celebrate and remember the veterans of the Civil War. I don't remember any mention of this during the Decoration Day observances of my youth. If a veteran had passed away during the year, he would be remembered with all the others. Even now, of course, though May 30 is now known as Memorial Day, people still take wreaths and flowers to the graves of family members and friends who have passed on.

Wakes and funerals in the mountains were attended by almost everyone, including small children. One of my earliest memories is standing in the sunshine beside an open grave looking down at a dead baby lying in an open, homemade casket. The baby's blue eyes were wide open. The young parents kept crying and touching the baby's face. I never got over the horror of that experience. Even today the memory makes me want to cry.

I remember another funeral in the springtime on Ben's Branch, at a small hilltop graveyard. Pines grew near the edge of the clearing, and green moss covered the ground under the trees, the rocks, and the old wooden benches where people sat. I was five years old by that time, and do not remember much that was said or done, but I do recall the way the moss and wildflowers looked, and how the soft wind stirred the pine branches silhouetted against the clear sky, and how the carpet of pine needles covered the ground. I wondered if this was the heaven people were talking about.

When I was six, while we still lived on Coon Branch at the head of Stoney Fork, I experienced new life and death for the first time. Martha Jane, Mama's sister, lived on Punkin Knob to the north of us. She had six children and was soon to have another baby. One day in August word came that she was in labor and having trouble. The midwife sent word for Mama and the other sisters to come and help out. Dad was on a hunting trip, so Mama had to take us with her. A number of relatives were already at the house when we arrived.

Aunt Mossie was bossing all the children around and trying to get dinner dishes washed and supper on the table. We went in to see Martha Jane. She didn't speak; she just kept moaning and saying, "Lord have mercy." The adults were all kneeling around the bed and praying for her. I remember her husband, Uncle Dewey, kneeling between the bed and the wall, crying and calling to Aunt Martha Jane to get better. They said "Amen," and the Holy Ghost blessed Martha Jane; she began waving her arms about and shouting.

I quietly slipped outside and walked around in a daze. I did not know what was happening and what it meant when a baby could not be born. I tried to say a prayer and grieve like the others were doing, but I just couldn't. I picked up a fork from the kitchen floor. "Poor Aunt Martha Jane, her fork is on the floor," I mourned aloud.

I heard a muted whimpering coming from underneath the house and crawled under the porch to investigate. Far back near the chimney was a little brown dog. I remembered that cousin Willie Gladys had told us that her mother was going to have a new baby and their dog was going to have new pups. I watched the dog to see what would happen. A wet little body emerged and fell to the ground. I started to move closer, but the dog growled and I was afraid of her. As I watched, several more pups dropped to the ground.

I heard someone call my name, and Aunt Mossie stuck her head under the porch and yelled at me. "Come out from under there, Sidney! You shouldn't be watching that dog. I'm going to tell your mother."

I felt scalding shame at this rebuke, and tears spilled down my cheeks. I grabbed up some clots of dirt and threw them at Aunt Mossie, fast and furious. She backed away from the porch and left, calling for Mama.

By the time Aunt Mossie got back into the house, the baby had been born. I heard it crying. I crept up onto the front porch and Aunt Bertha, the midwife, patted me on the head. "You children be quiet now, yore poor Aunt Martha Jane is dying," she said. "The Lord gives and the Lord takes away. Bless the name of Jesus."

Uncle Dewey had started out to get the doctor. I remember watching him running down the hillside and Aunt Bertha calling out that he didn't have to run. He walked all the way to Pineville and came back with a doctor who was riding a horse. They went on into the house. The doctor left after confirming that Aunt Martha Jane was dead.

Other people came out onto the porch, some of them sobbing. I heard Aunt Bertha say, "Children, keep praying; she might 'vine' up again." How could a poor, sick woman 'vine' up, I wondered. Years later I realized she had meant that Aunt Martha Jane might revive. I went into the kitchen where Mama stood. I remembered how Aunt Bertha said we must praise the Lord no matter what happens. "Well, then, praise the Lord," I said as loud as I could. Mama's face turned red and she slapped me. "Don't you ever say things like that!" she screamed at me. I ran outside and leaned against the front yard fence, crying in outrage and bewilderment.

At dusky dark Dad rode in and unsaddled his mule. He picked me up and carried me onto the porch. Sitting down in a rocking chair, he asked what had made me cry. In a jumble I tried to tell him about the pups, Aunt Martha Jane's fork on the kitchen floor, and Mama and Aunt Mossie making me mad. I nestled in his arms, safe and secure. Dad made everything all right.

Weeks later, I heard Dad talking to Grandpa about that night and the tragic loss of the mother to her family of young children.

"I'd been to Kettle Island," Dad said to Grandpa, "and when I come home Rachel and Mossie were gone; I figured Martha Jane was sick to have her baby. I didn't know at the time that she was already dead. Old Bob, my mule, is going blind in his old age, I reckon," Dad continued. "I have to make torches out of any kind of dry brush that I can find for him to see by, and lead him out of places. It's jist at night he can't see. When I am riding along and he starts snuffling the ground I stop, fer I know he can't see a thing and is trying to trail the road by smell. I started over the hill to Martha Jane's house and had to strike matches all the way and lead old Bob clear around to Punkin Knob."

I have no memory of Aunt Martha Jane's funeral. I never thought to ask Mama for details. After my aunt died, her older girls took care of their siblings, including the new baby. Eventually Uncle Dewey married again, and the family continued.

6
Growing Years

Those in my world who heard the mountains'
call told me about things that were past as well
as things yet to come.

When I was five and my sister Della was not yet four, Dad moved us from Coon Branch down to Straight Creek so I could go to school. Until Dad could get our new house built, we lived in a ramshackle two-room building at the back edge of the property, which faced a small hill called Little Knob. The roof of the building slanted all one way, with the front, high part facing Little Knob. The back wall of the house had no windows and no door, so from inside the house we could not look across the valley to the other side of the mountain.

I was sick for weeks that summer—Granny Brock said it was the "summer complaint" that killed so many children. I remember lying in bed crying because my stomach hurt. I must have dozed off one afternoon. When I awoke I saw that a door had been cut into the back of the house. The sun was setting, and I got up and stood in the doorway, looking at the sky. I ran to Mama.

"When did Dad cut that door out? Come look, Mama, it lights up the whole house."

"You've been dreaming," she said. "There's no door cut out in that wall." I argued with her until she grabbed my arm and forced me to look at the blank wall. "See there?" she said. "You were dreaming." But my vision was so vivid I decided that the new door was magic, that only I could see it. For the rest of the time we lived in that house, every morning when I awoke I would turn quickly to look at that wall.

I never saw the door again.

That same year, late in the fall, I saw another strange thing. Mama, Aunt Mossie, Aunt Laura, and I had walked over Birch Lick Mountain to the Red Bird Hospital Free Clinic. As we walked down Mud Lick I saw a square little house sitting in the edge of someone's yard. Laura and I ran up to it and tried to look through the doll-like windows. I remember how Laura patted the roof, asking who lived there. Its walls were green like jade and its roof was flat. Later, when I mentioned it, Mama said, "I didn't see that." Mama often accused me of telling lies, because she believed if you talked about something you only imagined, it was a sin. But I held stubbornly to what I had seen—both the little house and the doorway cut in the back wall of our house.

School Days

Even though I was not going to be six until October 30 that year we moved to Straight Creek, I was allowed to start school in August. I fell in love with school my very first day. The one-room school housed all eight grades. Each class was called to the front of the school to read aloud or work problems on the blackboard. I listened to each class all through the grades. I read ahead of my class whenever books were available. By the fourth grade I had practically memorized the eighth-grade reader because I had listened to the class read and recite so often. The teacher decided I was so far ahead of the other children I could skip fifth grade.

The first year I was in school, Dad began to build us a house down the hill from the old building. He cut and hauled in logs to build the house and got rough lumber from Sonny LeFever's sawmill. The new house had two rooms with a lean-to kitchen. Dad and Grandpa built a fieldstone chimney, daubing in the cracks with yellow clay, which they also used between the logs to help keep out cold air. The front porch extended across both rooms. The back portion of the foundation rested on the ground, but the front half was several feet off the ground, with the space underneath underpinned with rock. There was a small crawl-hole in one side. Sister Della and I would play in there on hot summer days.

One night Dad was gone on a trip to sell moonshine. We went to bed when it got dark; the younger children soon went to sleep. Mama and

I talked awhile; by around 9:30 or 10:00 we began to feel sleepy. Suddenly we heard a knocking under the floor right between our beds. Again and yet again the knocks came: knock-knock-knock-pause, knock-knock-knock-pause. There never seemed to be any change in the sound or the rhythm of the knocks. This continued until about midnight.

Mama and I lay there for quite a while, too scared to move. Finally we began to talk loudly so whatever, or whoever, was there would know we were awake. It made no difference; the steady knocks continued. Then Mama got her shoe and hit it loudly on the floor, hoping to scare whatever it was away. But the knocks kept on until about midnight, when they abruptly ceased. The next day Dad crawled under the house and looked for evidence of what might have been under there, but all he found was the rag doll Della and I had been playing with the day before. I always believed that either a real person or a ghost was under our porch that night.

A year or so after that, on a very dark night, when we were all in bed, another strange thing happened. I slept at that time on a little cot in a corner opposite to where the other two beds were in the room. All at once I felt uneasy. I felt as though something was looking at me. Then, on the end of my pillow, something began a soft tapping. It was just exactly the way a cat would do if it was playfully patting the pillow with its paw. This happened several times—pat-pat-pat-pause; pat-pat-pat-pause—before I screamed. Dad jumped up and lit the coal oil lamp on the table. There was nothing in the room that we could see.

I have always believed that what was patting my pillow was a big cat that Dad had seen one night playing with a bind of golden fodder in the moonlight around the structure of our new house. One night Dad rode in and was getting corn from the crib to feed his horse. He heard something making a rustling sound and turned around, facing the framework of our new house. He said he saw a big black cat walking along, tossing a bind of fodder up into the air and catching it with its paws. Dad said he started walking toward the cat, but as he got closer it went under the foundation and disappeared.

I believe there are supernatural beings and spirits. I believe there are physical and spiritual laws that we know nothing about. Who is to say for sure there are not unseen entities all around us? Perhaps there's a warp now and then in the curtain that separates our realm from other realms that allows us to catch glimpses of these other entities. Man has learned enough about the laws of nature to send ships into space and to enable men to walk on the moon—feats unbelievable to those who lived in an earlier time. Perhaps in the future we may use those same laws to usher us into infinity.

Games We Played

As the oldest child, it was my responsibility to bring the cow in for her morning and evening milking. At times I was frightened at having to do this chore, particularly when the fog was thick and tasseled in the trees, or if the cow was in the holler between Little Knob and Big Knob. Little Knob had a graveyard on its flat top, with some of its graves so old that the carving on the stones was half obliterated, and others so new that faded and stained crepe paper flowers would still be sitting there on the graves.

There was always so much work to be done that there was little time to play. But we kids were crazy for play and grabbed every opportunity. We played Ante Over—pitching a ball over the top of the house from one side while others tried to catch it on the other side. We played Drop the Handkerchief—standing in a circle with one person going outside the circle and quietly dropping a handkerchief behind someone and then running back to place as the person grabbed the handkerchief and chased after the one who dropped it.

As early in spring as we possibly could, we would go barefoot. Mama fussed that the ground was still too damp, that a misty rain could still get us sick, that we would catch cold. We paid no attention to her warnings, however, and by full summertime the soles of our feet were hard and tough.

The girls loved to play Hopscotch, with the blocks marked off in the hard dirt with a sharp stick. We girls dearly loved Hopscotch, Jump the Rope, and Drop the Handkerchief, but the boys did not like to play these games, preferring baseball and marbles.

The girls did not think playing baseball and marbles was only for boys, however. In early spring you could see tight little circles of children on the school grounds playing marbles. We played at morning and afternoon recesses and all through the lunch hour. The boys always played Keeps, drawing a circle around their hoard of marbles and with their "steelies" and "best shooters" gambled with their whole collection. If they won other boys' marbles they kept them. They scorned girls who wanted to play. But several of us girls were sharpshooters, and occasionally the boys would allow one or two of us to play with them.

One game that boys and girls played together was horseshoes. I was allowed to play because I had a strong throwing arm. The grown men in the community most often pitched horseshoes on Saturday and Sunday afternoons. The game is still popular; one often sees it being played at picnics and family reunions. There are even horseshoe leagues and national competitions.

Boys and girls also played baseball together. There was no money for store-bought baseballs, so we would compress and sew together pieces of cloth until we had a ball of material approximately the size of a baseball—and almost as hard if one hit you! I was one of the best batters and fastest runners among the girls, and it thrilled me when teams were chosen and the boys wanted me on their teams because they recognized my abilities.

No doubt many of the expressions we used in our games (like "fudging," "dibs," and "knucks down") as well as the rhymes we chanted as we jumped rope, or the song we sang when we played Drop the Handkerchief ("Skip to My Lou") would sound strange to children today. Some of the games that we played then have been relegated to the past.

The Cure for Freckles

In the spring, when sap rises in maple trees it also rises in wild grapevines. We would make a small cut in a big grapevine and set a tin can or lard bucket to catch the sap. Mama diluted the sap with a little water and used it as a hair rinse after our weekly shampooing. The water we used for our shampooing, and the water used for the clothes that were hand-washed was water that Mama would collect from a bucket she would set under the downspout when it rained. Mama's hair was a dark tawny shade, mine was a light blond, and my sister Della had Dad's dark chestnut shade of hair. The rinse highlighted millions of gold flecks in Mama's hair and brought out gold highlights in mine and red highlights in Della's. We all felt so proud and fine with our clean, shiny hair.

Being fair-skinned and blond, I freckled easily in the summer sun. I tried everything that was purported to be a cure for freckles—everything but one cure Aunt Mossie told me about.

Mama's sister Mossie married Dad's brother Squire, and our two families lived fairly close to each other. One day, my cousins were teasing me, pretending to count my freckles. Aunt Mossie said that if I could find a tree stump with a hollow in the top where rainwater had collected, and bathe my face in the stump water, my freckles would disappear. It took awhile but finally I found a stump with rainwater standing in it. But I was so repulsed by the ugly, scaly growths in it and the yellowish red color of the water, I could not bring myself to put that stuff on my face. I have some freckles to this day.

My life was crammed full those early years with family and friends. For a while my best friend was Lora Hoskins. We played together at her brother Jeff's house. Jeff and his wife, Minnie, kept Lora and Jeff's grandmother, Hettie Hoskins—everyone called her "Aunt Hettie" out of respect for her age. Aunt Hettie told us many stories of people and places she had known, and she had a trunk, which she allowed Lora to open once to show me what was inside. When I saw what was there, I was both attracted and repelled. Aside from a few keepsakes, the contents were a memorial to Aunt Hettie's only daughter, Julia, who had been married to Sam Nunn, a jealous and possessive man, with whom she had several children. One day in a jealous rage Sam Nunn shot and killed Julia, and then rode into Pineville, the county seat, and turned himself in to the sheriff. He was tried, found guilty, and served many years in prison. When he got out of prison he came to live with his son, Sonny Nunn. Sonny was a friend of Dad's, and I knew both Nunns.

It was a custom in Appalachia to keep the last clothes of the deceased. People also kept locks of hair (which were often woven into a brooch) and pictures of the deceased as they lay in their coffins. Sure enough, inside Aunt Hettie's trunk were the clothes Julia Nunn had been wearing at the moment of her death and a picture of her taken shortly before her murder. She was a pretty brown-haired woman with a shy smile and big dark eyes looking directly into the camera.

Two or three times a year Dad, Grandpa, and various cousins and uncles saddled up and rode away. Mama said they were going off hunting, but when I got older I learned that their actual destination was their hidden moonshine still, where they went to run off a batch of liquor. Usually at these times Mama and Grandma took the children and rode over Birch Lick Mountain and down Mud Lick to the Red Bird Mission. There we could go to the free clinics at the hospital and the used clothing sale at the Mission office.

One time late in October (two days before my fourth birthday) when the men rode off, Mama decided we would just go spend the night with Grandma. In the late afternoon when the chores were done, she got us ready. She said I was big enough to walk and she'd let Della walk part of the way. Mama fastened the Yale lock on our front door, picked up baby Clara, and we set out.

We walked alongside the creek, crossing it several times on foot logs and swinging bridges, and then we headed up Ben's Branch. Most of the way Mama carried both Della and the baby. It seemed to take us a long time to get there. We stopped to rest on the last hill before we turned down the other side to Grandpa's house.

Then we heard the strangest noise. Around the hillside to our right we heard a thump, as if a heavy body had jumped or fallen from a tree. Then came a cry, at first sounding like a woman's cry, then gradually rising to the sound of a train whistle, before cutting off abruptly.

Terrified, we ran down the mountain. Mama had the baby in her arms and snatched up Della. When I stumbled and fell headlong down the trail she ordered me to be quiet and not cry. Then somehow she had me in her arms, too. She ran down to Meadow Branch then up the road to Grandpa's pasture gate before she put me down. Sobbing for breath, shaking with fright, we hurried into the house. This was the first time I'd seen my mother afraid. We told Grandma what had happened, and she and Mama talked about what could have made those sounds. When the men came home we told them all about it.

For two weeks after that, the menfolk talked about hearing an animal on their way to or from work at the Ritter Lumber sawmill. Then, as suddenly as it had come, the sound was gone. Grandpa said it was probably some animal escaped from a circus at Harlan, Pineville, or Middlesboro. "We may never know for sure what it was," he said.

"What's a circus?" I asked, but Grandpa didn't answer.

Reading and Writing

I started out in life full of light and with the clearest vision. I loved everything about words. I remember my feeling of excitement when I learned how to paint pictures with words. I was ten years old when I began to write little poems and descriptive essays about the mountains. Words came easily to me.

There were no pictures in our house when I was small. One time, when I was around three years old, Mama got some used Christmas cards. I'd never seen anything like them. One card had a cluster of grapes on the front, and I tried to bite them off. Even then, I was trying to absorb words to describe those grapes.

I read everything I could get my hands on. Aunt Dellie, who loved to read, shared her books with me. Neighbors down the road from us— Annie LeFever; her divorced daughter, Liza Meredith; and Liza's two daughters, Lovella and Pauline—read romance magazines and comic books. They passed on copies to me after they read them.

Mama never approved of my reading. "Those old books are full of lies and will drive you crazy," she often said. Despite Mama's disapproval, I continued to cherish words and books. Every spare minute I was not working or reading, I was writing. I kept my writing bundled up and hidden in the loft. One day Mama found the bundle and read some of the pages I'd written. She burned them all and told Dad about it. She said I was losing my mind from reading sinful old books all the time. I was furious that she had found my writing and had dared to destroy it. For months after that both of my parents watched me for any "bad signs."

7

It Was So Ordered

*Even in the dead of winter the promise of
springtime lies just upon the horizon, ready to
nose out winter with its fine-spun radiance.*

Being the oldest, I became almost like a second mother to my siblings. I was bossy, telling them what to do and when. Della resisted the most, and told Mama everything I said or did. Then Mama would sit me down and tell me straight what I could and could not do. Clara, the next sister, was mild-mannered and cried easily. I remember one game we played often—Farmer in the Dell. We made a circle and sang about the farmer; his wife, Lillie; and his farm animals. One by one they all died, and Lillie was left all alone. We sang mournfully about poor Lillie. At this point Clara would start crying, and at that we would laugh with glee, trying to shame her for crying. Today I regret how cruel we children were, especially to Clara.

The fourth child, Hazel, was born during the year we lived with Uncle Squire and Aunt Mossie on Ben's Branch. Hazel grew up to be a tall, slender woman with blond hair and blue eyes. She knew a sad life when she grew up. She met a man in Indianapolis, who courted her and persuaded her to go with him to Georgia. The wedding he arranged was fake, which Hazel discovered only later, when she got pregnant and the man abandoned her. She returned to Indianapolis and worked as a waitress until her son, Steven, was born. Steven was born prematurely and was not fully developed. By the time he was three, he began having seizures and going blind. Eventually he had to be put in a home. This broke Hazel's heart, but she couldn't work and take care of him. She would bring Steven home for weekends and holidays as often as she could.

When Hazel was forty-six, she brought Steven home for her birthday. That Saturday, sometime in the night, she suffered a massive stroke. She lay on her bedroom floor until the next day. Steven was too handicapped to use the phone. Our youngest sister, Sharon Rose, tried repeatedly to call Hazel, and finally went to check on her. Hazel was still alive when Sharon Rose found her; Hazel was rushed to the hospital. That morning I was called; the family told me to get to Indianapolis as quickly as I could. Hazel died an hour before my husband, Grant, and I got there. We stayed with Sharon Rose and her husband, Joe, until after Hazel's funeral. It broke my heart to think of Steven alone with Hazel, not able to understand what happened to his mother. Now in his forties, Steven is still living in a home for disabled men in Indianapolis.

After Hazel was born, Mama had three boys—Jeems, Fred, and Lee Roy. Then she gave birth to three more girls, Minnie, Lola, and Sharon Rose. When they grew up, Hazel, Clara, Minnie, Lola, and Sharon Rose all moved to Indianapolis to work. Lola and Sharon Rose were the only high school graduates in my family; Lola and I were the only ones to get a college degree.

When Della graduated from elementary school, it was possible for her to attend the Red Bird Mission High School. I was jealous because I didn't get to go; I had had to drop out of school early, and by this time I was married. But Della dropped out of high school in her junior year to get married. I did my best to persuade her to stay in school, but to no avail.

In all, Mama and Dad had ten children. By the time Sharon Rose was born I was fifteen, married, and living in my own home. My sisters all got married before they were twenty.

Sharon Rose, the youngest, was Mama and Dad's favorite child. They named her for the Rose of Sharon, found in the Bible. She was musically talented: she sang with a voice clear as crystal and played the piano by ear. After I learned to read music, every time I went home Sharon Rose would have already picked out songs for me to play. After she'd heard them once or twice, she could play them by ear. For a short time I paid for her to take piano lessons, but Mama and Dad didn't allow her to do this very long. They told me they knew God had given her the gift of music, and were afraid God would take away her gift if she took music lessons. I tried to reason with them, but got nowhere.

Dad had a rule: as soon as each of us reached the age of six, we must learn fieldwork. Sure enough, when I was six, Dad took me to an old worn-out field high up the mountain above Grandpa Saylor's house in Bingham Hollow. He, my grandfather, and my uncle Andrew were preparing the field for corn, grubbing small roots and stumps and piling them up, along with dead limbs and dry leaves, then setting the piles on fire. Smoke drifted over the hills, and the spring sunshine was almost too warm at times. I tried to help, but I soon became bored with the whole process.

I knew then that I would never like to work in the fields. As I got older, when I had to hoe out a patch of corn by myself I would get so bored hoeing one row after another that I would invent different ways to get it done. Sometimes I would hoe several rows out halfway to the end, then go to the other end and hoe back a fourth of the way. I enjoyed hoeing those shorter rows.

On this particular day, my first one hoeing in the field, tiny ground squirrels were frolicking and scrambling everywhere in the woods. They were surely going to dig up the corn as soon as it was planted. To eliminate as many of them as possible Grandpa had brought his twenty-two rifle with us to the field.

The gun was pointed downhill, leaning across a rotted stump. It caught my attention, and I went over for a closer look. I touched the highly polished gunstock and curled my fingers around the trigger—I had seen Dad and others pull back the trigger to make the gun shoot. Was it hard to do? The others were cutting brush and digging up roots; Grandpa was just down the hill setting fire to a pile of brush. No one was paying any attention to me.

I was fascinated with the gun and pulled back the trigger just to see if I could make it shoot. It sure did, and with quite the reverberating detonation. Grandpa lurched sideways and almost fell. He was not shot, just startled—and angry. The bullet had missed him by inches. All eyes turned toward me; Dad yelled and Uncle Andrew swore at me. I was mortified.

After Grandpa got over his shock he evenhandedly ordered me never to touch his gun again. I promised; and I have never since tampered with guns.

By late that afternoon the sun was shining horizontally against Pine Mountain. The soft rays detailed every sassafras, every sourwood, and every gnarled oak on the mountainside. It highlighted the big rocks, and the dark mouths of caves in the higher limestone ridges. I knew that soon it would be dusky dark, and time to go home.

It Was So Ordered

In the Appalachian Mountains it used to be that a man's word was his bond. He would no more think about not keeping his word than he would turn his children away hungry. All through my childhood I heard adults in the community use certain words and phrases to indicate a course of action. If they said they would be at a certain place the next day at noon, you could count on the fact that nothing except death would keep them away from that place. But there could be extenuating circumstances, they realized, and they worked those into their verbal agreements. For example, Dad and Grandpa would make promises this way: "If the Lord's willing, I will." Sometimes they would say, "If the Lord's willing and the creeks don't rise."

Over the years it seems to me that a man (or a woman's) word has lost its seriousness and has become so watered down it almost has no meaning. Today people will promise you anything, but they are like the Don Juans of the world, eternally running here and there, never remembering from one day to the next, making promises but not keeping them. It hurts my feelings when I hear country people say flippantly what Dad and Grandpa used to say in earnest: "If the Lord's willing and the creeks don't rise."

I remember a saying my mama always had for certain events. When something of note took place, whether it was good or bad, Mama would say, "Well children, it was so ordered." For a long time I wondered what she meant. When I got older I understood that she meant it was God's divine will.

Wilburn Saylor (1911–1966)

In March 1966 Dad was admitted to the Appalachian Regional Hospital in Middlesboro, Kentucky. I traveled from Berea, where I was living at the time, to be with my family on the day he was to have surgery. He had suffered for months from prostate trouble. The doctor finally decided the only solution was surgery. I spent the night before his surgery with Mama, and we got up early in the morning to be at the hospital. Dad came through the procedure really well, the doctor reported. By this time it was raining hard. I spent another night with Mama. Creeks were overflowing their banks, and the roads were washed out in places between Pineville and Barbourville, on the way to Berea, where I lived. I felt I needed to get home as soon as possible. My son, Bruce Alan, was only three years old, and I did not want to be away from him any longer.

I stopped by the hospital to tell Dad I had to go home. We visited a few minutes, and I got up to leave. "I wish you could stay longer," Dad said. I told him the reasons why I had to go home. At the door I turned and looked back. Dad was looking at me so intently, and with such love blazing in his eyes. I felt uneasy and hesitated at the door. Then, telling him good-bye again and that I loved him, I left.

Dad died days later. Mama, Della, and Minnie had gone to see him at the hospital. They talked with him a few minutes, and he said he was hungry. Della and Mama went to speak with the doctor, leaving Minnie alone with Dad. Suddenly he had a convulsion. Nurses and doctors came running, but he was dead in a matter of minutes. Mama came back to find him gone. I can't imagine how she must have felt.

Through my own shock, and my numb grief, I felt a small measure of comfort because Dad's life for the prior two decades had been one of faith in God.

I dealt with Dad's sudden death the way I deal with most things: I wrote about it.

He Is Dead to the Hills He Loved
He is dead to the hills he loved
They cannot call him back to live again.

But I remember him
When the fields are turned for planting,
When I hear silver winds of summer,
See wood smoke in the fall of the year,
And wild geese honk south for winter.

And I remember him
When there is rain on Pine Mountain,
When foxfire lights up dead logs at night,
When his bees work in the red clover
And wind whispers in the corn.

I remember
The day after the night he died—
Frost-white fodder in the shock,
Sumac leaves red enough to bleed,
Yellow dirt where we dug his grave.

He is dead to all he loved
We cannot call him back to live again.

Though I worked and revised this poem over a period of two years, and though it was eventually published, I was always a little dissatisfied with it because it ended on a sad and hopeless note. Eventually I started working on it again, writing version after version, until I came up with a very different poem.

On Streets of Gold
Dad's dead.
He'll never walk up Stoney Fork again,
Or take his dogs foxhunting in the hills at night.
The preacher says so.
Dad's gone on before us to heaven, the preacher says.
We won't see him again until we meet him in paradise.
Right now, the preacher says,

Brother Saylor is shouting up and down the streets of heaven.
When he gets tired of shouting for joy,
    He'll play on his harp awhile.
The preacher says he can see angels leaning on gates of pearl
    To welcome Brother Saylor home.
        I try very hard to see Dad on the golden streets.
        I strain to hear the strings of the harp he plays
        While angels listen.
        I can't see or hear him anywhere.

I get up to run from the church.
"She's taking it hard," I hear a woman say.
Outside I look at the ridges and valleys,
The hills where Dad loved to hunt.
    White clouds
    Driven by April winds,
    Move across the valley
    And cloud shadows glide over the ground.

I see Dad on the hill back of the church!
He and the Lord Jesus are walking and talking together.
Dad pulls down a branch of dogwood tree
As he points to the crown of thorns in the center
And the bloodstains in the outer edges of the petals.
A little farther on Dad scoops away dead leaves
That have drifted against a fallen tree,
Jesus bends over to look at a cluster
    Of blue Sweet Williams.
They stop for a moment and Jesus points to the
Smoky distance of mountain ranges, to white clouds
In the blue sky. They both turn quickly
To watch a red bird fly across the valley.

    White clouds fly fast in April winds.
    Shadows move across the ground.

Dad and the Lord Jesus have gone out of sight.
I will see them forever in my heart.

Finally, I could let Dad go. I knew he was in the light with God. We are from the light, and sooner or later we will go back to that light. If getting there requires death, so be it.

8
Honeybees and Birch Trees

I am passionate about each of the four seasons
and have no difficulty finding reasons for being so.

Dad, Grandpa, and several of my uncles each kept five or six hives of bees. Most of Dad's hives were homemade except for one lovely blue one; it looked so elegant and out of place sitting there in the row. I have often wished that I had asked him where he ever got such a pretty thing as that blue hive.

I have read that one of the more important and ancient foods in the wild was honey. The English brought the honeybee to America in the early 1600s. The settlers took colonies of bees with them as they moved west, and some swarms escaped, returning to the wildnerness from whence they had been captured thousands of years before.

If you found a bee tree and you marked it, even if it was on someone else's land, it was yours. The mark of the Saylor men was two parallel vertical slashes cut into the bark of the tree. This mark let everyone in the community know that the Saylors had claimed this tree. You had to get permission from the landowner to cut the tree, but since most of the mountains where we lived was "company land," Dad did not have to get permission to use the trees he found there. (Rich corporations bought mineral rights to thousands of acres of land for as little as fifty cents an acre. Some of them also bought timber rights. This land was called "company land.")

In order to get the bees and their honey out of the trees, we made "bee gums"—homemade beehives. Black gum trees are almost always hollow near the ground and can be made into excellent bee gums. Dad would cut a black gum and saw the trunk into appropriate lengths for a hive. Then he would hollow out the pieces, using a long chisel to round out and smooth down the insides. After this was done he bored four holes, one at each point of the compass, and put two sticks horizontally through the gum at right angles to each other, the ends of the sticks resting in the holes. Then Dad made a flat head for the top of the gum and put a slanted lid above the flat top to keep rain from running into the gum. Last of all, he cut a small half-circle (somewhat like mouse holes in comic strips and Tom and Jerry cartoons) in the bottom edge, thus making an entryway for the bees. Though the bees would enter at the bottom of the gum, they always chose the top half for their honey, suspending their brood combs from the top and using the crossed sticks as supports. When he was done, Dad would set his bee gums on a raised platform several inches off the ground.

To fill his new bee gums, Dad would go "coursing" the wild bees. He put corncobs soaked in honey in a cleared spot in the woods, sat down nearby, and waited for the bees to find the bait. Soon dozens of bees were attracted to the spot. When they rose up to fly home he noted the direction and followed. It might take several baits placed out before he could find the bee tree.

Dad cut bee trees early in the spring when there were plenty of blossoms from which they could make new honey. Bees began to swarm around the first of April. If they swarm much later, say in late June, they will not have enough time to collect the honey they need to see them through the winter. The day before this targeted time he would take a new bee gum and set it in place near the tree. Early the next day he and his helper (who was I, when I got big enough) carried a crosscut saw, axe, and a tub or large bucket in which to place the honey from the tree. Dad would notch the tree to get it to fall in a certain direction.

After the tree fell, he used a bee-smoker, in which he burned old rags, to puff billows of smoke around. This would make the bees settle. He also wore a mask and gloves as protection, although I did not think the bees would sting him. Dad said that bees could tell if a person was afraid. I tried not to be afraid but never quite succeeded; sometimes I was badly stung.

Dad brought the bee gum and positioned it near the fallen tree. If a tree was hollow, sometimes it split lengthwise when it fell, making his task simpler. He usually made a cut two or three feet above the hole where the bees were and another the same distance below, then split a place along the grain to expose the honey. Inside would be nothing but chaos—dead bees, smashed honey chambers, and the frightened bees.

Lifting out a piece of honeycomb, Dad put it inside the bee gum. Then he took out what honey he could salvage. In the process he could usually find the queen bee; he would set her near the hole in the bee gum. The attendant bees swarmed around her, and soon they all crawled into the hole. We let the bees settle overnight and then early next morning Dad went for them. He plugged up the hole and put a sheet over the bee gum to keep the bees inside while he carried it home. It was marvelous how well the bees survived the trauma and how quickly they set to work building new combs and filling the fresh cells with honey.

When the hive got overcrowded the bees swarmed. One of the queens would leave, taking a portion of the worker bees with her to a new home. Dad always seemed to know when it was time for bees to swarm. I asked him how he knew.

"It's simple," he replied. "All you have to do is watch for the signs. Nothing happens in nature without a sign being given."

Taking me to a hive he said, "Look at the pattern of bees outside on the front." Looking closer I could see bees clinging to the outside in the shape of a horseshoe. "Within three days that hive will swarm unless something is done to relieve the congestion," he said.

With modern beehives another compartment, called a "super," can be set on top of a crowded hive, and the bees will move up into it and start making honey there. Homemade gums could not be adapted that way, so Dad watched for the bees to swarm and tried to settle them down near a new bee gum.

When we needed honey Dad took it from the hives, but seldom more than once a year. We spoke of it as robbing the bees, and in a way that is exactly what we were doing. Dad liked to take honey during the new moon in June. This gave the bees plenty of time to replenish the honey before cold weather had a chance to set in. Sometimes on a country road outside Berea I see bees around a water hole, and I watch them rise, circle to get their bearings, and then take off, heading for their hives or bee trees. Sometimes, feeling very nostalgic, I remember the many times Dad coursed the bees and brought wild honey to our table.

Birch Sapping in June

A favorite excursion when I was a child was to go birch sapping. Every year during the first new moon in June, Mama and Aunt Mossie took us to the birch trees. Mama said the sap was best if it was taken during the first new moon in June. We always looked for a tree that was at least twenty-four inches in diameter, because a smaller tree would die if you removed too much bark. (Dad always cut the bark and stripped it away in a complete circle around any tree he wanted to kill in order to clear new ground for a patch of corn.) We carried buckets, spoons, and a hatchet or long sharp knife when we set out.

Once we had found a suitable tree, using the hatchet or knife, we cut a square or rectangular outline in the bark. After the patch was outlined we took a flat knife and inserted it under the bark all along the edges. When the piece was loosened so that we could get our fingers under the edges we stripped it from the tree. Then, as soon as each piece was taken from the tree, we used a large tablespoon to scrape the fiber from the inside of the bark. We'd drop the long strips of sappy fiber into a pail where we had put a quart or two of clear, sweet, spring water. The fiber had to get into the water quickly in order to keep from turning dark. When we had enough for our purposes, we added half a cup of sugar and let the mixture stand for about an hour or so in a cool place (we did not have refrigeration at that time). Once we drained off the liquid we had a delightful summertime drink. We'd also chew the fiber strips after we'd drained the sap, in order to tease out their last bit of sweetness.

Birch Sap Candy

We did not often make candy when I was a child because we had little money to buy sugar. We used honey and molasses as sweeteners in most of our baked products. We made molasses taffy and molasses butter.

I had read about people tapping sugar maples in New England and boiling down the juice into maple syrup. This sounded fascinating to me, and because I always loved the delicate flavor of birch and wondered how the sap would taste boiled down into candy, one spring when I was about twelve years old I decided to tap a birch tree. Early one morning I made my way to a good-looking birch, bored a small hole into its trunk, and inserted a hollow tube I had made by slipping a round of bark from a tree limb. I hung a small bucket under the tube and waited patiently for the sap to start flowing. But it dripped so slowly that I lost patience; leaving everything in place at the tree, I went home. Several hours later I went back to check and found about half a cup of liquid. Carefully pouring this into a jar, I again went home to wait a while longer.

Just before it got dusky dark, I went back to the birch tree and found another half cup of liquid. I carried the liquid home. To make the candy I added about two cups of sugar to the cup of birch sap and poured it into a kettle to boil.

When a small amount formed a hard ball when the hot mixture was dropped in water, I decided the candy was ready. I poured it onto a flat, oiled surface, as I had seen Mama do when she made taffy. When the mixture was partly cooled but before it hardened, I marked the surface in squares. I made the cuts deep so that the candy could be broken along the lines when it was cold.

When the candy hardened, it looked like a clear sheet of ice. The result was great; my sisters and brothers loved the birch candy as much as I did.

Bloodroot

What an explosion of memories comes to me when I think of bloodroot. I remember how we picked bloodroot flowers to decorate our playhouses and ourselves in my childhood years on Straight Creek and Stoney Fork.

When I began working in the Special Collections Department of the Berea College Library, I had the chance to research just about any subject that I wanted to know about. I found out some interesting facts about bloodroot.

Bloodroot is named for the red-orange sap that flows whenever you break its thickened root. My sisters and I used the juice to paint our fingernails and toenails and anything else we wanted to paint. We were disappointed that it washed off so easily, because we wanted to keep our painted nails all day.

In the hills of Stoney Fork, sometimes bloodroot bloomed as early as February, but it usually was not among the first flowers of spring. Solitary flower buds emerge sheathed inside rolled-up leaves that gradually relax as the flowers open. Each blossom consists of eight to sixteen petals arranged in rows around bright-yellow stamens. After the flowers drop, rich, green, deeply lobed leaves carpet the ground until late summer.

I wanted to transplant bloodroot in my yard after I got married. I found out that fall and winter are the best times for transplanting bloodroot. But you can divide it in late summer or early fall. Make sure your soil is moist, well drained, and replete with organic matter. Set the root lengthwise into the ground, about one inch deep, with the buds pointing up. Space the plants about six to eight inches apart.

I read that American Indians used bloodroot sap in a number of ways. The men dabbed it on as war paint, while the women used it to dye baskets and cloth. The sap was also used as cough medicine. Considering that it contains a potentially lethal alkaloid, this seemed a bit like using a mallet on a mosquito, I thought.

Special June Days and July a Delight

In June we would begin to harvest produce from our garden. I will never forget the satisfaction of eating tender new beans, new potatoes, tomatoes and cucumbers, sweet corn, a pan of hot, golden cornbread, and cold milk or ice tea. Admittedly, if we'd had a cold spring we might not see tomatoes and green beans until July. But they will always be associated in my mind as June foods.

There are other special days in June, days that bring back memories of when I was a child. My mother was born on June 22, 1909, in Leslie County, Kentucky, on Laurel Branch. (Dad's birthday was in the summertime, too: August 12, 1911.) She and Dad were married in June 1930.

The middle brother, Fred, was born June 16, 1943. Other days in June are also memorable. Many people universally hold Father's Day dear. My husband Grant was born June 19, 1947. (When Grant and I married, my son Bruce suddenly had three presents to buy on Father's Day—one for his dad, one for Grant, and another for Grant's birthday, which often coincided with Father's Day.)

I always loved the month of July. It meant pure summer—generous sunshine—wondrous green leaves and grass. Perhaps because it is Independence month, it makes me think of the phrase "July Jubilee." In July especially, the landscape and sounds of the forest, the look of the moon at night, the slant of light during the day, and the falling rain all give me a deeper perception, a keener awareness of what the word has to offer. When we have a cold, wet spring, it is sheer delight to soak up July's warmth.

Blackberries

I have mixed feelings about berry-picking in June and July. On the one hand, I enjoy eating the ripe berries. But on the other hand, *they have to be picked first*. This was chigger feast time and also the time for wood ticks, which would become badgering pests if we were not careful. And we also had to watch out for snakes.

Granny Brock would carry a stout stick and walk ahead of us children, beating the weeds and making as much noise as she could to scare the snakes away. It was scary to be standing still while she did this, and then suddenly see the tall grass start swaying ahead of us or around the side of the hill, something moving through it. It might just have been a rabbit or other small creature. But we were convinced it was a snake Granny had scared into running away.

I tried to be brave as I poked my hands into the green-matted briars to grab those perfect, plump berries. Yet I spent so much time looking out for snakes Granny could pick two buckets for every one of mine. The blue-black berries often tempted us at first. But eating a few would usually sate our appetites.

Granny Brock or Mama would make the blackberries into a hot cobbler for supper, and would use them to make jam for future biscuits. After feasting on fried chicken, simmered green beans, tomatoes, and golden cornbread, blackberry cobber made a perfect finish to our July supper.

When huckleberries ripened, it was usually the men and bigger boys who went to pick them. Huckleberries grew on the top of hills and ridges, and they were difficult to find and pick. Huckleberry picking was considered men's work.

One day, however, Dad took me with him to pick huckleberries. I cannot quite remember what made him decide to let me join him, but I do remember how excited I felt and how I bragged to Della. She wanted to go with us, but Dad said no, it was too rough a trip for her. Dad and I climbed up the hillside and worked our way around the ridge until we found a growth of huckleberry bushes. I was not afraid of snakes or anything else because I knew Dad would not let anything hurt me.

We started picking, and the sun climbed higher and higher in the sky. By the time it was directly overhead I was tired, hungry, and thirsty.

Dad found a little cleared space in a sheltered area and built a small fire. He cut three or four limbs from a bush and sharpened the ends. Then he took a piece of lean bacon and a piece of cornbread out of his hunting pouch. He cut small chunks of bacon and speared them onto the sticks. We held these over the fire until the meat was cooked. A chunk of bacon broiled over a fire and eaten with cornbread, the hot grease soaking into the bread, made a tasty meal there on top of that hill.

One July day, Dad, my sister Della, and I were hoeing corn. The field we had planted was not far from a little country store. Dad said he would get us something to eat at the store. At noon, he bought "viennie" sausages (only years later did I learn about a city in Austria named Vienna), a can of sardines, and saltines. He got each of us a bottle of cold pop to drink, and we carried our lunch back to the edge of the cornfield to eat. Dad ate the sardines, but Della and I preferred the sausages. Nothing in this world has ever tasted any better to me than those Vienna sausages, crackers, and orange pop.

That store was my haven. Its nooks and crannies became as familiar to me as my mother's kitchen. We kids earned spending money by gathering bottles to return for deposit (five cents per bottle). Candy was five cents a bàr, bubble gum a penny apiece. Pencils also sold for a penny each, while Blue Horse writing tablets cost a nickel. I loved paper and pencils.

Recently some out-of-state friends came for a visit. We drove from Berea several miles out into the country to the Drip Rock Fire Tower. Stopping at a country store along the way, I bought an orange pop and a can of Vienna sausages, hoping to recreate that delicious long-ago lunch in our cornfield. But they tasted nothing like what I ate in the cornfield that July day. I was disappointed.

When I am in pain or feel the world is closing in on me, just one thing will make me feel better: to cook food like Mama did when we lived on Stoney Fork. Green beans, fried corn, biscuits, fried chicken and gravy, mashed potatoes, baked ham, homemade pickles, soup beans with ham—these are foods I take out and savor in my memory, even if I am not prepared to cook foods like that for my next meal. Usually, though, when I'm feeling low I wind up cooking at least one dish like my mother did.

Dog Days of Summer

The dog days of summer runs from July until mid-August, when the Dog Star rises and sets with the sun. The dictionary definition is that dog days are the stifling hot days of summer. It is a season of mold, mildew, and the pestilence of stagnant water.

Mama and Granny Brock warned us about dog days. We children were not to wade in the creeks because the stagnant water would make "fall sores" on our legs. I remember how impossible it was to stay out of the creek during the torrid days of summer, when every bug bite and scratch turned into a sore. There would be four or five sores on our legs and arms during late summer until cooler weather set in.

We were told that dogs went mad during dog days, so we were terrified of any strange dog that happened to wander our way. The rumor that a possibly mad dog was spotted in the neighborhood was enough to send us inside, locking the doors and vigilantly guarding the windows. We were also told that snakes went blind during dog days, striking out savagely at anything that moved.

During dog days, in addition to hot, sultry days there were days of rain. I thought of rainy days as days of freedom from the sweat bees, briars, and the duty of hoeing corn in the hot sunshine. I would take a book to the corncrib or barn, where I could spend hours in another world, reading and being comforted by the sound of rain on the roof. To this day, when it rains I feel an urge to snuggle up in a dry place with a good book.

9

Transition to Harvest

Sometimes it almost seems a burden to realize
the promise of summer when red and white
clover blooms and green corn uncurls, when
butterflies come in clouds of color and a misty
rain washes the earth.

Always in early spring, Dad began clearing off new ground in preparation for a field of corn. He liked to plant a new field every year, along with the old ones. We planted corn as early as possible and by the middle of May, if the weather was good, it was ready for the first hoeing. When the rows of corn were shoulder-high, Mama would stick in half-runner beans, which would grow up and twine around the cornstalk. This kept the beans off the ground and made picking them easier. The beans never hurt the corn.

Dad said that corn must be hoed three times, the third (and last) time called "laying it by." If it was a good growing season, the corn could be laid by before the Fourth of July. In fact, it was a matter of pride for every household to have their corn laid by before the Fourth.

When I was a child, we might have to chop the weeds from between the rows of corn after laying it by, but we'd never have to hoe it again that season. When green ears appeared on the stalks, we could hardly wait for the corn to mature so we could eat it in a variety of ways.

Jarflies

When I was young, every summer I would hear the queer, metallic whir of the jarfly in the mountains while waves of heat shimmered from the fields and pastures.

Usually jarflies start their hollering in the summer, around the last days of June. It was a signal that the plowing and hoeing of corn could be laid by. "There used to be a lot more of them," Granny Brock said. "They hollered so loud people couldn't hear the cowbells."

Occasionally I would hear the high-pitched cry of a seventeen-year locust, or cicada, from a distant treetop. I was fascinated with the story of the seventeen-year locusts—how they lay dormant for seventeen years, then move in clouds, thousands and thousands of them devouring all the fruit, berries, and garden produce in their path. I read about them in the *Farmer's Almanac,* and I asked Mama to tell me everything she had ever heard about them. I sometimes found empty shells of these insects beneath the apple trees, with a split down the backs the sign of their freedom. I thought of all the years that they lay dormant, waiting for their summer of release. One day when we heard the locusts' shrill cry, I said to Mama, "They must be cries of victory."

Predictions of the Weather

Of course we had all sorts of sayings about the weather. Early mornings in the mountains, tendrils of fog would often curl their way into the sky from the hilltops. When the mist rose a certain way, it was believed to be a sure sign of rain. The old mountain saying "Fog on the hills brings water to the mill" was often repeated.

There is an old rhyme about St. Swithin's Day, July 15: if it rains on St. Swithin's Day, it will rain for the next forty days; if it is fair on July 15, it will be fair for forty days.

Another saying was "Rain before seven, quit before eleven." There was also an old Indian saying, "Cloudy all around, pouring down in the middle."

I was taught to believe in signs, sayings, and predictions, and when it came to the weather, I believed them all.

Heritage Seeds

Dead leaves, stems of dry plants, and yellow and brown grass all told of cycles and seasons. I am glad when the time of mold, mildew, and stagnant water has passed. Even if I hold a thread of regret that summer's promise is almost over, I look forward to gathering and storing in preparation for the winter months. Each season of the year brings blessings and gifts.

I always long to hold on to the crisp, refreshing air of early fall, the white morning mist, and the golden dust of fall evenings. I wish I could hoard those days in a treasure chest so that in the dead of winter I could take them out and enjoy a day of sunshine and blue skies. Part of the melancholy we feel in autumn is knowing that summer has gone; and when autumn ends then come the gray days and cold rain of November and December.

My mother always saved seed from each year's crop to plant the next year. She would plant some "seed hills," let the beans dry on the plant, and save them for seed. She grew "greasy-back" beans, which we loved. They grew six or more beans to a pod. Mama kept her own seed from year to year from the tender plants, and never took a chance on store-bought seed because, as she said, "they might have tough seed mixed in with the tender seed."

Mama and Dad raised bushels of potatoes and onions to store. They had turnips and mustard greens and pumpkins and cushaws ready just after the first frost. And sometime around the middle of the growing season, Mama would plant several rows of late beans. I love green fall beans when they first come out of the kettle, especially if they have been seasoned with a piece of well-cured, dried-out, properly aged fatback. But they are even better when they have been warmed over a time or two until the cooking water gets good and thick. If you pour some of that thick "pot likker" over a chunk of cornbread and let it soak in a bit, you have a wonderful accompaniment to the beans. These late beans Mama simply called "fall beans." She kept the seed for them alive year after year. I depended on Mama to save seed for me.

Mama would also save a few of the biggest, most perfect tomatoes. When they were fully ripe, she scraped out the seed, which she dried in the sun and then stored in a jar until early spring. She planted the tomato seed in a galvanized washtub, which could easily be covered during frosty nights, and set out the transplants when the ground got warm.

Every year we would find tomatoes growing in the places where a tomato had rotted, or tomato peel and seeds had been dumped. These we called "Tommy Toes," and it was incredible how strong and vigorous the plants were and how the small, round tomatoes would be bursting with flavor. Today at the farmers market, I buy cherry tomatoes. But they never taste as good as the sweet, sound flesh of the Tommy Toes in our garden, and the skins of the cherry tomatoes are tougher.

Canned tomatoes were a beautiful sight on the pantry shelves. But they took a lot of peeling, coring, seeding, cooking, stirring, sterilizing, and processing. It is much easier to freeze tomatoes. But frozen tomatoes are watery by comparison with canned, and they are not as tasty or versatile. However, when we got electricity on Stoney Fork and purchased a freezer, I began freezing most of my tomatoes. I like having tomatoes for soups, catsup, and juice in the winter, and the steam that's generated from making catsup and juice is always more welcome in the house at that time of the year than it is in the summer.

I am glad that there are gardeners today who continue to preserve specimens and seeds of many of the old plants our forebears loved—delphiniums strong enough to stand alone, dianthus that smell of cloves, and tomatoes that taste like Tommy Toes. Tommy Toes are probably growing in somebody's garden or field even as I write.

The last few years when I have bought half-runner beans, I have been disappointed with how tough they are. They must have been from altered seed—not heritage seed like Mama's.

Rachel Saylor (1909–1986)

My mother died in 1986 at seventy-seven years of age. She never remarried after Dad died and cherished memories of him all of her life. For a long while she suffered with congestive heart disease, but the day she died was one of the best days she had had in years.

Brother Jeems said she cooked a good dinner that Sunday. She was cheerful, laughing and talking with him. She told him she would like to go to church that night. Jeems drove her to the little Holiness Church on Stoney Fork, which they attended when they were able.

During the service Mama gave her testimony, and asked for special prayers for her children. When Jeems and Mama got back home, she began having an attack of shortness of breath. Immediately Jeems took her to the kitchen door near where the car was parked. At the door, she put her hands on the doorframe and wouldn't go outside. Jeems asked her if she wanted to go to the hospital; she shook her head no. He half-carried her to her bedroom and put a blanket over her. He called Della, who lived only a few doors up from them. Della came immediately, and Mama died in her arms. When Jeems called me to tell me what had happened, I said, "I'm glad she won't suffer anymore." I felt at peace about her transition.

Brother Jeems's Green Thumb

My brothers Fred and Lee Roy both married young, but Jeems did not marry until he was older, and then, after the birth of a daughter, got a divorce.

When he was twenty, Jeems was diagnosed with juvenile diabetes. Every day thereafter, he had to inject himself with insulin. He did a poor job of controlling his sugar, and by the time he was in his late thirties he had eye damage. This forced him to give up his job as a county school bus driver, and it was almost impossible for him to find another job.

His health kept failing; he developed heart trouble and suffered a series of prostate infections. Jeems lived with Mama and helped care for her until her death. She took care of him when he had bad spells, and he did the same for her. Eventually he was entitled to receive Social Security payments.

After Mama's death in 1986, Jeems lived alone. He could not see well enough to drive and was dependent on others to take him where he needed to go. Mostly he just stayed home alone.

At first he continued to live in the little house Mama had left him, but the mortgage payments got to be more than he could handle. Eventually Jeems sold the house and was able to move into a government-subsidized high-rise apartment complex near Pineville, Kentucky. His apartment was tiny, consisting of a galley kitchen, a living room, a bedroom, and a bathroom. There were sliding glass doors in the living room and bedroom.

Mama had a green thumb; anything she stuck in the ground grew vigorously in her care. When Jeems moved to the apartment, he brought with him some of Mama's houseplants. He took delight in and cared for the plants just as she had. Every plant stayed healthy and proliferated.

Jeems and I both took after Mama when it came to plants. I grow plants and trees in every room of my house. In my kitchen window I have pots of geraniums and petunias, which are in full bloom as I write. During the recent snow and ice, I would stand and look at the pink and white petunias and the red geraniums and marvel at the fresh beauty of the delicate flowers. I love each plant, and I'm glad to have them in my home.

I started taking Jeems any extra plants I had on hand. Other women in our extended family would bring their puny, sick plants to him, and invariably Jeems would coax them back to health. Sometimes their owners would take them back home, but every once in a while they would tell Jeems to keep the plants. Soon his apartment was crowded with plants. The plants were his family, his children. He loved each one and spent many hours working with them. People who visited him for the first time were always surprised when they came into his living room, because it looked like a greenhouse.

I was proud that Jeems had found a love for trees and plants and kept busy caring for and loving them. Lord knows he had little else. He could not read or watch much television because of his eyesight. He was not able to go places and do things physically, but he kept his mental health.

Meanwhile I kept adding to his collection. Anytime I found a particular type of plant that Jeems did not have, I got it for him. Other family members would smile indulgently at Jeems and all his plants, and said they could never get plants to grow that way. Jeems just grinned at them; he would not even try to verbalize his love and commitment to his plants and trees.

I once gave him a deep pink hibiscus that had eight to ten blooms at a time all summer long on my front steps. I really did not have a good place to keep it over the winter, so I offered it to Jeems and he readily accepted it.

Several weeks later in a phone conversation he told me all the leaves were falling off the hibiscus. I reassured him as best I could, suggesting that the climate change may have been a shock.

The next time we talked, he told me sadly that he thought the plant was going to die. I said rather flippantly that he should start talking to it. He should tell it to live and bloom or he would throw it into the trashcan. Jeems had never heard about talking to plants, and I know he thought it was a weird suggestion. A couple of weeks later I asked if the hibiscus plant had died. He was silent for a moment, then said, "I reckon I've been talking to it, telling it what you said."

"Can you tell any difference?"

"It put out green shoots and now it's full of buds!"

When still in his fifties, Jeems moved like a much older man. He talked about his impending death. His dearest wish was that people take his plants and care for them as he had.

When Brother Jeems died in 2001, in a way his going was a relief to us. He had suffered so much and lived such a lonely life for so many years. He had told me on several occasions of his wish to die. He really had no quality of life because of his illness and handicaps.

My youngest sister, Sharon Rose, took most of his plants home to Indianapolis with her after the funeral. The remainder his former wife shared with her friends.

I used to call Jeems every Sunday. I miss those talks. But I believe that he is at peace and happy to be home with the family members who left before him.

10

Sweet and Meat

*Making molasses is a ritual of autumn as old as
any civilization that has endured in the hills.*

We always had molasses at our house because almost every year Dad
and some of his brothers, along with Grandpa, planted a cooperative
crop of cane. From this one patch they would get enough molasses to
supply their families for the entire year. And, like other of their recipro-
cal understandings, if they did not plant cane one year, they helped their
neighbors cut, gather, and process their crops through the stir-off process
and received gallons of molasses in return.

Molasses: Amber Magic

Early in the fall when the cane was ripe, Dad and his brothers cut it and
separated the stalks from the blades. Sometimes they cut a piece of cane
into joints and gave them to us children to chew for juice. The juice was
wonderfully sweet and satisfying, but we had to be careful not to cut our
lips on the sharp and biting edges of the bark.

When the cane was harvested, the men dug a trench, built up low rock
ledges on each side, and set in place the long cane press vat they used to
boil the juice. Not everyone could afford a cane press; usually one man in
the community would buy one and loan it out for use.

A toll of a quart of molasses was the fee in Stoney Fork for using the
cane press. When the vat was in place, Dad cleaned the cane mill and got
it ready for use the next day. Last of all, the helpers cut enough wood to
feed the fire several hours. Word would already have gone out that a big

stir-off was taking place the next day, and everyone in the neighborhood felt free to drop by.

Early the next morning Dad hitched Old Bob, our mule, to the cane mill and delegated Jeems to watch him and see that he walked at a steady, even gait. He hitched Old Bob to a long pole, or "sweep." A rod had been mounted horizontally in, and at right angles to, the butt end of the sweep and a line tied to it, which ran to Old Bob's halter. When the sweep was pulled forward, the line connected to the butt would keep pulling the mule around in a circle. The sweep turned a crusher roller in the mill, which in turn engaged another roller, forcing it to turn also. The men fed the cane in between the rollers.

The cane was fed into the mill on one side, the rollers crushed it dry, and green juice came out the other side into a trough that ran down to a covered container. From there it was taken to the boiler and poured through several layers of cheesecloth to filter it before it entered the vat. They would fill the vat to within two or three inches of the top. The vat held about eighty gallons of juice, which boiled down to eight to ten gallons of molasses.

Neighbors up and down the road gathered, eager to sample the molasses and have a good time. They brought buckets, jars, and bowls to carry home some of the finished product. As the juice boiled down they skimmed off the rich, yellow foam with wooden paddles or spoons and ate their fill as they sat or stood in groups and talked, or joined in singing, square dancing, or playing ball.

I have since learned that for hundreds of years molasses was considered a poor substitute for sugar, its pungent flavor being found unsuitable for the finer tables and the more developed palates in the land. Only wealthy people could afford the expense of sugar; the less affluent had to rely on other means of sweetening their food, such as using molasses and honey.

The early settlers in America had little choice when it came to sweetening because until the mid-nineteenth century refined sugar was prohibitively expensive and difficult to obtain. Maple sugar and maple syrup were available in some areas, but by the eighteenth century most families in America used molasses in a variety of ways—to moisten their hoecakes, in baked beans, to sweeten pork dishes, and to make steamed Indian pudding palatable.

Pioneer women found that because molasses had such an intense flavor it stood up well to heavy spicing in foods—ginger in gingerbread; allspice in rich, moist fruitcake; mustard with tender baked beans; and cloves in succulent cuts of pork. Another good companion to molasses was whole grains, such as water-ground cornmeal, stone-ground whole wheat, and tangy rye, which women used to make loaves of chewy, nutritious bread.

When sugar-refining methods were developed and the price of sugar went down, more and more housewives began to relegate molasses to the category of specialty foods. In Appalachia, molasses never lost its important place on the pantry shelves. Women could be more lavish in its use in baked goods because it was made at home and therefore relatively inexpensive. It is ironic that molasses, so long out of favor with the average cook because of its humble connotations, is now much more expensive than refined sugar.

I think of autumn as stir-off days. During the summer months the mountains seem to sink in hazy sleep, their topmost peaks wrapped in blue smoke. But when fall weather comes they wake up and explode in color. During this pause between sleepy summer and shivering winter, when the nights turn cool but the sky is blue in the daytime and the sun shines warm and bright, mountain people would harvest their crops and make molasses, just as their forefathers did in the oldest of times.

Butchering Time

Memories of fall seasons of my childhood bring back thoughts of pawpaws and persimmons, walnuts and hickory nuts, potatoes and cabbages, late apples, and other delicious things to gather and eat. For us children, autumn also meant looking forward to the first snowfall and to the holidays of Thanksgiving and Christmas.

At this time of year, we would be getting ready to butcher the hogs Dad had been fattening in pens for a few weeks. The hogs ran wild in the mountains. Dad and Grandpa caught them and put them into pens to harden their fat before they were butchered around Thanksgiving when it just had begun to get cold enough. We had no electricity to run refrigerators and freezers, so the weather had to be cold enough to chill the meat.

Mama, my sisters, and I dreaded this chore. Dad usually just had a handsaw and a sharp butcher knife to cut the meat. Everything was done the hard way. Mama used a hand grinder to grind all the fat for lard and to use in sausage. She depended on the children to help do the major part of this arm-wrenching, backbreaking chore. Mama would start rendering kettles of lard, then frying the sausage before canning it. I remember all too well the feel of the greasy handle of the sausage mill and the smell of hot grease.

Since the pork sausage, chops, and tenderloins could not be kept in the smokehouse with the rest of the meat without spoiling, they were cooked and canned with lard, rendered out from the same hog. Mama would also can the ribs and backbone. It was good to have hot pork, sauerkraut, and a square of cornbread to eat on a cold winter's day.

Dad would cure the hams, side meat, and shoulders in a brown sugar and salt brine, and then he would hang them up to smoke in the smokehouse. This was the hard way to do it, but modern meat-processing methods can never produce the flavor of that pork.

We used every scrap of the hog; nothing went to waste. Mama would make souse out of the head, cooking it until the meat fell off the bone. The pig ears were cooked tender and chopped along with the head meat. The chopped meat and broth were then mixed with fresh chopped garlic, onion, dill pickles, sage, a little vinegar, and salt and pepper. The mixture was placed in loaf pans and chilled overnight. It could then be turned out on a platter and sliced. The feet (minus the hooves) were scraped, cooked tender, and pickled.

It shocks some people when I mention some of the things we used to eat. Chicken feet, for example. Mama would chop off the toes, parboil and peel the feet, then dip them in seasoned flour and fry them. We children never fought to get a fried chicken foot, but we ate them if we were told to do so. We were never allowed to waste a scrap of food.

Winter's Counsel

Mama and Dad were married during the Great Depression, but they knew before then that life was hard and everyone had to make do with what they had. I remember how I detested garden peas. If I ate just one or two peas, I would get a headache. It was a point of contention for a while between Mama and me, but eventually I outgrew my dislike, and today I love fresh garden peas.

There was never any problem getting us to eat what was set before us. There was no "I don't like that" or "I'm not going to eat this" at our house—we knew we could either eat it or go hungry.

I used to think the November hills always had sad faces, and I was always glad to see December spread out a white veil to cover the mountains when winter was upon us. When the snowy days of winter file across the land of the summer's dead, I think of gray nuns walking through an orchard counting the seasons lost while prepensely counting those ahead.

During this time of year we hear the word "season" more than any other time of the year. There is the "holiday season" leading up to New Year's Day. We also speak of the "cold season," the "flu season," the "rainy season," and others. When I was young, I felt the turning seasons of the year in my heart, and now, as I get older, I feel them also in my bones!

Hearing Colors, Making Wreaths

The fall and early winter season brings me thoughts of warm, fuzzy things. I yearn for cozy places, good books, and the company of loved ones. Nature brings a wide selection of colors in the fall, and technology brings vivid hues as the holiday season approaches.

I love the colors of things. I invite colors to drift before my closed eyes, holding each for a deep look, then sending it along to make room for others. At the same time I "hear" the colors, as if each were spoken aloud. Each color seems to have its own resonance, its own glowing health.

In school I could hardly wait for the teacher to give us pictures to color for the holidays. My favorite pictures were of Christmas wreaths.

When I got older I researched how wreaths came into being. I found out that they existed in ancient cultures and were a symbol of royalty when worn around the head. They were called diadems—from a Greek word meaning to bind around. Fresh laurel and oak leaves were used for garlands, which became symbols of power for political and military leaders. Leaves were used as prizes to recognize athletes. This practice probably brought about the phrase "to earn your laurels" or "Don't rest on your laurels." The olive branch also has become a symbol of peace.

Head wreaths became status symbols, which led to the development of ornate crowns for the elite. A crown of thorns was used when Christ was crucified as an act of ridicule and humiliation. Wreaths also became a symbol of love. An unending circle that symbolizes eternity, the wreath was used to commemorate the missing spirit at the most somber of events, funerals.

History does not tell us when the wreath as a head adornment was adapted to a wreath as a door or wall decoration. Traditionally in our country, wreaths have hung on entrance doors or over the fireplace. They seem to reflect the mood or ambience of whatever the occasion happens to be. Wreaths are used today to beautify as well as to reflect personality and color.

Barbara Power is the head of the circulation desk at the college library where I worked for twenty-four years. She and her late husband, Paul, lived in Berea. Barbara is a talented gardener, clever with needle and thread, and skilled with various handicraft materials.

One year she made a large dried wreath that she hung over her buffet in the dining room. The wreath was composed of various kinds of dried materials, including tiny pink rosebuds. When the library staff gathered at her house for a Christmas potluck, I stood for several moments, admiring the flawlessly crafted decoration.

Mountain craftspeople use dried nuts, pinecones, and other materials to make wreaths in natural shades of brown and sand, which they sell in craft shops every Christmas. One year I decided to make one just like theirs, although I was neither as skilled nor as talented as they in being able to capture the mood of the season using such items. Nevertheless, I made a wreath and hung it in my house. All through that Christmas season, whenever it was quiet and peaceful, we'd hear a sharp crack or a dull thud, depending on whether it was a nut or a pinecone falling to the hardwood floor, bouncing and rolling.

I discarded that poor wreath, and never tried to make another with nuts, pinecones, and a hot glue gun. Of course, my son Bruce has managed to introduce suggestions and comments about "Mom's Christmas wreath" every Christmas since, warning others in the house to watch out for "Mom's wreath" or they might get poked in the head with a buckeye or pinecone.

II

Winter's Hunger and Cold

*When winter comes the ground freezes, and all
signs of growing things are removed.*

The winter months always remind me of cold and hunger. I don't
know why this should be because even in Appalachia we always had
food to eat. It may have been only a kettle of pinto beans cooked with a
ham bone, a bowl of fried potatoes, and home-canned pickles with a pan
of hot cornbread, but it was filling, and we never went to bed with empty
stomachs.

Perhaps the memory of cold and hunger has a racial or ethnic origin.
Through stories and accounts handed down from one generation to another we all knew of starvation, the inability to pay rent, and being cast
out into the cold by ruthless landlords.

Grandpa told me that our ancestors were forced to leave the Highlands of Scotland and go to Ireland, where they lived and intermarried
until the great potato famine came, driving some of them out of Ireland,
leaving them with no choice but to immigrate to the New World. When
they arrived, the more accessible parts of the country were already settled
and turned into towns and cities. My ancestors kept moving until they
arrived in western North Carolina. They found the mountains to be somewhat similar to the land from which they had come, making it seem natural to settle there.

Eventually half the group went into Virginia and the other half came
into the Kentucky mountains, where they homesteaded in the hollows and
valleys with no one house in sight of another. My many-times-removed
great-grandpa cleared land at the head of Stoney Fork. His children settled

in hollows around him and their children did the same, until Stoney Fork was populated with Saylors.

Irish Potatoes

In the Kentucky mountains where I grew up, some farmers planted their potatoes on March 17 through swirling snowflakes, because St. Patrick's Day was the traditional potato-planting day. Others waited until the hundredth day of the year (April 10) to put out their potatoes. I don't know what special significance was attached to that day.

We called white potatoes "Irish potatoes" and, along with dried beans, they composed the backbone of our diet. Perhaps because of our Scots-Irish inheritance, we had an inborn love for potatoes. But then good country grub has always included beans and potatoes. Sunday dinners always featured a huge bowl of fluffy mashed potatoes, and through the week we ate potatoes boiled, fried, baked, and creamed. Our favorite potato dish was the tiny new potato that we "graveled" out with a fork early in the growing season, after which we covered the hole. Mama served them with a white sauce. Dad fussed that we were destroying his crop by graveling the new potatoes, but he always ate them as eagerly as we did.

Anytime we went on a picnic we packed Mama's big iron skillet and some potatoes. To my way of thinking there is nothing in the world half so good as potatoes fried in an iron skillet over a campfire, along with boiled coffee.

Another favorite was Mama's potato cakes. She would use leftover mashed potatoes, mix in one or two chopped onions, add an egg, and mix well. She fried the little round cakes in bacon grease until they were golden brown. I make potato cakes that taste like dressing by adding chopped celery, a pinch of sage, chopped onion, and an egg. Another variation: instead of patties I put the mixture in a buttered casserole dish and bake it in the oven until lightly browned on top.

During winter days and evenings when we wanted a snack, we would put potatoes in the hot ashes in the fireplace and roast them. This gave them a wonderful taste, far superior to baked potatoes. Perhaps the wood ashes and smoke were responsible for the flavor. When they were done we would rake them out, peel off the skins, season them with butter and salt, and eat them hot. When the potatoes that we had planted had matured and were dug up in the fall, Dad put them into burlap sacks, hauled the sacks to the corncrib, and spread them out to dry. Just before cold weather froze the ground he would "hole them up" for winter.

First he dug a big, round hole in the garden nearest the house. He would line the hole with straw and add enough potatoes to make a big mound above the ground. Then he put straw over the top of the mound, packing it carefully along all the edges. He covered the mound with a layer of dirt. Last of all he would put flat boards over the top, slanting them toward the ground at one end to drain off water. During the wintertime, we would dig in the side of the mound and reach through the straw to take as many potatoes as were needed.

Potatoes holed up this way kept sound and good through most of the winter. They did not shrivel or rot, although they did begin to sprout when the ground warmed up in early spring. Dad holed up cabbage the same way when we had a good crop, and sometimes apples, too, although they did not keep as well as cabbage or potatoes.

Corn to the Gristmill

Dad took our corn down the creek to Morgan Helton's gristmill to be ground. I always begged to go with him, but usually Mama said no, because the men were apt to drink and play cards while they waited for their corn to be ground. It was awesome to me how the waterwheel turned the stones to grind the grains of corn.

Early pioneer farmers had to grind their grain by hand, with mortars or hand-stones called "quern," until the arrival of the waterwheel in the late 1700s revolutionized the process. The first millers brought the knowledge required to build gristmills with them from England. Soon, many small towns and communities in the region had their own gristmills.

The gristmills in the mountains varied in size and efficiency, even though the waterwheel was the core of every mill. Some mills had waterwheels outside the building; when they were inside they were called turbines or "tub" wheels. Buckets or troughs attached to the wheel filled with water, which spilled into the next bucket, causing the wheel slowly to turn. Wheels of this type, where the water flows from the top, are referred to as "overshot"; those using water that is carried upward from the bottom is described as "undershot."

I learned that there were two ways of powering the mills. Logs or stones might be stretched across a stream to create a millpond. Water rushing through a controlled sluice (a boxed-in channel) in the dam passed over or under the wheel. The water turned the wheel, thus setting in motion cogs, shafts, and pulleys in the mill that powered the grinding stones. Another way was to divert water from nearby streams and channel it through pipes to the edge of the mill, then shoot it into buckets in the waterwheel.

Millstones usually came from local quarries, but a few "French bur" stones were imported from France. Two stones four feet in diameter were placed one on top of the other; the bottom stone was stationary. Half-inch grooves cut in the center of the stones enabled corn fed from a hopper down between the stones to grind the corn and pass it outward into a pulley-operated conveyor that moved it to a box ready for sacking.

Back in pioneer days, the miller would set certain "mill days" when settlers could bring in their corn to be ground. The trip could be dangerous because of the Indians, but the pioneers would make the trip nevertheless. The gristmill was both a social meeting place and a necessity.

Fire was one nemesis of gristmills, and floods were another. Some mills burned to the ground, and others washed away. Civil War armies burned hundreds of mills to deprive communities of their food. A few were rebuilt, but many were not.

When Dad took corn to the mill he described it as "taking a turn of corn to the mill on grinding day." The miller performed his services for a "toll," usually a gallon of corn for two bushels of ground meal.

It is sad to me that waterwheels, and gristmills, once so important to the survival of many, are now tourist attractions. Gristmills that once ground corn into meal now simply grind out dollars for their owners.

The Old Moon in February

Grandpa and his pa before him on Stoney Fork each set store by the moon and the stars and other kinds of folklore. They would be quick to explain the reason why floors buck, doors warp, shingles curl, and fence rails rot. They would say, "They went agin the moon. When the moon is full timber, fibers warp and pull." According to them, there was a difference in wood cut three hours before the new moon and that cut six hours after.

Dad held to certain beliefs about the weather. Sometimes on a winter night the fire in the grate would make a noise like someone whose boots went "scrunch" through the snow. When the fire made sounds like this, Dad would say it was going to snow. It always did.

I have since learned that as early as 1300 B.C. people believed there were intimate connections between man and the celestial bodies. Astrologers used the zodiac as a guide to nearly everything—butchering hogs, pulling teeth, fishing, forecasting the weather, milking cows, baking, cooking, and all phases of farming and wellness.

Grandpa always said, "The old moon in February is the right time for cutting timber that will stand forever straight and true." In the old days in Appalachia, men knew how to hand-cut timber and rough lumber. When Grandpa and other old-timers in the mountain cut down trees, rived shingles, or even cut firewood, they did it according to the signs of the moon. Today, much of their lore is looked upon as mere superstition. Perhaps that explains why today's lumber is considered inferior to that used in the old days.

When Dad rived out boards for our house roof, as well as for the barn, crib, and smokehouse, he was careful to go with the grain because "shingles split with the grain shed rain" while shingles cut across the grain hold water and rot. He also believed that boards and shingles should be put on when the horn of the new moon points down. "Then they won't cup on you," he would say. "When you see a roof with the boards all cupped up, they were put on in the light of the moon." Grandpa said one time that firewood should be cut at the quarter of the moon to prevent it from snapping and throwing embers beyond the hearth.

The old-timers had learned from experience that it was best to cut wood from the north side of a tree, because it was not as susceptible to warping from dampness or milling. When they cut a pine to get lumber for flooring, they first split the tree in half and kept the northern half, using that half for wide, flat boards. They quarter-sawed the southern half for lumber to be used where warping was not as important.

Today's furniture is often made from just one kind of wood, but in the old days a simple rocking chair might contain as many as seven kinds of wood. Dad and Grandpa, as well as several of my uncles, were excellent chair makers.

They knew that wood breathes with the weather, warping, contracting, or expanding with each change of humidity and temperature. If your house creaks and cracks during weather changes it is built of healthy wood.

If you believe the old-timers were backward and superstitious when it comes to working with wood, you should have had a chance to sit a spell with them on Stoney Fork, especially during the 1930s, 1940s, and 1950s, and learn the wisdom handed down through generations of mountain pioneers.

Following the signs of the zodiac was common in the mountains when I was a child. I loved reading in the *Farmer's Almanac* about signs and wise sayings. I looked at the stars on clear nights and believed they were friendly to us. I made up stories about the stars, fairies, and devas (wood spirits) of the natural world.

12

Family and Friends

The mountains taught me just about everything
I needed to know. My family and friends taught
me the rest.

When my youngest grandson, Eric Lawson, celebrated his eighth birthday, I went to his house to pick him up. When he answered the door, I announced to him that I had been "instructed to come kidnap a little blond-haired, blue-eyed boy who was eight years old!" His blue eyes opened wide, and he looked toward his dad. I hurried him out of the house without telling his parents specifically where we were going.

When Eric was younger, we would go shopping together. He loved going to the grocery where they had a big, round sun face as part of their decorations. He would climb up into the cart so he could be sure to see it. I used to marvel at the look of pure delight on his face when he saw that sun face.

Sometimes I would take Eric to the flea market at the Boone Square mini-mall. As we browsed up and down the aisles, he would ask ten thousand questions. "What is that used for?" "How did they make that?" "Why is that painted blue?" "Who owns all those books?" And, of course, the most popular question: "Will you buy this for me?"

When I picked Eric up for his eighth birthday I was not surprised when he requested that we go to the Boone Square mini-mall flea market. We walked up and down the aisles, as he selected small items he could not live without. Then we discovered two bicycle helmets, one in good shape. He had received a brand-new bicycle for his birthday, but no helmet. I bought one of the helmets for him, and he promised to wear it every time he rode his bicycle.

Something about our shopping trip was different this time, and it took me a little while to realize what it was. Eric only occasionally asked questions about the items. I realized that since he was four or five years old, he had acquired a lot of information about things in general from school and television, and he did not need to ask as many questions. He was growing up, and I wanted to hold him and savor every moment with him.

Today his family lives near me, and Eric is seventeen years old. He rides his bicycle to visit me. We have always been close. But now that girlfriends and learning to drive keep him busy, I don't think I will see him as often now. Time changes people, but you can still love them as before.

Beloved Maple Tree

My favorite tree on High Street in Berea is a huge old maple that stands in the corner of my yard. Fortunately it survived the 1996 tornado—which did uproot a fifty-foot white pine growing near the edge of my front porch. The maple, however, was unscathed. I am so grateful it is still alive.

My son Bruce loved that maple tree. He would climb up and be hidden by the thick limbs as he watched people walk or drive by. If the passerby was someone he knew, he enjoyed making noise and watching the person on the street try to figure out where the noise was coming from.

In the fall when full color comes to all the trees, the maple lights up my living room and the bedroom upstairs above the living room. It makes the room look sun-filled even when the sky is overcast.

My husband Grant's mother, Jeanette Farr, opened her heart to six-year-old Bruce the first time Grant took us to her home in Black Mountain, North Carolina. One year she visited us in October, just when the beauty of our maple was at its peak. The leaves were abundant that year and generously carpeted the whole front yard.

Bruce introduced Gran to "his" tree, and it is a wonder we did not find her up in the tree with him! It was curious how, when the two of them were together, Bruce seemed older and she younger. They had grand times together. She often did things that made the rest of her family fear for her safety, and got Bruce's promise not to tell Grant or anyone else.

She did not try to climb the tree. However, she could, and did, play in the leaves with him! I have photographs of the two of them on the ground, covered up with leaves, just their heads sticking out. Grant both laughed at and scolded his mother for lying on the cold ground "at her age." But I thought it was wonderful that she, *especially* at her age, *could* get down on the ground and romp and play in the leaves with Bruce.

Every fall after that, when the maple tree shed most of its leaves, I could not help but go walking through them. Leaves make such a satisfying crunch. I hope I never get too old to feel the urge to play in them—or, when October's burnished gold spills over into the brown of November, ache to be one with Indian summer days.

I will always be grateful that Bruce had those years with his Gran. She taught him that some adults could be trusted to keep secrets; she taught him how to use his imagination; she gave him lessons on how to look to nature for the simple truths, and to trust the world of spirit for eternal values.

Gran passed to the world of spirit in 1979; and though a bright light went out in the universe, its radiance still shines in our hearts and memories. She took Bruce and me in and made us feel part of her large family. And even though Grant and I are now divorced, other members of the family stay in touch with both Bruce and me, and we continue to visit them.

Brother Fred

My middle brother, Fred, died in 1995, when he was fifty-two. I married and left home so early that I did not get to spend as much time with Fred as I would have wished; and then he married and began raising his own family. After he became terminally ill, however, I saw Fred often, and we shared some good talks about our lives in the mountains, our parents, and each other.

Our youngest brother, Lee Roy, wrote a tribute to Fred that is as eloquent as anything I could say about him, and I believe his remembrance is worth quoting in full.

> My brother was diagnosed with cancer in April 1994. His wife, children, our remaining brother and six sisters, all went through alternate stages of hope and despair in the next year and a half.

I spent many days at his bedside talking, listening, and praying for and with him. Through this process I found myself changing—certain beliefs, old habits, acquiring more patience and a deeper spiritual attitude. His faith and strength were shining examples to me.

He was in charge from Day One. He decided when to stop painful treatments, and when to declare he wanted to die naturally at home.

He asked forgiveness and achieved peace with God and other people. He thought of many details that he could take care of to spare his family after his death. He planned his funeral and picked out the burial plot, made a will, and took care of many other details, including adoption of his two stepdaughters.

His wife Jackie became even more his partner, his helpmate, as he talked everything over with her. She kept a cheerful countenance for him, encouraging him, telling him little anecdotes about family, friends, and church. She kept demonstrating her love for him and taking care of him day and night.

Through spending time with him I managed to see my recent past in perspective, to realize how small my troubles were compared to his. He talked about our lives as boys, about Mama and Dad, about his children.

One day when he was very sick, he seemed to be in our childhood again. He replied seemingly to a question that he was seven years old. The most moving part of this was when he turned over on his side and began singing part of a gospel song with phrases like "I'm going to a better place, where there's no more pain, no more sorrow, no more death."

I am thankful that I got to spend as much time as I did with him. I witnessed how real and close God and the angels were to him and to us.

Appalachia–Alaska Connection

When I first met Ginny Carney in 1991 I had no inkling of the friendship we would come to share. Ginny Carney, an RN and a native of East Tennessee, moved to Alaska to live for almost two decades with her husband and three sons. At one time they had lived in the Bahamas and befriended a young native woman, who became their cook and house-keeper. They kept in touch with her after she married and bore four children, two sons and two daughters. Then their friend was tragically murdered. After a frustrating time working through all the legalities, Ginny and her husband adopted the four children and started raising a family again.

During those years in Alaska she lost touch with what was happening in her native region. One winter day while in the library at the University of Alaska at Anchorage (UAA) she found a copy of my bibliography on Appalachian women and was "thrilled to see that someone was doing something about Appalachian people." Though we had never met and did not know each other, Ginny called to tell me how much she appreciated my bibliography.

At the time, Ginny was teaching two English classes at UAA and, using my bibliography and other lists of materials I had sent her, she wrote a proposal for a grant to teach a course on Appalachian women in literature. She received the grant, along with permission from the university to teach the course on a one-time-only basis. Fourteen women and one man enrolled.

Ginny called me when the course was assured. She invited me to come to Alaska and lecture on Appalachia at the university. With my son Bruce, I flew to Anchorage on September 25, 1991. Over the next two days, I spoke to Ginny's class and another class on American women writers, as well as at a colloquium and a town forum.

I have never been more warmly welcomed in any place than I was in Alaska. Bruce and I were invited to dinner by several of Ginny's class members, and we enjoyed a potluck supper one night, where we sampled some native dishes, including moose stew. After I spoke to Ginny's class, the students presented me with a picnic basket full of small gifts—a dream catcher and homemade mincemeat, Alaskan cookbooks, a cassette tape, and other delightful surprises. The students said they had been reading about Southern hospitality and wanted to make me feel at home. Somehow they found out my birthday, and the following October, back in Berea, I received a dozen roses from the class. I also received letters and telephone calls from them during the holidays.

Word got around about Ginny's class, and other students became interested. A petition asking that Professor Carney be allowed to teach the course again was circulated, and it garnered 224 signatures. The university complied, and Ginny taught two more classes on Appalachia, one of them focusing on contemporary Appalachian women writers.

Ginny and I kept in touch. She asked me about the doctoral programs at the University of Kentucky (UK). She planned to drive to Berea to meet me when she came to visit her mother in Tennessee later in the spring. I made telephone calls to UK and set up appointments for her; during her visit she spent a day on the UK campus. She then applied and was admitted to the doctoral program.

Ginny, with her four adopted children, moved to Berea in July 1993. Her husband remained in Alaska. I helped her find a big house for rent in the country. She and her landlady, Etta Anglin, became good friends and allies as they pursued their higher education goals and cared for their children. Ginny's children enrolled at Silver Creek, Foley Middle School, and Madison Southern High School.

Living out in the country, Ginny says, enabled her to get in touch with her roots again. She talks about sitting on her front porch and listening to the evening and night sounds, watching the moon come up and millions of stars light up the sky. She says this healed her body and soul. She in turn has formed an amazing network of teachers and writers throughout Appalachia.

Going to Alaska was a tremendous boon in my own life. It also enabled Bruce to fulfill a longtime dream: to walk on a glacier. While in Alaska, we saw two big glaciers; we saw salmon trying to swim upstream—though they were dying because it was late in the season. We saw a huge iceberg near one glacier but were barred from going any further because bears had been spotted nearby.

Ginny Carney is one of the strongest women I have ever met. Knowing her has made me stronger and renewed my enthusiasm for being a writer and member of the Appalachian network of educators and writers.

While she was living in Kentucky, Ginny told me she wanted to visit Stoney Fork and meet some of my relatives who were still living there. We drove to Stoney Fork on a Sunday. Our first stop was at a subsidized highrise building for incapacitated and elderly people. My disabled brother

Jeems was living there in a tiny apartment that shone with cleanliness. Several of his foliage plants and smaller dish gardens were in his living room, and family photographs were hanging on the walls.

After a short visit with Jeems, we drove up the Right Fork of Straight Creek to the mouth of Stoney Fork to visit with my sister Della and her husband, John. They lived in the old Ritter Lumber Camp, which was built in the early 1950s. When the mill closed down, the company offered to sell the houses on an individual basis. Della and John bought one, and their house is neatly painted and tidy.

While Della and I caught up on family news, Ginny and John talked. John had to quit school after the eighth grade because there was no high school close enough for him to attend, nor school buses to the county high school fifteen miles away. Perhaps as a result of his lack of formal schooling, John does not read much except perhaps a weekly newspaper, but through television he keeps up with what is happening politically in the nation. He talked with Ginny about local, state, and national politics and their impact on Appalachia.

We drove up Stoney Fork and turned into York Branch, where my childhood home used to be, and then up Bingham Hollow to the place where my grandparents had lived. Relatives of mine still lived in small homes along the road from York Branch to the head of Bingham Hollow. To my surprise, what had always been a dirt road was now paved. "Somebody around here must know the right politicians," I said to Ginny.

My paternal Aunt Betty and her husband, William, still live at the old home place. Betty is now in her eighties; William is a decade younger, but has been on crutches for many years, having lost a leg as the result of a timber-woods accident. The road literally stops in their front yard. When we drove up, we saw that they had planted flowers everywhere—alongside the little creek, beside a dead stump, at one corner of a shed, among rows of corn and beans, in back of the kitchen—each plant looking as if it had grown there naturally. Their five-room house was neat, the front porch and yard around the steps were swept clean.

We noticed a field of corn on the hillside opposite their front porch. We asked how they had cultivated the ground; William said they dug it up by hand, using only hoes. I could not picture a man on crutches, standing on a steep hillside using a hoe.

Aunt Betty wanted to show me her garden, so we left Ginny and William to enjoy the shady front porch.

William told Ginny about his earlier life in eastern Kentucky—and how, after meeting and marrying Betty, he has lived in Bingham Hollow ever since. Ginny told me later how William shared his philosophy of life, his views on people in general, and what he thought of living conditions for people in specific locations around the world. He told her he had never learned to read.

At the end of our visit, as we drove back to Berea, Ginny told me she could live in a place like Bingham Hollow or Stoney Fork forever!

Through Ginny, an educated and worldly woman whose vision is unclouded by stereotypes, I saw Stoney Fork and my people with a new appreciation: my brother Jeems, living in three tiny rooms, unable to get outside on his own, still managing to surround himself with life and love; and William and John, as politically and socially aware as anyone I know.

We are constantly bombarded with stereotypes, both blatant and subliminal, all stemming from supposedly informed sources. Stereotypes have shadowed the Appalachian people from the first accounts. Too often the media, without knowing the people they are describing, look for the unique, the grotesque, or the tragic, because that is what the tabloid mentality seems to find most appealing.

Marijuana in the Mountains

When their family was almost grown, Grandma and Grandpa Saylor moved from the head of Stoney Fork down into "civilization" at the head of Bingham Hollow. Two of their children—my Aunt Betty, who was thirteen years older than I, and Aunt Laura, who was only four years older— were playmates of mine when I was a child.

It was a snug, safe place surrounded by folds of hills and valleys, and we were surrounded by kinfolk. My family worked hard raising corn, potatoes, and a big garden every year. We got milk from our one cow, and eggs from a dozen or so chickens. Grandpa had a few apple trees, and we always picked huckleberries and blackberries and gathered black walnuts and hickory nuts to eat. We lived in our own little world.

On one hand not much at Stoney Fork has changed, but on the other everything has changed. When I was young, there was a rough dirt road for jeeps and trucks from the mouth of Stoney Fork up to the beginning of York Branch, and elsewhere there were only narrow footpaths. Today there is a paved road all the way up to Aunt Betty's house. The number of houses and trailers alongside the creek, and in any level spot to be found, has tripled since I lived there.

There is still grim poverty, but the people do not seem to dwell on that. They do what work they can find and eke out a subsistent living as best they can. They have hopes and dreams, just like most people do.

And they have marijuana!

I was aware that marijuana was grown in the hills. I can recall numerous stories of marijuana crops destroyed by the state police, and of people being arrested—or killed—in the process. A talk with Betty and William brought it home to me.

Two summers before Ginny and I visited, their garden was destroyed when a helicopter flew over the hills and dipped down into the hollows, searching for marijuana. Their corn was shoulder-high; staked tomato vines were loaded with green tomatoes just beginning to turn color. The wind-blasts from the helicopter blew down the tomato vines, even sucking some of the plants up by the roots, and the cornstalks were uprooted, twisted, and flung about. Even the onions and cucumbers did not escape damage. The helicopter flew over again and again as it crisscrossed the area.

William complained to the state police office in London, Kentucky. Later state police from both Frankfort and London came to look at the damage. The Frankfort police wrote down accounts and estimates and promised that something would be done.

William asked the London policeman just what would be done. The officer told him, "The reports will be filed in Frankfort, and that's probably all that will ever be done." Then he added, "Sorry for your loss," and walked away. Betty and William never heard again from officials in either London or Frankfort.

An old cornfield sits near the top of the mountain in back of Betty and William's house. They said marijuana had been grown there before the raid, but not by anyone they knew.

Odd things began happening at night around their house and out-buildings after the raid. For example, in the early morning hours they would suddenly hear knocking on a back wall of their house, loud and insistent. They would get up and look everywhere but could find no one on the premises.

Aunt Betty is very superstitious, and she concluded that this incident was a supernatural warning of some impending disaster. William, how-ever, insisted that human beings did the knocking. Their disagreement over the cause of the occurrence went on for several weeks.

Finally, William decided to take matters in hand. He knew some men in other communities who had been involved with marijuana crops. Two or three of them were casual friends and happened to be in Bingham Hol-low one day. William cunningly invited them to have dinner with him and Betty. They came to the house and enjoyed the good midday meal of fresh, homegrown vegetables and cornbread.

While they sat around the table Betty mentioned the harassment they had been subjected to and her opinion that it was some supernatural warn-ing. William jumped in with strong words about his guns and what he was going to do the next time it happened.

As Betty and William told me the story, Aunt Betty said, "I can't help but believe that it was a warning of some kind and that we've got to be ready for whatever comes."

"Yeah, it was a warning all right," William said. "They wanted to scare us into moving out of this hollow. Then they could plant marijuana in here."

"Is the harassment still taking place?" I asked.

"No. Not since I let it be known what I was ready and able to do," William said.

Although Aunt Betty was very superstitious, William was more prac-tical about human nature. He was strong and active even though he was handicapped. It was amazing to see him and Betty on a steep hillside hoe-ing corn.

13
Foods We Loved

As I look back over my life, I am impressed with
how many memories I have of foods we gathered,
prepared, cooked, and ate.

Perhaps it is my memories of early childhood, warm kitchens, and
scrumptious food that has made my kitchen the most popular place in
my house today. When friends come to visit inevitably we end up settling
down to talk in the kitchen. Each of us has different types of memories and
recollections from childhood to call upon, but food often figures largely in
those memories.

After I married, my husband and I had two sons, Dennis Wayne and
Bruce Alan. Wayne is eleven years older than Bruce. We lived on Stoney
Fork when Dennis Wayne was small; Bruce Alan was born in Berea. Each
of them has different memories about home cooking, perhaps because our
lifestyle in Berea turned out to be very different from that in Stoney Fork.
Wayne always wants me to make chicken and dumplings, banana pudding, and molasses pie. Bruce wants hamburgers, chili, French fries, and
chocolate cake.

I see little reason in taking all day to cook something that can be done
just as well in thirty minutes. At the same time I value the knowledge and
survival skills that were handed down from the pioneers to my ancestors
and, through them, to me. These skills, and the knowledge and wisdom
that accompanied them—hunting in the hills, tending the garden, feeding
the family, and providing a warm kitchen—are all part of the Appalachia I
knew and still love.

We worked sometimes from early morning until it got too dark to see
outside. We also played hard. Three meals a day were never enough for us,

and we looked for snacks in the afternoons and at night before bedtime. We had breakfast before daylight, dinner in the middle of the day, and supper in the early evening.

During the winter we snacked on walnuts, hickory nuts, beechnuts, and hazelnuts. Dad often gathered hickory nuts while he was out squirrel hunting (squirrels were found most easily where hickory trees grew in the hills). Sometimes he would come home with his hunting pouch full of hickory nuts instead of wild game. Walnut, hazelnut, and beechnut trees grew close to our cabin and alongside fences and roads. We children eagerly gathered the nuts.

I remember the golden days in October when we used to take coffee sacks made of burlap and head up the smaller ridges and coves to gather walnuts. The ground would be covered with leaves as rich in color as an Oriental rug. When we reached a walnut tree we would rake back the leaves with our hands and feet and find green-hulled nuts covering the ground.

For days after gathering the walnuts, we had the task of hulling them. I remember how embarrassing it was to go to school being one of only a few girls with my hands stained brown from the walnut juice. The stains could not be washed off; they had to wear off with time. We stored walnuts and hickory nuts in the loft of our house or in the hayloft of the barn. The smaller nuts we stored in jars and cans in the kitchen.

A favorite snack of mine was black walnut kernels and cornbread. We kept a sack of walnuts near the wood box in the corner and a hammer by the hearth. We'd crack a bowlful of kernels, sprinkle them with salt, and eat them with a piece of cornbread.

Chicken and Dumplings

A favorite dish at church suppers and family reunions was chicken and dumplings. (Pork, wild game, and chicken were the most commonly served meats.) This dish can feed fifty people, or just a few. Many Appalachian cookbooks contain basic recipes for chicken and dumplings, using various ingredients.

No one knows when chicken and dumplings was first served in Appalachia, but it became a welcome dish in big-city homes and mountain kitchens alike. Cooks varied the taste by using sherry, lemon peel, parsley, and pepper in stewing the chicken. Some added butter and chopped giblets as well as boiled eggs to enrich the broth. There were two kinds of dumplings: fluffy round balls and slick dumplings rolled out flat and cut into strips.

Up until the 1950s mountain people lived closer to pioneer times than did their city cousins. They dressed chickens and made dumplings the way their mamas and grandmas had always done, still using wood-burning stoves and cast-iron cookware.

In my childhood Mama filled her cast-iron teakettle with water to heat on the cook stove, then caught a chicken (usually a hen). She killed the chicken, either by wringing its neck or chopping off its head. She then put it in a number two–size galvanized tub. Picking up the boiling teakettle, she walked outside to the tub and poured water over the chicken. After the hot water loosened the feathers she plucked and saved them for pillows and feather beds. Mama then brought the chicken inside and held it over a flame in the stove to singe the remaining pinfeathers and hairs.

After Mama washed and dried the chicken, she cut it into serving pieces and boiled them in a cast-iron kettle. When the chicken was fork-tender she removed the kettle from the fire to cool. After deboning the chicken she put it back into the broth and moved the kettle back onto a hot part of the wood-burning stove.

Then Mama made dumplings. Hers were always fluffy and tender. She shaped them into round balls and dropped them into the rich, boiling chicken broth where they cooked until they were waxy on the outside and fluffy and tender on the inside.

Our family did not like flat dumplings. These had no baking powder and little shortening, and were rolled and cut into strips like wide noodles; when cooked, they were firm and bumpy. I believe that fluffy round dumplings are more old-fashioned, while flat dumplings are somehow more sophisticated. The preference for one version over another tends to run in families.

I grew up believing my mama's dumplings were perfect. I knew I could never improve on her basic recipe, so I never tried. I no longer use a wood-burning stove or a cast-iron teakettle in which to heat water. I also buy chicken from the supermarket. But I still shape dumplings by rolling a wad of dough with my hands and cooking them just the way she did. People rave about my chicken and dumplings almost as much as they did about Mama's.

Dried Apple Stack Cake

Mama's dried apple stack cake was a low-fat, nonsweetened, many-layered cake. It was made with stiff, cookie-like dough flavored with ginger and sorghum molasses, and a sweet, spiced apple filling. When served, the cake was tall, heavy, and moist.

The dried apple stack cake was a favorite pioneer wedding cake. In the mountains, weddings were celebrated with "in-fares," where people gathered to party, dance, and eat potluck dishes. Because wedding cakes were so expensive, neighbor cooks brought cake layers to donate to the bride's family. The dough for the cake was rolled or pressed out into very thin layers and baked in cast-iron skillets. The family of the bride cooked, sweetened, and spiced dried apples to spread between the layers of the cake. The number of layers in the wedding cake was a gauge of the bride's popularity. Sometimes there would be as many as twelve layers; the average was seven or eight. Stack cake was also served at family reunions, church suppers, and other large gatherings.

The dried apple stack cake is the most "mountain" of all cakes baked and served in southern Appalachia. The story goes that James Harrod, one of Kentucky's early pioneers and the founder of Harrodsburg, Kentucky, brought the stack cake recipe with him when he traveled the Wilderness Road to Kentucky. Whether this story is true or not, this cake has remained popular with mountain people.

Wherever Appalachian people migrated—to Washington, Florida, and Arizona, for example—they took along recipes for their favorite version of old-fashioned stack cake. Called by different names—dried apple stack cake, apple stack cake, Confederate old-fashioned stack cake, stack-cake, and Kentucky pioneer washday cake—all had two constant ingredients: ginger and sweet sorghum molasses. (While sorghum molasses was considered not suitable in most cakes and pies because it was too heavy, it worked very well in the stack cake, with the dried fruit and spices. Sometimes cooks varied the amount of sweetening by adding brown sugar to the sorghum molasses: one-half cup of sugar to one-third cup of molasses.)

The original method is a long, tedious process, with the cake taking as much as three hours to assemble. Some cooks just use regular cake layers and plain applesauce or apple butter, or a combination of both, as the filling between the layers. While stack cake made this way may be tasty, there is no comparison between applesauce or apple butter and the strong apple flavor that dried apples give.

One method of preserving foods in Appalachia was by air and sun drying. After coring and peeling, apples were cut in half, then in quarters. Each quarter was cut into two or three thin slices. When the apples were ready they were spread on a large white cloth and placed on top of a shed or other flat area to dry in the sun. A fine wire screen put over them kept out flies and bugs. This method was chancy because of cloudy skies and the chance of rain. Apple slices can also be dried near a wood-burning stove, in a sunny window, or in the oven at a low temperature. Stringing the slices with a needle and stout thread and hanging them can also dry them. As they dry, the apple slices shrivel and turn brown. When completely dry, they are stored in cloth bags, glass canning jars, or the freezer.

Not many mountain families still dry fruit in this old-fashioned way, although they still love dried apples and dried green beans. They are more likely to use a dehydrator or barter with local florists for room in a greenhouse where they can spread out their apples and beans to dry.

Although today's cooks may use different methods for drying fruit, and different versions of stack cake can easily be found in recipe collections and cookbooks, mountain cooks still prefer the old-fashioned recipe for apple stack cake, handed down for generations.

Roasting Ears

Mountain cooks have many ways to prepare corn, including roasting the ears and using the ground cornmeal.

To roast corn, turn back the husk to expose the ear of corn, but do not break it loose from the ear. Inspect the corn for worms, bugs, or rot-ten spots. Clean away all the silk. Turn the husk back over the ear of corn, and tie some of the husk ends together. Dip the corn into water to wet the husks so they will not burn. Place them on hot coals. Turn them once or twice while cooking. Leave them in the coals until they are tender. Then peel back the husks and eat the corn on the cob with salt and butter.

Johnnycakes and Hoecakes

Granny Brock told me how johnnycakes got their name. The story goes that one time a little boy called Johnny was crying for his supper. His pioneer mother told him she'd fix him a little cake of cornbread, and it would be "Johnny's cake." She heated a bit of bacon grease in a skillet and spooned a mound of cornmeal dough into the skillet, where it quickly spread into a pancake shape. Later, the thin, crisp corn cakes baked in a skillet or on a griddle on top of a hot stove came to be called "johnnycakes."

The early settlers in Appalachia often cooked bread at noon in the fields. Usually the cornfields were high on a steep hill, a good walk from the house. If the corn needed to be hoed out quickly, the men would take their lunch with them—cooked vegetables and a piece of ham or shoulder meat. They would build a little fire and, using a sharpened stick, broil the meat while baking their bread. Tradition says that these early settlers never bothered using skillets for the bread they cooked in the fields. They cleaned their hoe blades, made up the dough, and baked bread on their hoes. They called this kind of bread "hoecakes."

When he was working, Dad would take along a cast-iron skillet and a coffeepot. He would make a fire and put bread in the skillet and coffee and water into the pot. The aromas made even the weakest person feel glad to be there under the shade trees, high upon the mountain.

Gritted Cornbread

"When the corn is too hard for the table and too soft for the cow," Mama used to say, "it's just right to make gritted bread." This was a delicious way to prolong the season for eating wholesome, garden-grown corn at the end of the summer.

First, you must have a homemade gritter with which to grate the raw corn kernels from the cob. To make a corn gritter, Dad would open a tin lard bucket at the seams, and flatten it out until he had a piece of tin about six or eight inches wide and sixteen to twenty inches long. He used a number 10 (medium-size) nail to punch holes at close intervals over the surface of the tin. Then he would cut a flat one-by-six-inch board twenty-four inches long, and nail two one-by-two-inch strips lengthwise along the edges. Then he stretched the piece of tin, smooth side down, across the board and nailed it to each strip. This left a space between the tin and the board for the gritted meal to slide down into a pan as the cob was raked across the gritter. Mama would bake the bread as she did any cornbread. Yet it tasted wonderfully different. We loved to eat gritted cornbread at the end of the growing season.

Spoonbread

In 1996 I was invited to compile a cookbook of spoonbread recipes for the first Spoonbread Festival in Berea, planned for the last week of September. I was pleased to hear of the plans to make this event an annual affair. I agreed to do the cookbook.

People around the world bake and eat some kind of bread every day. Bread, they say, is the staff of life. In Appalachia we ate hot bread three times a day—biscuits in the morning, cornbread for dinner in the middle of the day, and a pan of cornbread or a skillet of cornpone for supper. This routine might be varied for special times, such as when we had company.

At times our flour supply ran low and there was no money to buy more. Mama would use the flour very sparingly, keeping it for breakfast biscuits and cream gravy. She did not mix flour in with cornmeal when we were short, but made cornbread with boiling water. This gave the bread a completely different texture and taste, soft and savory. Only later did I learn that bread made in this manner was called spoonbread. After I moved to Berea and experienced Boone Tavern's version of spoonbread, I had to admit that their spoonbread was richer than the kind Mama made back in the mountains.

At an early age, I became fascinated with collecting as many different recipes as I could. It was a special delight to find copies of very old cookbooks, and cookbooks put out by small organizations and churches. I discovered that some of these newer cookbooks contained recipes gleaned from much older cookbooks (the newer book always credited the name of the original group and the title of the old cookbook). In one old cookbook, the *Cook-Book of Southern Recipes,* published by the Woman's Club of Charlotte, North Carolina, in 1908, I found a recipe for "mush bread," which has to be an early version of spoonbread:

> Sprinkle slowly half a pint of white cornmeal into a pint of hot milk.
> Cook until it is a smooth mush. Take from the fire, add the yolks of
> four eggs, and then fold in the well-beaten whites. Turn into baking dish
> and bake in a quick oven for 30 minutes.

Spoonbread resembles what you might call a cornbread soufflé. It is the richest, lightest, and most delicious of all the cornmeal recipes I have ever tried. It makes a good accompaniment to country ham and red-eye gravy, or any meat and gravy dish. It is a good match for seafood, too, and is wonderful with fresh garden vegetables, salads, and fruit dishes.

As far as it can be determined spoonbread probably originated in Virginia, perhaps with Mary Randolph in 1824. Some authorities maintain that spoonbread originated with the Indian porridge called *suppone* or *suppawn,* and consider that the true ancestral source of spoonbread. Others say that the butter, milk, and eggs, which made spoonbread such a special dish, probably were added after the Civil War. Spoonbread was most likely first made in Virginia, Maryland, the Carolinas, Kentucky, or Tennessee; some say Virginia is most likely.

The basic ingredients of spoonbread are very much the same from one recipe to another, the major difference being between those who use baking powder and/or sugar, and those who use neither.

Blackberry Dumplings

In the summertime we looked forward to fresh fruits and berries. Mama canned dozens of jars of blackberries every summer. She would use the canned berries to make a blackberry cobbler, or sometimes she just put them in a bowl for us to eat. Best of all was when she made blackberry dumplings.

BLACKBERRY DUMPLINGS

    1 quart blackberries, hulled and washed

    ½ cup hot water

    1 cup sugar

    Dash of salt

    2 cups sifted flour

    4½ teaspoons baking powder

    1 tablespoon sugar

    ½ teaspoon salt

    1 cup milk

Combine the berries, hot water, sugar, and salt and cook in large kettle with tight-fitting lid over medium heat until boiling point is reached. Reduce heat and cook until the berries are tender. Sift together flour, baking powder, sugar, and salt. Put in enough milk to make a light dough. Drop dough by heaping teaspoons into simmering berries. Cover tightly and reduce heat to low. Cook for 13 to 15 minutes or until dumplings are done. Serve with cream. These dumplings will keep in the refrigerator for four or five days, and will still taste fresh and look good when served warm.

Spring Greens

"Wild sallet is good for you," Granny Brock was fond of saying. "It is rich in vitamins and it tones up the system." Granny always said you can find wild lettuce, pepper grass, sheep's tongue, poke, creasies, and crow's foot in almost any field. She would add a basket of curly dock, dandelion leaves, watercress, wood sorrel, and a few wild onions, chopped. The greens would then be doused with oil and vinegar dressing or smothered with red-eye gravy. Either way is delicious.

In researching the subject, I found that most of the lore of wild sallet came from the Indians. It is said that in addition to greens, they knew and ate over two hundred different kinds of berries and fruit. One of their sweets was called "serviceberry" cake. They gathered the delicious, edible red berries and pounded them into a paste; after pressing the paste into cakes, they dried them in the sun. They also made blackberry cakes in this manner. Early white settlers learned from the Indians how to do this and many other things.

Many wild greens, however, like wild berries, are not safe to eat. Plants such as poison ivy, nightshade, and many more are poisonous. If you do not know wild greens, do not take a chance picking them yourself.

Granny Brock and I would go into the hills and hunt lamb's quarters, woolen britches, and what she called "shouny" (it takes land facing north to grow shouny). Dock is good, too, but you must pick it very young. There is yellow dock, narrow dock, and burdock.

A favorite green was poke. It comes up early in April and must be eaten while the plants are young and tender. Poke was cooked and fried different ways by different cooks. I always thought the way my mama fixed poke was the best way of all:

> Gather poke shoots, cut them off above the ground because the roots are poison, and cook the leaves and stems together, parboiling two times and pouring off the water each time. Fill the kettle with fresh water the third time, add salt to taste, and cook until tender. Mix lard and butter half to half in an iron skillet, then add the cooked green poke and heat it again. Break three or four eggs over the top (adjust to amount cooked) and scramble with the greens. To serve, pass white vinegar as dressing, if desired.

Poke cooked this way tastes a bit like very good, very tender broccoli.

Mountain Morels

One of the treats of springtime in the mountains was when Dad found hickory chickens and brought them home. I asked him once why he called them "hickory chickens."

"I usually find them growing under hickory trees," he said, "and the way your mama fixes them they taste like chicken, only better. They have a proper name, I guess, but I don't know what it is."

Later, when I went to college and researched the topic, the first thing I found out was that they were called morels. Finding out what I could about them was a pleasing job.

Morels are conical, honeycomb-like mushrooms that sit on fat stems, with the cap and the stem a continuous piece. In Appalachia, besides being called "hickory chickens" as my dad did, they are known as "dry land fish," "markels" (*Morchella esculent*), and "big-foot." Morels are the easiest and safest mushroom to hunt, but mycologists say they have a dangerous look-alike: the helvella, or beefsteak mushroom, easy to identify because it is squatty and thick, with a brainlike head on a short, stick stem.

Morels grow in rich soil mixed with ashes in burned-over ground and in old fencerows and orchards. They grow from an inch to a foot in height and are spread by spores. Cutting the stalk with a sharp knife is the best way to gather morels, as this does not damage the underground growth and enhances the likelihood that the morels will come back in the same area year after year.

Dedicated morel hunters know when the time is right to gather morels in Appalachia—in April, after a warm rain, when blue violets are in bloom. As one moves north, or at higher elevations, the morel season gets later, even into early June. Morel hunters recommend that a person look for mushrooms while walking uphill, because they will be at eye level and easier to see.

Morels are cooked in a variety of ways by professional chefs; Appalachian people think the best way to prepare them is simply to drain them well and sauté them in butter or bacon grease.

I have been told one can freeze morels, but doing so often makes them lose flavor. Drying morels, and reconstituting them in warm milk or water, is a better option. Probably the best way to deal with a surplus is to invite your friends and neighbors in for a mushroom feast.

Shuck Beans

In some states in the Appalachian region dried green beans were called "leather britches"; in other areas they were called "shuck beans" and "shucky beans." Most people knew them as "shuck beans"—and dried green beans have been a traditional food from pioneer days.

The Cherokee Indians cultivated beans long before the European settlers arrived in the early 1700s. Like maize, beans were nutritious and fairly easy to grow, particularly in the rich valley bottomlands in the mountains. For most Appalachian families, green beans, served from the garden, canned, pickled, or dried, became a staple food.

In pioneer days drying beans was a necessity, but people liked dried shuck beans so much that even today some mountain families who raise bean crops dry them for winter eating. They crave the intense flavor of the dried shuck beans. Appalachian natives who migrate "up north" carry fond memories of dried beans and dried apples, and it is not unusual for boxes of dried beans or apples to be shipped to Phoenix, Detroit, Indianapolis, or Cleveland, where they are eagerly received by those who are homesick for the old-time cooking and traditions.

In the Big Sandy region of southeastern Kentucky, some families would wait for the first deep snow to cook the first mess of shuck beans. This was an annual ritual for many generations. Favorite beans for drying were the mountain white half-runner, the striped cornfield bean, and the Kentucky Wonder.

A bean stringing was a popular social event in the first part of the twentieth century, as were apple peelings, corn shucking, and quilting bees. This was a way for neighbors to socialize even as they got needed work done.

Word would go out to neighbors that a bean stringing would take place at a certain home on a certain date; everyone was welcome to come. Family, friends, and acquaintances came from near and far. Someone might bring a guitar, fiddle, or banjo and provide music. The music provided entertainment for youngsters not old enough to string the beans. They would frolic and play games while the music rang out. Many hands made short work of readying two or three bushels of green beans for canning or drying.

There were two methods for drying beans. (Neither method was used for "shelly beans," which mature and start to dry on the vine before they are shelled.) When the beans matured but the green pod was still edible, they were picked from the vines. Each end was broken off and the strings removed. A big darning needle was threaded with heavy thread; the needle was then carefully inserted between the two middle beans in the pod. It was like stringing popcorn for Christmas trees. When the string of beans was three or four feet long, the thread was knotted at the ends and the string hung on porch rafters or on walls behind the wood-burning stove in the kitchen. The beans would slowly turn straw-colored as they dried and shriveled up. After the beans were dry, they would be put into cloth sacks or glass jars for storage. (A later method was to put the dry beans in the freezer to keep out bugs and insects.)

The second way to prepare beans for drying was to break off the ends and strings from both sides, then break each pod into bite-size pieces, usually between each bean in the pod. The bean pieces were then spread out on white cloths and put in a sunny place to dry. Many women preferred to break their beans before drying because, they said, it was easier to prepare the dried beans for cooking. It was, for one thing, almost impossible to pull out the threads after the strings of whole beans had dried.

The best method for cooking dried beans is to soak them overnight in a kettle of water (or put them into boiling water and soak them for an hour), then rinse and cook them with a piece of smoked slab bacon for two hours or more until the beans are fork-tender.

When I was growing up on Stoney Fork, families ate what they grew on the place or found in the hills. In the years before and during World War II, before the timber and coal companies came and stripped the land, the hills brought forth all kinds of berries. In addition, we had both orchard-grown and wild fruits such as apples, plums, grapes, persimmons, and pawpaws. There were fish in the creeks and wild game in the hills.

Each little homestead had its cornfield, its patch of cane, and its beehives. Somewhere along the creek there would be a water mill, where corn was ground into meal. And somewhere in the hillside thickets would be moonshine stills where corn liquor was bottled, sold, and drunk.

In any culture people's activities concerning food often reflect their social customs and beliefs. In our community it was considered bad manners to eat a meal without inviting anyone who happened to be on the premises to eat with us. The invitation would be extended several times, because it was not good manners for one to accept the first time offered; and the response, worded differently each time, made it perfectly clear to each party just what the result should be. They had to go through the ritual because it was the custom, the traditional thing to do.

The ways of cooking and eating in Appalachia have changed. My son Bruce, who grew up in Berea, has never tasted birch sap, or corn parched in an iron skillet, or potatoes roasted in the hot ashes of a wood-burning fire. On the one hand, I am sad that Bruce is missing so many of the things I took for granted as a child. On the other hand, I like my electric kitchen. Both Bruce and Wayne now can cook a meal in their own kitchens as well, and certainly in less time than I could in the kitchen on Stoney Fork. Who can say the old-fashioned ways are the best? There is value in both old and new.

14

Moonshine and Celebrations

When the screech of dry leaves on bone-hard
ground told us winter was not far away, we
knew it was time to dig the potatoes, gather the
corn, and get ready to celebrate the harvest,
Christmas, and the coming year.

As part of my work for the Council of the Southern Mountains, I read articles and books about Appalachia and talked with people working in community action programs in communities across the area. In this way I learned that land grants brought the Scots-Irish mountain folk to the hills of southeastern Kentucky. Marooned in their mountains, they were generally isolated and were spread out as political minorities among the states that share Appalachia geographically. Grandpa told me that he and his people felt hardly any loyalty to North Carolina, Virginia, and the other states they lived in when they first settled there.

When the Civil War came, a majority of mountain men supported the Union. During the Reconstruction period, ex-Confederates were considered to be traitors and were left mostly to themselves. The mountain people's land was almost worthless for tax purposes, their roads were little more than trails along rocky beds of streams, their families were outgrowing the capacity of rugged mountain farms to sustain them at subsistence levels, and the wild game was mostly gone from the coves and ridges.

The mountain people thus became burdened with terrible poverty at a time when there was inadequate tax support of public education and the construction of roads. The culture turned inward upon itself in an over-crowded land; and the people, old-fashioned even when they arrived, now depended upon the ancient oral culture their ancestors knew to sustain rigorous life on a static frontier.

By the early twentieth century the Appalachian Mountain range held nearly half of the coal the world would need. Coal and virgin timber were discovered in the late nineteenth century. Powerful timber and coal enterprises sent representatives to purchase rights to these resources.

"Land given to us as land grants was sold for as little as fifty cents an acre," Grandpa told me. "Fifty cents an acre seemed big money back then—especially when people were told they could still live on the land." Grandpa's face turned red with anger and his voice got loud. "They lied to us! They got the coal and timber out, no matter what destruction it caused."

Fortunately, the skills possessed by the pioneers were taught, father to son, mother to daughter, on down through the generations. People who live in the mountains still know how to raise gardens, tend small orchards, and plant and raise corn on steep hillsides. And some carried forward the knowledge of how to make moonshine. That was the only cash crop Grandpa, Dad, and his brothers and cousins ever knew.

Moonshine Whiskey

Moonshining in Appalachia has been romanticized in so many books, songs, and motion pictures that many find it difficult to differentiate between fiction and the true role the production of illegal alcohol played in the lives of mountain people.

There were legal whiskey makers in Kentucky, but Appalachian men made illicit whiskey. It was part of my heritage. My ancestors made liquor in Scotland and Northern Ireland. In the 1600s they had been forced to hide their small stills in wild, inaccessible places to avoid the despised British tax collectors. Making whiskey was considered to be a man's own business. Why should he have to pay tax on a product made on his own land?

When the Scots-Irish poured into America in the 1700s, they brought with them both the knowledge of whiskey making and a contempt for government taxation. Their protests about taxation were loud and angry. In the rugged regions of Kentucky, Virginia, Tennessee, and North Carolina, the moonshiner practiced his ancient art long after it had died out in other parts of the country.

When national prohibition was passed in 1919, the moonshine trade increased considerably. The price of alcohol rose dramatically after Prohibition, and this brought criminal elements into the industry, ruining the reputation of the proud old-time mountain moonshiner. The newcomers, often lacking know-how or concern for their customers, sometimes produced bad whiskey. Dad always spoke with scorn about people who would do that for money.

Dad, his brothers, and Grandpa all made moonshine, primarily to sell for cash, but they also drank their own product. The Saylor men all had good reputations as moonshiners. They did well during the years before and after World War II. It was said they made the purest and best-tasting moonshine of anyone in Bell County.

Mama, however, grieved that Dad made whiskey and sold it to people who would then get drunk. She felt he was breaking two laws, that of the land and that of God. But Dad could make more money selling moonshine than any other way, and we needed the cash. He could sell a bushel of corn for $2 or $3; but he could take a fourth of a bushel, turn it into mash, and make a run of moonshine, which would bring in about $100.

Dad's still consisted of two main parts, the top and the bottom. After he put fermented mash in the bottom part, he'd seal the top with a flour-and-water paste. He never sealed the top tightly because he wanted it to blow off if necessary. This was a safety measure in case the fire got too hot and built up too much steam.

A copper pipe, called an "arm," projected from the top of the cooker and over to one side, where it tapered down to about an inch and a half wide. It needed to be the same diameter at this end as that of another copper pipe called a "worm," which met it at this juncture. The worm was made by taking copper pipe about fifteen to twenty feet long and filling it with sand, stopping up both ends, and wrapping it around a fence post to make it coil. The sand kept it from kinking in the wrong places. The worm was then cleaned of sand and attached to the arm in such a way that the rest of the coil ran down inside a barrel. The barrel was kept full of cold, running water. Dad said it was best to have the water running in at the top and out an opening at the bottom of the barrel; this way it circulated around and over the copper worm.

To make the moonshine, Dad took a peck of shelled corn and put it in a cotton flour sack. He poured warm water over the corn to wet it, then put the sack in a warm, dark place. Several times a day he wet the corn with warm water. In just three or four days the corn sprouted, but he would let the sprouts get about two inches long before he spread them out flat to dry. After the sprouted corn was dry, he ground it up in the meat grinder and added it to twenty-five pounds of cornmeal and twenty-five pounds of sugar. He added boiling water and mixed the dry ingredients into a mush—which he called mash. After letting the mixture cool down, he added one-third of a pound of yeast to a gallon of lukewarm water and poured this into the mash. Last of all, he added enough water to make thirty gallons of mash. Fermentation could take up to ten days without yeast; Dad's adding yeast shortened the process to four days. When the mash had fermented and then settled down it was ready to be run. At this stage the mash was very sour.

Dad's moonshine still was hidden in the hills near a running spring or stream of water. It was no easy job getting the still set up, the mash poured into the cooker, and a run of moonshine started. The fire had to be carefully tended all the while so that it did not burn too hot or too slow. The heat caused the spirits to rise in the vapor along with the steam. It went into the arm and then on to the worm, where cold water caused condensation. This liquid was collected into a container.

The first runoff was weak and impure and had to be redistilled to rid it of water and oils. The cooker was cleaned out in preparation for the second runoff. The first run was then put back in, some water was added, and the liquid was turned to steam, condensed, and collected again.

The first quart of the second run was always far too strong—about 200 proof; toward the end of the run it was too weak—about 10 proof. This was where the skill of the moonshiner was called for: to mix the two to make 100 proof whiskey. Dad always knew when to stop a run: if a tablespoon of moonshine did not burn when tossed on the fire it meant there was not enough alcohol to burn and therefore not enough to continue the run.

Dad tested for the right proof by putting some moonshine in a quart jar, covering it tightly, and shaking it a few times. If the bubbles rose and sat half above and half below the top of the liquid he had the right proof. After the right proof was obtained, Dad, being a good moonshiner, always filtered his product through charcoal to improve the taste.

Other moonshiners were not always as careful with their whiskey as the Saylor men were. Sometimes very bad whiskey was sold in the mountains, and we would hear of someone getting deathly ill. We knew this was one of the reasons why moonshine was illegal according to the laws of the land and also why the revenuers were so diligent in searching out and destroying moonshine stills. They never found ours, but their presence loomed over us with an impending threat.

It became a matter of pride and took skill to outwit the revenuers. We lived at the head of the Stoney Fork Valley, and we'd often hear from the grapevine that revenuers were on their way. One time Dad was away from home after he had run a still of moonshine. Mama walked about, wringing her hands and saying, "Lord-a-mercy, Sidney, what are we going to do?" But after a few moments she figured out the answer to her question and told me to get her a hoe.

We had just planted a big garden with a dozen or more cucumber hills, each rounded with a smooth, flat top. Mama carried the jars of moonshine to the cucumber hills. We made a hole in each hill and buried a jar there.

The revenuers did not come that day, but I wished they had. I wanted them to look but never find where my clever Mama hid the moonshine.

First Christmas Tree

When I was young, nobody on Stoney Fork put up Christmas trees. The first decorated tree I ever saw was at the one-room school when I was eight years old. I thought it was the most beautiful thing in the world. I begged Mama to put up a tree, but she said there was no room in the house. Our home was a three-room log house with a front porch, and there were five children living there at the time.

But I was determined to have a Christmas tree. I took the axe and went up on the side of Pine Mountain to look for a small tree. I found several small pines and cedars, and selected a cedar to cut because it had the prettiest shape. Dragging it down the hill got the branches muddy, but mud could be washed off.

Positioning the tree on the porch by the side of the front door, I drove a nail into one of the house logs and tied the tree so it would not blow away. The other children helped me make paper chains, wrap sycamore balls in silver paper, and string popcorn, all of which we tied to the tree. We loved our first Christmas tree!

Every year before Christmas, Mama warned us ahead of time that Santa Claus might not make it this time. But we hung up our stockings just the same and hoped for the best. The spirit of love never forgot us, however, and we awoke each Christmas morning to see our stockings bulging with apples, oranges, English walnuts, and hard candy.

We celebrated Christmas, New Year's, and the Fourth of July by shooting off firecrackers and other kinds of noisemakers. The men and boys could not always afford firecrackers and larger fireworks. But Dad, his brothers, and Grandpa made their own. They got baking-powder cans and punched holes in the bottoms. After putting a few grains of carbide in the can, they sprinkled in drops of water and pressed the lid down firmly on the top. (Clabber Girl baking powder cans always had nice, round lids for the covers.) When a carbide light ignited the wet carbide, the lid was blown off with a loud noise and flew several yards away.

Besides setting off fireworks, the men enjoyed drinking and playing cards, and having shooting matches. Sometimes a chicken, turkey, or ham was put up as a prize. The men would take turns shooting at a tin can. The best marksman got the prize for the day. There were shooting matches at other times of the year, but especially during Thanksgiving and Christmas holidays.

For holiday dinners the women cooked whatever they had on hand. When Mama and Dad were young there would be wild turkey and venison for holiday meals, but in my day it was more likely to be ham, or simply chicken and dumplings. Sometimes just the immediate family gathered around the table; at other times there would be six to eight distant relatives and neighbors.

Mama never drank a drop of whiskey in her life; neither did Grandma, Aunt Betty, or Aunt Laura. But Granny Brock loved her hot toddies made with moonshine whiskey, and she always fixed a special Christmas drink. She would fill a half-gallon canning jar with oranges, sliced very thin. After adding a cup of sugar on top of the orange slices, she would pour moonshine in to fill the jar. She did this a day or two before she planned to drink it. When the liquid had been drunk down to about halfway in the jar, she would refill it with more moonshine.

The Christmas when I was twelve, Granny Brock invited our family to spend Christmas at her house. Granny's last husband, Andrew, and his adult son, Judge, were there. Granny had prepared most of the food the day before and left it pretty much up to Mama to get Christmas dinner on the table. Granny stayed by the fire in the front room, talking and drinking with the men.

We ate ham, baked sweet potatoes, canned corn, shuck beans, cornbread, and sweet pickles. For dessert there was dried apple stack cake.

Judge gave me a sip of Granny's Christmas drink, and I liked it. During the afternoon I managed several more sips. During one trip to the kitchen I found Judge. He knew I'd come for another sip. He put his arms around me and gave me a half kiss on my lips (it was a half kiss only because I was startled and turned my head). Judge looked just as startled as I felt. I hurried back into the front room. Granny looked at me and frowned, and Mama said it was time for us to go home.

View from the front porch of the cabin on Coon Branch, 1935.

The earliest picture of me. *First row, left to right:* Andrew Brock (Granny Brock's husband), Annie Farmer (Granny Brock's daughter), and Granny Brock; *second row:* Green Hoskins (Minnie Hoskins's first son) and I; *third row:* siblings Della, Hazel, Clara, and Jeems; *fourth row:* Minnie Hoskins (Andrew Brock's daughter), Rachel Saylor (my mother), and Susie Saylor (my paternal grandmother).

My maternal grandfather, Willie Saylor.

My paternal grandparents,
Solomon and Susie Saylor.

Sarah and Dewey Saylor. Dewey was my mother's brother.

My paternal grandfather, Solomon Saylor, and all of his brothers, the sons of Squire and Margaret Saylor (*l to r*): Will, Lloyd, George, James, and Sol.

My youngest sisters (*l to r*)
Sharon Rose, Lola,
and Minnie.

Newly wed, I am standing next to my friend, Matilda Swain. The woman on the porch of my house is Hazel Richter, a missionary from the Red Bird Mission.

Leon Lawson.

Reverend Herman Siedschlog,
Leon, and I, 1958.

Sidney Lawson, age eighteen.

My parents and my
brother Lee Roy, 1964.

Pregnant with Bruce,
1962.

Leon and I with our sons, Dennis Wayne and Bruce Alan, 1964.

At work with Bill Richardson (*l*) and Thomas Parrish (*r*), Council of the Southern Mountains, 1968.

The Reverend Don Graham pronounces Grant and me husband and wife, 1970.

Grant's parents, Jeanette and Mack Farr.

Sidney Farr, 1972.

Grant and our dog, Taylor.

Posing with one of my first books, *More than Moonshine,* 1983.

My sister Hazel Saylor, who died in November 1984.

My brother Jeems, 1991.

Jeems, my sister Sharon Rose Clark, and my brother Fred.

My son Wayne, my mother, and my grandson Richard, 1985.

Richard Lawson,
1975–1990.

Tom Sawyer and I at a book signing, 1993.

Friends and colleagues:
James Still (*front row, seated*)
and (*back, l to r*) Lee Smith,
me, and Silas House.

The New Opportunity School for Women Writers, 2003.

Berea College Archivist Shannon Wilson and I, November 2006.

15

Snake-Handling Saints

And these signs shall follow them that believe.
In my name they shall cast out devils; they
shall speak with new tongues, they shall take up
serpents; and if they drink any deadly thing, it
will not hurt them. They shall lay hands on the
sick, and they shall recover. —Mark 16:17, 18

My dad, grandpa, and various other relatives used to sit on our front porch or around the heating-stove in the living room and critically examine the subject of snake handlers in our community and in other parts of the mountains.

History tells us that snake handling as a religious practice started with a man named George Hensley in 1909. He was "searching the Scriptures for a text for a Sunday sermon," he told people. He came across Mark 16:17, 18. He read the verses again and again, and testified that it was like a bright light being turned on in his head. Could a person, filled with the spirit of God, actually handle deadly serpents and not be harmed? He decided to test (or confirm) the Word. Various people told us Hensley's story. Grandpa and Dad knew these reports by heart.

I listened to my elders' talk with horror and fascination. I never actually witnessed a snake-handling service, but my imagination made it seem real to me.

George Hensley climbed up White Oak Mountain in Tennessee and returned with a big, black rattlesnake. He handled the snake during services at his church. Soon other members began to handle snakes also. Eventually one man was bitten and nearly died. The church members then became doubtful and hostile toward Hensley; he left Tennessee and came into Bell County, Kentucky, where he started a church at East Pineville. Soon people in this church were handling snakes, and the practice grew and spread.

Hensley handled snakes for many years, until he was finally bitten and died in Florida in the 1950s—"which goes to show you that if you play with fire long enough you'll get burned," Dad said when he and Grandpa talked about Hensley's death.

The Holiness Church people I knew when I was young did not necessarily handle snakes, but they did believe in glossolalia (speaking in tongues) and various other gifts of the spirit. Some of this group did in later years go across the mountain to Blue Hole in Clay County and join a snake-handling group. A favorite saying among some of these Holiness people was "We are in the world but not of the world, children, praise God! We're not long for this world, little children; we're just strangers a-passing through."

The snake-handling sect has proven itself to be a durable one. It has been outlawed repeatedly in many places only to spring up somewhere else. New devotees are drawn in frequently. At the present time there are snake-handling churches in Kentucky, Tennessee, Virginia, West Virginia, North and South Carolina, Georgia, Alabama, Florida, Ohio, Indiana, and Michigan. (Snake handlers in the last three states mentioned are probably former residents of Appalachia.) In an age when there is ever-increasing skepticism and secularization, the faith of these people who say that they are "confirming the Word of God" is remarkable.

When the mining and timber corporations came into the mountains in the early part of the twentieth century and strip-mining operations began, the mountaineers engaged in a head-on collision with them. In addition, a large number of mountain men were active participants in World War II, and thus encountered some aspects of technology they could never have imagined back home. When these soldiers came home it was inevitable that they would feel marooned, abandoned, and perhaps God-forsaken. When faced with such conditions, people tend to devise religious practices that will dramatically prove that God is still with them, that he will still protect them. Scholars tell us that snake handling did not arise until mountain culture was in decline.

Since 1910 dozens of people in the United States have died from snake bites received during religious services. Scholars see snake handling as an aspect of what is called crisis theology, and find similarities to the Ghost Dances of the American Plains Indians in the late nineteenth century and the cargo cult science of the South Pacific Islanders, both being cults that arose after the natives' initial contact with the superior technology of the West.

Perhaps as a result of the encroachments of modern civilization on the mountain people's way of life, several new practices took hold in some churches, including handling poisonous snakes, talking in unknown tongues, and sometimes handling fire and even drinking strychnine. Although these practices have received widespread attention and much media coverage, only a very few mountain people participated. Those who did held services in different places with others who held similar beliefs.

My experience with Holiness people was limited to attending their church services with Mama occasionally. She believed in the Holiness way. Dad, however, believed in the Southern Baptist Church. I was never allowed to go to a snake-handling service, so my knowledge is limited to what other people told me about it.

My mother's brother, my Uncle Dewey, was a Holiness preacher. He was the kindest, most loving person to everyone he met. I thought he was a saint.

The Holiness people I knew rejected the existing social order as being corrupt and beyond redemption. Their moral code was rigid and ascetic. Dancing, movies, tobacco, alcoholic beverages, patent medicines, and drugs were strictly forbidden. The women did not cut their hair, use cosmetics, dress immodestly or extravagantly, or wear jewelry. Some of them did not drink coffee, tea, or soft drinks, and did not chew gum. They believed in the witness of the spirit within and felt a person should show by outward signs—be witness to—his or her religious beliefs. They always said you could tell good Holiness people by the way they dressed and by the way they abstained from things. But hypocrites can be found everywhere, as this Holiness mountain preacher knew: "They is a false religion that can handle snakes. They is a false religion that can pray for the sick. They is a false religion that can speak in tongues. What I'm a-saying is that there's a counterfeit for everything that God's got. . . . If you didn't have the spirit of God, you'd think it was the Lord shouting. . . . The next day, they'll fight, cuss, and chew tobacco, smoke cigarettes, drink liquor, steal anything. And that's the way you'd extinguish [*sic*] the difference between a Christian and a devil-possessed person." As one Holiness woman testified in a church service: "To confirm the word means to practice anything you preach or teach. That is what we're doing. . . . This is to let people know what can be done through the anointing of God. Most people come to see the serpents taken up. But when you get them there, you can preach the word of God to them."

Mama once told me the story of what happened to a man named Jim Helton. He and his wife, Edna Mae, were acquaintances of my parents. Jim's nickname was "Butter Eye."

"Did you hear about Jim Butter Eye?" Mama asked me one day when I was home for a visit. "Well, Edna Mae is just tore up something awful about it. She said she had a warning about it one night the week before it happened. She was out bringing in the cows, and why she seed an old black ram on its knees up at the top of the pasture. She said hit was on its knees a-prayin'. Said she went up to see what was wrong, but it jumped up and run away. She said it was just a-moaning and a-going on, like someone a-prayin' to the Lord. She knowed then it was a sign that something bad was going to happen.

"Well, Sunday night Jim went off to Blue Hole to a church meeting. Edna Mae didn't go. She never goes to any snake meetings. She's a good Holiness woman and loves the Lord, but she don't believe in handling snakes any more than I do. Well, she said, they brought Jim home late that night. A big rattler bit him. Edna Mae said that man did suffer awful. Why, she said he'd get up and kneel by his bed and moan and go on just exactly like that old black ram did. She called the ram to mind when she seed how Jim was actin'. She knowed this was the sign coming true.

"Jim died on Monday, and they buried him a-Wednesday. Edna Mae is just awful tore up."

"Mama, I'm awful glad you never did get in with that snake-handling bunch," I said.

"I never believed in it. I know they have scripture that says that about taking up serpents and things like that. But they's another scripture that says you shall not tempt the Lord. Poor old Edna Mae. Her children all grown and gone off and left her, and now her old man is dead."

Later that weekend I was talking with Old Widow Cane, who belonged to a branch of the Holiness Church that practices the handling of snakes. She was testifying (witnessing) to her faith to me on a street corner in Pineville. I asked why she believed people had to handle snakes to prove their religion.

"My religion, I've got to see it, praise God," she said. "I've got to feel it, too, praise the sweet name of Jesus. God, he gives us the word and then the evidence, and we must act on it in faith if we're ever gonna get anywhere in this world and the next one too, praise Jesus. God, why he can lock the jaws of them snakes; he can draw the burn out of the hottest fire. We have Shadrach, Meshach, and Abednego in the Old Book to witness to that, praise God. What's good enough for them is good enough for us saints today."

The people of the Holiness Church call each other saints. They interpret Mark 16:17, 18 and Isaiah 43:2 literally. Some of them drink poison, some of them handle snakes and fire.

"I seed that man, Raymond Hayes, handle fire one time," Grandpa told me. "He got one of them there blowtorches and held it right up close to his forehead and it never singed a hair, not nary one."

"I recollect one time me and Otis and Ed Brock was out, foolin' around, you know," Dad said, "and we took a notion to drop in and observe one of them snake-meetin's. They's already shoutin' all over the place time we got there. We kept one eye on them and the other on the place where we thought the box of snakes would be. One old man—he put me in mind of Old Man Andrew Brock—he got happy. Now it was wintertime and the heating stove was red-hot in places. That old man run up and just hugged that stove like it was his old woman. And he didn't even scorch a stitch of his clothes or burn a red place on his skin. Now what about a man doin' that and not even getting burned?"

"I've studied on it and studied on it," Grandpa said, "and I can't figure out how they can do it and not be hurt a-tall. Some of 'em do get snake bit and some die after they drink strychnine. But they's others who don't suffer ary bit from any of it. I don't understand it."

Most Holiness members believe in a special anointing of the Spirit; they believe that when they receive this anointing they can speak in tongues, heal the sick, and experience extreme danger and not be harmed. Sometimes unbelievers say they can do these things also, and some do try—to their sorrow.

"You recollect what happened at Arjay last year?" Grandpa asked. "They's having a snake-meetin'—I believe Shilo Collins was the preacher."

"Yeah, I remember," Dad chuckled. "That's when that 'sinner-man' got a little too much from the moonshine jar. He went to that service and said if the saints could handle snakes, he could, too,"

"He did, too," Grandpa laughed. "He reached out and took a big copperhead from one of the brothers. The snake was quick as lightning, they said. Soon as he took a-holt of it, it bit him on the hand. Did you ever hear what happened to him?"

"He lost his hand," Dad said. "Delmar Rice worked the same place as he did. Delmar said the man was off from work for ages of time and lost his hand to boot."

The snake handlers could have told this man that he did not have the anointing, or the faith, to do what he attempted. Even the handlers admit they are afraid of snakes when they are not in the spirit. As one Holiness preacher put it, "When the anointing is on me, I'm not afraid of the serpents. Other times I'd run. I've taken up as many as six serpents at one time. . . . I've not ever been bitten. There's something there that you know, without a doubt, that it won't harm you."

In spite of popular belief, snake handlers do not worship the snake. Snakes are never the objects of worship, but rather they are an element of worship. The believers do not have snakes at every service, either, as some people think. As one preacher put it, "We can have a good time without snakes. Someone asked me if we worshipped the snake. No! We surely do not! The snake represents evil, the Devil. We just show that God, the good, has power over the Devil."

Those who handle snakes do so for several reasons. They believe they are subduing the devil when they take up serpents. They also believe they are confirming the word of God when they carry out the (implied) injunction in Mark 16: 17, 18.

Scientists tell us that the reason the snakes do not bite more often probably lies in the way they are taken up and handled. The snakes lose their sense of balance, become disoriented, and are utterly bewildered when they are moved through the air to another pair of hands, or draped or twined around a body. But this does not explain why the snakes do not strike the moment the box containing them is opened.

Time after time, in the books and articles I have read on the subject, there are recorded instances of people at the snake meetings kicking the box during the course of the service. When the time comes to handle the snakes, the box is picked up and shaken vigorously in order to irritate the reptiles before the box is opened. The box is then put down and the lid opened. At this point the snakes should be frightened and apt to strike out at anything that moves. Sometimes people do get bitten when the box is opened but, more often than not, they are not harmed at all.

As mentioned earlier, some scholars believe that snake handling is an aspect of crisis theology. The people I knew in Bell County led a drab existence; they were desperate for something, anything, to break the monotony of their lives. Snake handling did that for them to a certain extent. It brought excitement, danger, and bravery into their lives. For a few moments, each time they handled a snake in front of an audience, they were in the limelight. They proved, at least to themselves, that God was still with them, that he was still protecting them. At those times when the anointing was taken away and they were bitten, they still maintained they were doing God's will, and that it was the will of God for them to be bitten in order to prove to the world that the snakes were really dangerous.

In more recent years, a large number of women have become snake handlers. I suspect that these women also crave excitement, danger, and attention. They have long been treated as second-class citizens, bound by rules and restrictions that do not apply to the men.

I remember hearing about one particular snake handler when I was a child. His name was Lee Valentine. "That man has suffered about as much as ary man put on this earth," Dad said. Valentine had been a moonshiner years before, and perhaps his path had crossed Dad's and Grandpa's from time to time because they also were moonshiners. People said that eight of Valentine's ten children had died of various painful diseases. He worked in the mines after he gave up moonshining and was almost killed in a slate fall. It was reported that his body was crushed under the slate and he was given up to die. A Holiness preacher named Willie Simms prayed for him, and he was healed. They said you could hear the bones snapping back into place, and then Valentine got up out of bed, sat down at the table, and ate a hearty meal.

After his accident in the mines, Lee Valentine joined the Holiness Church and became anointed to preach the gospel. Mama and her friends hero-worshipped him. (I never saw him in person, but I have seen pictures of him; he resembled Jim Backus, the actor.)

Time passed, and we heard that Lee Valentine had joined Shilo Collins's snake-handling church at Blue Hole. Mama and her friends, who did not believe in snake handling, grieved for this man, who had suffered so much and, they felt, had been led astray.

Years later, word came that Lee Valentine had been bitten during a service in either Alabama or Georgia and had died. They brought his body to his old home place near Harlan, Kentucky, for burial.

One notable thing about the snake-handling saints in Bell County was that they did not kill the snake that had caused the death of one of their members. They believed they would receive some kind of special grace if they handled the same snake. At the graveside services for Lee Valentine there was almost a riot when the believers fought to handle the snake that had killed him. The police broke up the gathering and killed the snake. Later Dad said to Grandpa, "Old Man Howard told me that the man who killed that snake had it skinned and a belt made out of its skin. He wears it ever' day, Old Man Howard said."

The Holiness faith and the Southern Baptist Church were the only religious services I attended as a child and young adult. They taught that God was a fire-and-brimstone God, and they preached about the wages of sin and other evil things. I could never accept what they preached. If God was like they said he was, I wanted nothing to do with him. Later, the Evangelical United Brethren Missionaries established a church in Stoney

Fork; sometime after that, this denomination joined with the Methodists and became United Methodist. I joined this church as an adult.

One of my most heart-breaking experiences happened after I had grown up, when Dad was saved and baptized into the Holiness faith. When Dad joined her church, Mama was thrilled and shouted her praises in the church services as she testified. Dad, as a new convert, became a zealous worker in his church. One day he came to my house and started telling me about the Holiness Church, comparing it with the mission church to which I belonged and urging me to leave my church and join his. I could not be persuaded to renounce my church. Dad pleaded with such fervor that he started crying. This I can never forget.

16

Marriage and Life after That

When the mountains spoke to my soul I knew I
was fated to hear them forever, no matter how
far I wander from home.

My parents took me from school when I was eleven years old and in the seventh grade—I never graduated from seventh grade.

"You are only eleven years old, Sidney, you can't stop school now," my teacher, Miss Howard, said.

"I have to, Miss Howard, there's no one to help Mama."

"What's wrong with your mama?"

"Mama has a bad heart. The doctor ordered her to bed. I have to help."

It became my lot to cook and housekeep for my family. I never got to attend classes again as a child or adolescent. I used to dream at night about being back in school, but that dream never came true. The nearest high school was fifteen miles away, and there were no school buses at that time.

First Marriage

I married shortly after I turned fifteen; there were no other options. I wanted to go back to school, but Dad said no. There was no money for me to be a boarding student at the Red Bird Mission School or the Pine Mountain Settlement School. "You are needed at home to help your mama take care of the young'uns," he said.

Dad worked as a timber cutter for the Ritter Lumber Company off and on until the first-growth timber had all been cut and shipped out of the area. By then, when the Ritter Company relocated their mill, Dad was in poor health and not able to move his large family anywhere else.

Around that time, when I was fourteen, Wilburn Helton, the brother of my best friend Tilda, came home from World War II. I fell in love with him. He had blond hair and bright blue eyes. In his right cheek he had a dimple, which came out when he smiled. For a day or two Wilburn hung around our house, talking to Dad. After he left one evening, Dad scolded me. "You made me ashamed of you, the way you looked at him!" he said. Later he told Mama, "She's growing up, Rachel. You'd better keep a sharp eye on her."

Other young men began to hang around our house, but I was too naïve to think it was because of me. Wilburn left the community to work in another state. Then we got word that he had married and fathered a son. I mourned for the loss of this first love. The last time I saw him was several years after he'd married and divorced. I was by that time married. Some of Wilburn's relatives lived just below our house on York Branch. Wilburn was visiting with them; two or three came out in the front yard as he was leaving. I watched from my house as they all got into a pickup truck and drove away. That was the last time I saw Wilburn alive. Later the neighbors said he had gone back into the army and was shipped out to Korea. Before the war ended he was killed in action.

Leon Lawson, the man who became my first husband, was in the Navy during World War II. After the war ended, he came back to Stoney Fork and his family, who lived on Birch Lick. I got acquainted with him at the post office, and he came several times to our house. He was a really handsome man, even more so when he smiled. I just wish he had smiled more often. He was quiet and serious, and he often would say cutting words about something or someone of which he did not approve. He had the reputation of being a hard worker and held others to his own high standards. He was also a talented guitar player. Leon and I went to church services a few times together, but mostly he came to the house and we sat on the front porch or in the backyard and courted. When he asked me to marry him, I said yes. I thought if I was ever going to have any life of my own, what else was there except to get married?

I was fifteen years and three months old on February 23, 1947, my wedding day. Leon was twenty-five. It was a gray, cold day—the sky looked hard as slate, and you could see glints of frost in the air.

My parents had to sign permission for me to get married because I was underage. Later I was angry because Mama and Dad had not had more foresight and had not taken better care of me. Why did they let me get married so young? But because most mountain girls married when they were thirteen, fourteen, and fifteen years old, Mama and Dad didn't see anything unusual about it. We really didn't know the Lawson family that well, though, since we lived on York Branch and they lived on Birch Lick. Because our houses were in different valleys, we had little association with the Lawsons.

On my wedding day Leon's sister Helen and my Uncle Andrew, who had agreed to go as a witness for me, accompanied Leon and me. Because Mama had so many younger children, it never occurred to me that she and Dad would go with us. We rode the bus to Pineville, our county seat. Back then you applied for your marriage license and then immediately went to a justice of the peace and got married. That is precisely what we did. I wore a cotton dress with sprigged flowers and a blue sweater for my wedding. Leon seemed embarrassed.

After the justice of the peace pronounced us man and wife we walked out of the courthouse, and Leon and Uncle Andrew just seemed to disappear, leaving Helen and me. I remember it was cold, and I was shivering because I was not wearing warm clothes. Helen and I walked down Main Street in Pineville and looked in the store windows, then we started looking for Leon and Uncle Andrew. We passed a little restaurant and through the window we saw them at a table, eating.

I felt embarrassed that my new husband hadn't said anything to Helen and me about eating. We went inside, and finally Leon looked up and said rather sheepishly, "Do you want anything to eat?" Helen firmly said "Yes," and we sat down at the table. It was a small restaurant, just three or four tables. I was so miserable I could hardly swallow my hamburger and Coke.

Leon didn't say anything directly to me the whole time we sat there; he and Andrew talked. After that, we went to the bus station. While we waited for the Straight Creek Bus, Allifair, a girl that I had gone to school with, came up to greet me. She came from a family whose older members had died from tuberculosis, one by one. We talked for four or five minutes until the bus came.

Leon said he reckoned we had better stay at my house because there was not much room at his parents'. (It was the custom for young newlyweds to stay with their parents for a few weeks.) There was one bed in our living room where Mama and Dad slept, and two beds in the bedroom. The younger children piled up in one bed. I remember getting in the other bed that night, wishing somebody would tell me what to do.

Sometime that night, Leon got on top of me and pushed at me. I froze, because I didn't know exactly what to expect. I remember he did invade me, and I remember that it hurt very badly; the next morning there was blood on the sheet. All I felt was the pain. After a while, he rolled over to his side of the bed and went to sleep again. I tried to sleep, but I felt like my world had ended. The next day, suddenly he decided we would go to his parents' for a while after all.

We walked a couple of miles up the road to Birch Lick. We came first to his Uncle Brad's house. Brad Lawson had married a young woman from across the hill when he was in his forties. They had four or five children—little boys, I remember, just like peas in a pod. Leon wanted to stop and visit with Brad before we went on to his parents' house. So we stopped and stayed a while. Then he and Brad went off somewhere to another house in their community. I waited and waited for Leon to come back so we could go to his parents' house, all the time dreading it and wondering why he had gone and why he was staying away so long.

Ethel, Brad's wife, talked to me and was very warm and welcoming, but I still keenly felt Leon's abandonment. I could not relax for even just a minute. Eventually it got dark and they still had not come back. By that time I had really begun fretting. I said to Ethel, "Do you suppose he has already gone home and will he expect me to come?" She calmly said, "Oh, I don't think so. Why don't you just relax and wait here until he comes for you."

Leon and Brad finally came back about 9:00 that night, and Brad said, "Well, you might as well spend the night—it's dark outside." So Leon and I spent the second night of our married life at Brad and Ethel's house. We slept in the same bed, but this time he did not touch me.

The next day we went on up to Leon's home. He had told me that his parents never spoke to each other, that they'd been married for a long time and had several children, but it was like they hated each other. I found Leon's family very strange. They greeted me when we arrived, though, and to my satisfaction Leon's father seemed to like me. During the following days he spoke to me more often than the others did.

Leon had several younger brothers, and his mother was very pregnant. I remember thinking, "Well, they must communicate some way for her to be pregnant." We settled in for the night; I remember how lonesome I was. I listened to the ticking of the Lawsons' grandfather clock and felt sad.

Several days went by, and then one evening Leon went down to Brad's grocery store and didn't come back that night. I couldn't understand it; I was embarrassed that he would stay all night away from his new bride. Again I laid in bed listening to the grandfather clock in the living room. Leon came back the next morning and didn't say a word about where he had been. I did not dare ask.

Helen and some of the younger boys had planned to go see a radio show put on by Wilma Lee and Stoney Cooper and their band of musicians out of West Virginia. They were appearing at the school near the mouth of Stoney Fork. Helen asked if I would like to go with them and I said, "Sure!" She asked Leon to go but he said no. He refused to tell me whether he thought I should go or not. I decided to go. We got ready and walked to the school. There was already a big crowd of people. I had listened to music shows on the radio many times, but had never seen a live performance. I thought they were wonderful and enjoyed them immensely.

We got home that night to find that Dora, Leon's mother, had gone into labor and that Leon had asked Brad to take her over Birch Lick Mountain to the Red Bird Mission Hospital. Leon stayed at the hospital until the baby was born. My mother-in-law was fifty-one years old, but she had no trouble giving birth to her last son, and she was back home in a week.

Then I got fever and chills; I had no idea what was wrong with me. I was sick a day or two and then one morning I got up and had bumps all over my chest, throat, and face. Leon's mother recognized the symptoms. "You've got the measles," she said. I was sick in bed for two weeks. Before I recovered, Leon's brothers and sisters started coming down with it, one by one. Even the new baby got the measles. Dora said I had brought the measles in on the family. I felt terrible and extremely blameworthy. Sometime later I heard that Allifair, the girl I had talked with at the bus station, had had measles. I must have caught them from her. I tried to apologize to Dora, but she just sniffed and left the room. It seemed to me it took all that winter before the last person in that house got better. Leon acted indifferent to how I felt.

By the time we had recovered from the measles, Leon had made arrangements for us to live in an old house that was down the creek from where his parents lived. Some of his family had lived in that house years before. I remember that it was a nice, big house with several rooms. In fact, it was so big that in the winter we shut off part of the house to conserve heat. But I didn't like living there, for I always felt afraid of something intangible. The floor would creak, and a door would close by itself. Now that I am older and more sure of myself, I would like to live in that house again. But back then, when Leon wasn't home I was frightened to stay there by myself. Of course nothing ever happened.

When springtime finally came, delightful plants sprouted up all around the old place, and it was an adventure to see what would come up where and try to identify it. There were also fruit trees and a garden; that first summer we planted vegetables and I picked blackberries. I canned berries and apples, and made sauerkraut and pickled beets, like my mother had always done.

We lived there for a year, and then we bought a house and a small bit of ground, just flat enough to have a garden, on York Branch. From this little house I could look across the creek and see my parents' house on the hill. Mama and I could stand out in our yards and holler back and forth to each other.

The house we moved into was just a one-room house built with rough lumber. The roof leaned all one way, high in front and down in the back. It had windows at eye level that opened and closed. For a while we lived in that one room. In the wintertime we had a Warm Morning heating stove in one corner of the room, our bed in another corner, and a wood-burning cook stove in the third corner. The homemade kitchen table stood in the center of the floor.

Leon got a job at the William Ritter lumberyard and began earning money. For the first time I knew the joy of having more than one new dress at a time. We bought a set of pretty new dishes with peach blossoms around the edges. They were beautiful.

Leon had to walk to work, which meant that he had to leave when it was just barely daylight. I'd get up at 4:30 in the morning to bake biscuits and fix a hot breakfast before he left for work. I knew that I would have the whole glorious day to myself.

That summer I began listening to soap operas on the radio. I would rush out in the morning to pick beans and gather other vegetables for supper. I prepared the vegetables when the radio dramas came on the air. I appreciated the little bit of freedom I had living away from my childhood home and at least somewhat on my own.

I always found it exciting to listen to the radio. I imagined what the different actors looked like as they talked and tried to envision everything about the setting. It was much more exciting to listen to the radio and imagine what things looked like than it is to see everything on TV today.

Eventually Leon was able to get some lumber and materials to add on a room to our house. His dad and other men in the community helped to build a kitchen onto one side of our house. It was great to have a kitchen. Then after that he built a porch across both rooms so that we had a front porch. Later he boxed in half the porch. This new, extra room was just big enough to get one double bed in. You could barely get around the bed. A door opened out onto the porch, and one opened from the kitchen into the room.

That room became my refuge. Sometimes at night I'd wait until Leon went to sleep, then I would ease out of bed, go into that room, and stuff towels around the door so the light wouldn't shine through. There I would read for hours. (By that time, the Red Bird Mission Bookmobile came to Stoney Fork every three weeks.) Sometimes I would listen to the radio, but I had to keep it turned down so low I could barely hear it. I was always afraid that it might awaken Leon.

Almost from the beginning my husband abused me verbally and physically. If I tried to express my opinion and at the least hint of arguing with him, even if it was just to pacify or explain, he would slap me and tell me to "shut up." I could never win an argument because the more I stood up to him the more violent he would become. So early on I began to withdraw to a place inside where his blows and words no longer had power to hurt me.

I was ashamed for anyone to know about my fantasy world and how Leon treated me. Soon enough, however, my family and friends became aware of how things were between us, since he would scold and belittle me in a lordly sort of manner in front of them. But he would physically abuse me only at home.

17

Missionaries and Books

After all is said and done, the mountains are
still there. They are the backbone of my life.

At times I yearned to know what lay beyond the mountain ranges. I dreamed of cities, towns, lakes, and oceans, which I had only read about in books. When missionaries from the Evangelical United Brethren Church at the Red Bird Mission in Beverly, Kentucky, came to Stoney Fork to hold Sunday school classes on Sunday afternoons, I felt blessed. This was my first experience with people from outside the region, and they changed the world for me. I thought they were perfect.

The Red Bird Mission had centers in several other communities that they called outposts: Beech Creek, Middle Fork, Jack's Creek, and Mill Creek. They opened a center at Stoney Fork in 1949. The preacher at the Red Bird Mission Church, Reverend Ira Wilson, and two high school teachers, Iona Wendland and Hazel Richter, arrived and began holding Sunday school classes in the one-room schoolhouse. Leon and I started going to the services; it gave us something to do, and there were no regular church services in the community at that time. We and our neighbors filled the one-room school every Sunday afternoon, where we were divided into classes.

I was learning a lot just by associating with the missionaries and seeing how they related to other people and to each other. After a while, though, I began to feel ashamed of my mountain ways in the presence of the missionaries, ashamed of our poverty and lifestyle, which seemed so different than theirs. I worked hard to talk like they did and grew obsessed with making myself commendable and "worthy" so as to be accepted by people who were beyond the hills. By that time I had decided that if I were to live in a big town or city someday I would need to talk and act like city folks did. This annoyed my family and friends. They accused me of trying to get "above my raising," of being "stuck up," and of throwing away my heritage for a much more cosmopolitan style of life. Little did they know that I was even more driven to "get above my raising" than they even imagined!

At the Red Bird Mission, Esther Elmer was the high school librarian. The mission outfitted a bookmobile, and she began traveling up and down the hollows around each outpost. Esther came to Stoney Fork every three weeks. Patrons were allowed to check out three books at a time. Gradually that changed when she realized how much and how quickly I would read the books I borrowed, so she started bringing extra books just for me. She asked me to read them and tell her if I thought they were the kind of book that she should carry in the bookmobile. This gave me the chance to read all kinds of books on all kinds of subjects. I gladly read them all and dutifully reported to Esther.

In one carton of books Esther brought me was a magazine containing an advertisement about the American School in Chicago. It said students could take high school courses by mail. I was excited by that idea, especially when I read that the school was accredited and one could take college preparatory courses from them.

I wrote the American School for more information. They replied that it would cost $198 for three courses per semester, and that payment could be made by installments. I wanted to enroll more than anything. There had to be a way.

Around that time a full-time minister was sent to Stoney Fork. Morris Bauman arrived with his wife, Kathleen, and their two children, Sandy and Danny, in 1950. They rented a storefront house alongside the main road that went through the community. The building, with its sloping roof, had been hastily built. At one time it had been a store, where you could get gasoline or kerosene and groceries. The house had no electricity and no running water when the minister and his family moved in. I felt sorry for Kathleen because she looked too fragile to be the mother of two children, to keep house, and to help her husband in the church.

I prayed that the minister's wife would be able to read music and could give me music lessons. I played music by ear on a reed organ I had bought from a neighbor, but I wanted to learn to read music so that I could play songs I had not even heard before. After the Baumans arrived and we got acquainted, I found out that Mrs. Bauman could read music, but could not play very well. She used one hand, playing only the melody and the alto part of hymns. Still, she agreed to teach me at no charge if I would promise to play the piano for Sunday school and church. I agreed and further vowed that if she gave me lessons I would learn to play using both hands.

I went to Kathleen's house once each week for lessons on her piano. At home I only had the reed organ on which to practice. Then one week Reverend Bauman drove to Ohio and brought back a truckload of used pianos, one for the church, one for me, and several for some neighbors. Leon, who liked music, was very supportive of my getting the piano. He even paid the $40 charged to help pay the expense of the trip. My friend Tilda, who bought one of the used pianos, also wanted lessons from Mrs. Bauman.

I was still waiting to enroll in the American School. How could I pay for it? I went to Mrs. Bauman and asked if I could do any work for her. After thinking about it, she said I could do her ironing. (This was the day of cotton and almost everything had to be ironed.) She said she would pay me $3 a week. I wrote the school asking if I could pay $3 each week by installment. They agreed, and I enrolled.

Doing the Baumans' ironing turned out to be a terrifying job for me. I was accustomed to using irons heated on a stove, but the Baumans had a gas iron. Its pilot light, when lighted, burned with a blue flame that bubbled and hissed all the time.

After a year or so, the mission told us they had plans to build a new church at Stoney Fork. The mission leadership said they would match us residents dollar for dollar in getting the church constructed. They told us that the congregation could work on the construction and they would figure out what our contribution was according to how many hours we worked. This seemed like a really good deal. Dad, Grandpa, and some of my uncles all helped. The mission decided the church should be built of native stones gathered from the creek. I remember Dad with his horse, pulling sleds full of rocks. There was a lot to do, and quite a few people worked on the church.

The mission brought in a man, from near Toledo, Ohio, to supervise the building project. He had spent his life as a builder. He volunteered his time to come and supervise the construction. I liked him; but Leon was possessive and jealous if I even spoke to this man or any other of the workers. At home he would slap me or yell ugly names at me, claiming he had seen me looking at them. My friends who hear this part of my story inevitably ask why I stayed in the marriage. My answer is that there was no work for women, and I had no place to go. All I could remember at the time was Grandma Saylor saying, "You've made your bed and you have to lie in it. There's nothing you can do."

The music lessons gave me something else in my life, and Leon was proud that I was learning to play the piano. It was one of the few things that I ever did on my own initiative of which he approved. He played the guitar and sometimes in the evening would play and sing, and sometimes I would sing along with him. But for some reason I never tried to play my piano with his guitar.

A local preacher, who had a radio ministry over the Pineville radio station, asked Leon and me to sing and play for his program. We began practicing in the evenings and on weekends. We sang for our church services first; then we went to do the radio program. We began getting invitations to sing at other church services, revivals, and funerals. The funerals were difficult, especially when the deceased had left specific requests that we sing certain songs at the funeral.

I enjoyed everything about our singing together. I would have to say that those times of traveling and performance were the happiest times we spent together in our marriage. Leon, who usually criticized everything I did, did not criticize my singing, which encouraged me. We became well known in the region for our singing.

I also did some songwriting. During both World War II and the Korean War mothers hung stars in their windows to denote how many sons were in service. I wrote a poem entitled "God Had a Son in Service" and sent it to a radio program called *The Midday Merry-Go-Round,* which was broadcast over station KNOX in Knoxville, Tennessee. One particular group, Carl Story and the Rambling Mountaineers, liked my poem and composed music for it. They made a recording of the song, and I heard it played on several local stations. I even received two royalty checks: together they amounted to $150. I was well pleased.

Leon hated my reading books. Many times he jerked a book out of my hands, ripped the pages, and threw it into the fire. Because of this, I was afraid to tell him when I enrolled in the American School. I knew he would forbid me to do it. For a while I managed to keep my schoolbooks hidden from him, but one day when I was away from the house he found where I had hidden them. It was wintertime, and our Warm Morning heater was keeping us warm. How easy it was for him to burn those books. I was desperate when I returned home and discovered what he had done, and I wondered how in the world I could ever replace them.

Finally, in desperation, I wrote a carefully worded letter to the school. I never told a lie if there was any way around it. I wrote that my books had been destroyed "by fire." A person from the school wrote back to express their condolences for my home's having burned, and they replaced the three textbooks without charge.

At this point I told Leon I was taking correspondence courses and why. I said if he ever touched another one of my books I would make him very sorry. I finally had mustered the fortitude and stood up to him about this. I was firm and quiet on the outside, but inside I was boiling mad, just daring him to ever destroy another book. After that, he left my books alone.

Of course there were other things to keep me busy. Our little house on York Branch had no running water. I had to go down the road a quarter of a mile, where someone had put a pipe into the hillside where there was a natural spring. I would go down, fill two buckets with water, and carry them home. I asked Leon repeatedly to dig us a well close to the house so I wouldn't have to carry water. He always promised that "one day soon" he would get started.

Finally, after hearing "one day soon" once too often, I said, "If you're not going to dig a well, I will." Leon laughed. While he was away at work that day, I got a shovel, marked off the place in the yard where a well would be handy, and started digging a hole. Every morning, after breakfast and household chores were done, I would go out and dig before the sun got up high and hot. Day after day I dug, and day after day Leon would taunt me: "When are you going to reach China?"

I was stubborn and would say to myself, "It doesn't matter what he says, I will do this one way or the other." Pretty soon, the hole was waist deep. Then, when it got still deeper, and I was still digging and shoveling, Leon got worried because I didn't know anything about how to shore up the walls. He hired a man in the neighborhood to finish digging the well. Eventually two more men came to help. They took turns digging.

When the hole got very deep, the men reached some clay-like rocks, which they would pitch up and out of the hole. Some of these rocks would have imprints of leaves and ferns on them. They were beautiful; I marveled at the thought of how many millions of years ago those plants had been alive. I kept some of the rocks for a long time. Eventually the workers struck water, and it came in strong and cold. I was so happy.

They shored up the sides and built a wall about three feet high on top of the ground. They put a pump in and then cemented rocks into place so that the top was smooth all around the well. All I had to do was go prime the pump until water gushed out, and I had all the water that I needed.

Up until this time we did not have electricity. It wasn't until the early 1950s that our house was finally wired. On the day that Princess Elizabeth was crowned Queen of England—I remember listening to the coronation ceremony on my battery-operated radio—men were stringing electric wires into the house. We finally had electricity! We had bought an electric wringer-type washing machine, and the first thing I did once we had electricity in the house was get water from the well, heat it, and do a load of laundry. It was wonderful to watch the machine run by itself and to feed the clothes into the wringer. And all of this on that famous day! I listened to the radio the whole time.

Of course, we also quickly bought other electric appliances, such as a refrigerator and an electric radio. (Back then, in 1953, there was still no television.) Having electricity and water in and near my house turned out to be great, because I now had a baby.

18

Love for a Child and a Man

They brought joy and sorrow, contentment and
pain, growth and stillness. They illuminated my
soul. One stayed, and one left without warning.

In February 1950 Leon's unmarried fourth cousin had a baby in the
Red Bird Hospital. Reverend Wilson and Dr. Schaeffer, the mission
doctor, said she couldn't keep the baby, and they asked Leon and me if
we would consider adopting him. We had been married three years, but
had no children. After much discussion we decided we would, and I rode
across the mountain to the hospital to get him. In hindsight the thought
of riding a horse and carrying a baby sounds terrifying, but that day it just
seemed the ordinary thing to do. I rode my father-in-law's workhorse. It
was a big horse but very gentle.

I rode across Birch Lick Mountain and down Mud Lick to the mission hospital. When I got there a nurse met me at the door and said, "The
baby's not here. The mother came last night and took him home. She
changed her mind."

I was so disappointed as I rode home. When I came across the mountain and down Birch Lick, I began to think about how shy and modest
my mother-in-law and Leon's sisters were, and here I was riding a-straddle
this big old horse. When I dismounted, what if my skirt came up? To avoid
any chance of embarrassment, I decided to get off the horse before I got
to their front yard. In the process of getting off the horse, I slipped, and
my foot caught in the stirrup before I got to the ground. The horse ran
sideways, dragging me for a few steps before he stopped. Later I realized
that I could have been killed had he not stopped.

But he did stop, and I just sat there on the ground for a little while, trembling. Eventually I was able to work my foot loose, but it was hurt. I took hold of the bridle, then limped along, leading the horse on up to the house.

For the life of me, I cannot remember how I got home. My house was a mile down the road from where Leon's parents lived. Maybe somebody gave me a ride in a truck. People in the area had pickup trucks and jeeps, and there were log trucks active by that time, so somebody must have given me a ride to the house.

My right ankle was sprained, and for two or three weeks I could hardly bear to put it on the floor. I remember thinking, "It's a good thing I didn't have the baby with me!"

On March 23, a gray, cold day, I thought I heard a baby crying. "No, I'm just hearing things. That's not . . ." Then there was a knock at the door.

I went to the door, and there stood the preacher with a bassinet in his hands. It was an old bassinet that his children had used, he said. He told me that the baby's mother had changed her mind yet again and had realized, after all, that she was unable to keep the baby because she did not have enough money even to buy formula.

His mother had named the baby Dennis Wayne. He was exactly a month old the day he appeared at my door, having been born on February 23, 1950. (I turned eighteen years old that October.) He had lost weight since his mother took him home and didn't weigh as much as he did at birth. I remember how tiny his hands and feet were.

I could not wait for Leon to come home from work that afternoon. When he did, he was as pleased and surprised as I was, and immediately began talking to the baby. It seemed natural to me to take care of a baby because I'd had plenty of experience taking care of my younger brothers and sisters. Wayne seemed to thrive in our care. He immediately started putting on weight.

We had to wait three months before we could have the adoption hearing, and every day of those three months, if I heard a vehicle in the road below the house, I would run and look because I was so afraid that Wayne's birth mother had come to get him.

The mother had already had one illegitimate boy, who was four years old when Wayne was born. I heard later that while she was going through the process of deciding whether to give Wayne up, the older child would wake up at night crying, having nightmares that his mother would give him away, too. The girl's mother later told us that story, and I found it heartbreaking.

Wayne's mother decided to go back to Chicago, where she had been living when she had gotten pregnant. She left with her four-year-old, Dean. Her mother found out later that while on the train to Chicago, she got acquainted with an elderly gentleman who was on the train with her. She found out that he owned a railroad or two and seemed to love children. She gave Dean to this man and slipped off the train, leaving the sleeping little boy behind.

I used to have nightmares about this little boy waking up with his mama gone. We heard that the man adopted him. He lived in Moose Lake, Minnesota. That's all we ever heard about Dean. Wayne knew that he was adopted and he knew about his brother from the very first. I had always determined that I would tell him the truth about anything he asked. I did not want him to start school and then have the other kids surprise him with information like this. So Leon and I talked to Wayne about his adoption and tried to make him feel that he was ours because we wanted him.

For a little while being a father seemed to make Leon more calm and gentle, but old habits are hard to overcome. Soon he went back to calling me "stupid" and saying I was a "worthless Saylor." After hearing these things over a period of time I became brainwashed and began to think I really was stupid. Of course I realize now that this was Leon's way of intimidating and controlling me.

I went through these years being a wife and mother and feeling like nobody. I had little self-esteem. I remember one time when Wayne was five years old. Leon was raging at me about something and hit me. Wayne grabbed the broom, hit Leon across the head, and cried, "Don't you hit my mama! Don't you hit my mama!" This made Leon ashamed of himself. After that he tried to pacify Wayne and treated me better for a little while.

Unfortunately, I was making mistakes with Wayne. When Leon was harsh and threatened to punish Wayne, I always showered him with love and shielded him from his father as much as I could to keep him from getting a spanking. When Wayne got a little older, whatever was the worst thing Leon could think to say to him he would say repeatedly. Over the years, anytime Wayne was being stubborn or not obeying, Leon would yell at him, "You will mind me! If you won't mind me, I know where they will make you—I'll send you to reform school." That was the threat that he held over Wayne's head all the time: "I'll send you to reform school."

I turned more and more to the Red Bird Mission Church, which is now the United Methodist Church. (Back then it was called the Evangelical United Brethren Church.) The mission church was more liberal than the old-time Baptist and Holiness churches, the only ones with which I had had any experience. Eventually we got the church at Stoney Fork built, but we held services in the old school building for a number of years. Every year we had a revival, at first in the school and then, later, the church.

Eventually, with the help of the lessons I took from the minister's wife, I learned to play music well enough to accompany the singing of the old gospel church songs. I played the piano for the church services and the Sunday school.

A man named Edd Taylor came to live in the community; he could play the piano. His mother, Rendy, was a widow who moved into the house Reverend Bauman's family had first lived in, the Baumans having moved into the new parsonage. Rendy's daughter, Molly, was Edd's half-sister. She was married to John Lawson, Leon's uncle, and lived across the road from Rendy.

Edd had lived away from the area for years. He had gone away to college, served in the Marine Corps, and worked outside of Kentucky after he got out of service. A bachelor, he came home to spend some time with his mother. He started coming to church services while we were still in the schoolhouse. Edd had studied music for a number of years, so he was asked to play for church services quite often. I saw him every time I visited Molly that summer. What I did not realize at the time was how vulnerable and desperate I was for some real romance in my life.

One day I was in the schoolhouse before the service started. I looked across the room and spotted Edd talking to somebody. Suddenly I felt a strong desire to just walk over and put my head on his shoulder while he put his arms around me. This shocked me; until that moment I had not realized my feelings for him.

I started daydreaming about Edd. Although I was scared that Leon would find out about it, I visited Molly's house almost every day, hoping I would see Edd. I was, after all, still a teenager at the time.

Stoney Fork was a "gossipy" place. Just a look or a smile exchanged between a man and a woman was enough to make people talk. One day after Leon had been particularly hateful toward me, I wrote a letter to Edd. I told him that I loved him. I did not even think of what the consequences might be. I just wanted him to know.

Several days after that Leon and I were in Pineville. We had finished our shopping and were waiting at the bus station for the Straight Creek bus. Edd walked in, evidently planning to catch the same bus. Just then, Leon took Wayne to get some bubblegum out of a machine next door. Edd came up to me and spoke to me quietly. "The other day I got a letter which I shall always treasure," he said. I smiled at him but did not reply.

Later Molly told me that Rendy got suspicious about the letter Edd carried around in his pocket and read time after time. When he was sleeping, Rendy got it out of his pocket and read it. She told Molly she was afraid I was going to get Edd in trouble; she was going to keep the letter just in case it was needed.

Somehow word got out that I had sent a love letter to Edd. Somebody told Leon, and he became very upset. I remember he cried the first time we talked about it. It was nighttime and we were sitting on the front porch of the little house on York Branch. I remember him crying in the dark. I felt so terrible and wicked. Leon asked the Baumans to come talk with me. They asked me if it was true and I said, "I guess."

Leon wanted us to repeat our wedding vows; he thought we needed to do that. The preacher and his wife went along with it, thinking it would be a good idea. I felt such guilt that I did not dare refuse, but I also felt heartsick about it. The following Sunday in church, Reverend Bauman announced to the congregation that Leon and I were going to repeat our vows. He asked us to come up and stand before the altar.

Edd was in the congregation that day. I wondered what he could possibly be thinking. Leon and I stood there and repeated our vows, and I just wanted to die.

A few days after that Sunday, Edd left Stoney Fork. I was devastated. I felt so ashamed that I stopped visiting Molly. I repented and promised God I would be good. I was so involved in the church and prayer at that point that somewhere along the way I became convinced that if only I would be a good girl, doing everything according to rule, that God would someday let me be with Edd.

19
Endings and Beginnings

People with histories like mine have experiences
and memories that are rich and fertile. That
richness can make amends for the disadvantages
of poor educational opportunities, intellectual
isolation, and other hardships.

Time went by, and the gossips in the neighborhood told me that Leon was seeing a girl named Lizzie. I got to watching him. He would go to her house, and they would go for a walk together. This made me angry, because it was he who had insisted that we repeat our vows. I thought this meant that we were making a new commitment to try to make our marriage work. Yet now he was openly seeing Lizzie. Seven-year-old Wayne was with them once and later told me that he had seen Dad and Lizzie kiss each other. At the time Wayne thought all this was funny and innocent.

Then after Lizzie there was somebody else. It was almost as though Leon felt he had to get revenge against me for my having dared so much as to look at another man, let alone express myself to him. I wished fervently that I had had the foresight and impudence to have hatched some sort of plan and run away to be with Edd.

I didn't seem to get as much satisfaction from attending church services that I once did. I didn't find myself praying as often as I had before. There was no joy, no spark of anything in me. I had been a good girl, but God seemed to have let me down, and my heart hardened.

Two or three years went by; then I got a letter from Molly. She wanted me to come and see her. She said she had a pair of shoes she wanted me to try on. The next day I went to see her. As soon as I got into the house, she said, "I don't have any shoes. Edd's come back. He's sick, and he wants to see you."

"What's wrong with him?"

"He has cancer of the liver and has come home to die. Ever since he got here he keeps saying, 'Sidney will come to see me, I know she will.' It breaks my heart."

We went across the road to his mother's house and found Edd in bed. I walked into the room. I was not prepared to see him; he had lost so much weight. Edd told me how he'd gotten sick and what the doctors had told him. I asked if there was anything that I could do, and he said he had been craving macaroni and cheese. He said that Molly had made some, but that he "had never liked the way she fixed it." He then described the way he liked macaroni and cheese prepared.

"Well, that's the way I fix it. I'll bring you some," I promised.

"That will be good. I'll try to eat some of it." He smiled.

Going home, I felt so desolate because I realized my dream had ended. I had dreamed for such a long time about going away to live with Edd. I could not believe God would let him die now, nor could I believe that God was going to take him so soon because I had been good. I had gone out of my way to be good to Leon. Times when I should have been angry, I was good. I'd been a good mother. I'd been a good church worker. But now it looked as though God wasn't going to reward me for having been good. I felt nothing but confusion and pain. I also felt overwhelmed with grief and sadness for Edd. I fixed a dish of macaroni and cheese and took it to him later in the afternoon. He thanked me and reached out for my hand.

"I'm glad that things turned out the way they did," he said. "You are young and have your life still ahead of you." He squeezed my hand and looked at me lovingly. "I would have left you too soon."

Leon heard that Edd had come home to die. That Friday, when he came in from work, he said, "After supper, let's go see how Edd Taylor is doing." I hadn't dared tell him that I'd been going to see Edd. So we went to pay a neighborly visit, and sat around Edd's bed and talked. Edd told Leon he couldn't eat and that he was losing weight because he just couldn't keep down enough food. It was a painful visit and we didn't stay long. We took our leave, and when we got to the door, I looked back. Edd was looking at me with such longing in his eyes and such love; it was almost like beams of light came from his eyes toward me. It was a look I will never forget. After we got outside, Leon, upset, said, "Why did he look at you like that?" I said, "I don't know." But of course we both knew.

The next morning, word came that Edd had died that Friday night after our visit. The cancer didn't kill him, but a heart attack did. I was thankful that he didn't have to suffer any longer, because I'd heard that cancer of the liver can be a very painful death. I was glad he had the heart attack. Molly said the doctors had told them that something else would probably end Edd's life before the cancer did. I was glad that he didn't have to suffer anymore, but I felt as though the world had just collapsed around me.

They buried him at the top of Birch Lick Mountain, just on the other side as you start down. That was the old family graveyard, and that's where his mother wanted to bury him. I remember the way that graveyard looked. I remember Rendy, his mother, holding on to my arm as we walked up the footpath. And as we stood for the service she kept hold of my arm, and I took care of her as I knew that Edd would do if he were there.

Edd's mother had told me earlier that their family always dug the mountain graves so that they faced east, "so that on Resurrection Morning, they will come up out of the grave and be facing east, where the Christ will come." They buried Edd facing east. Thoughts of Edd and his grave site stayed with me, and sometime later I wrote a haiku about him:

> Facing east he lies
> Morning sun touches his grave
> My heart is still dark.

After the service at the graveyard, we went back home. Rendy and Molly were grieving for their son and brother, and I was grieving over the fact that Edd and I had never gotten to really be together; we had never even so much as kissed.

For years after that, and even to this day, sometimes I dream that Edd is alive again. I go to that little house by the side of the road and he is alive.

Or sometimes I dream he has just died. Or I am trying to get him to come back. Or I am trying to talk to him and yet never quite able to do anything but feel grief, frustration, and regret.

After Edd died, my heart became very hard.

WAYNE WAS NINE YEARS OLD when Leon wanted us to move to Indianapolis. His sister and other kinfolk of his had all relocated there, and they all had good jobs, so Leon wanted to go see if he could find a good job too. By this time I had completed my correspondence courses and had received a high school diploma. For five years I had fought Leon for the privilege of studying and having books. I had also taught myself to type. I thought that if we did go to the city, maybe I could get a job as a clerk or some such position and help earn money. We closed up the house on Stoney Fork and moved to Indianapolis.

With my high school diploma, I got a job in a very short time in an insurance rating bureau, which was housed in the Chamber of Commerce building in downtown Indianapolis. It took Leon longer to get a job, but eventually he was hired to work in the Beverage Paper Mill. He worked on the eleventh floor where they mixed the formula for paper. He soon came to hate his job because the work was hot, smelly, and backbreaking. He said it was much worse than the job he'd had at the sawmill because at least there he was working outdoors and had fresh air to breathe. He seemed to resent that I had a job in an air-conditioned office. I tried to explain to him that I got the job because I had a high school diploma. He became furious when I pointed out this fact, and told me to shut up.

We had been in Indianapolis for only a little while when I met a man in the neighborhood. When he went to work in the morning he drove near the building where I worked. I rode the city bus most of the time. But he started coming by as I was waiting for the bus, offering me a ride to work. Before I knew it, I found I was attracted to him. I was a mountain girl, but I was not entirely naïve. One morning when I started to get out of the car he took my hand, leaned over, and kissed me. Wow! He called me a very pretty woman.

Suddenly I had somebody else to daydream about. I felt rebellious and angry at life. After all, when I had been a good girl, God had let Edd die. For a long time after that, I wished I had made love with Edd, wished I had memories of a real love affair instead of just fantasies of him.

In short, I was ripe for an affair. Andy and I had the right chemistry, and the sex was satisfying in a way that I had never experienced before. I was overwhelmed with emotion as I tried to conquer my fear.

Several months went by, and then I discovered I was pregnant. Our adopted son, Wayne, was almost ten years old by this time, and I had been married for over thirteen years. The doctor I had been seeing at the clinic I had been going to for minor illnesses confirmed that I was pregnant. "I'm not surprised," he said. "The medicine you've been taking for the last month to help regulate your periods can also act as a fertility drug." He also said that a change of climate, a different lifestyle, and changes like that could also help some women get pregnant. That is the story I told Leon and his sisters.

For a time I think Leon actually tried to believe I was carrying his child. But every so often he would suddenly lash out at me with jealous fury, accusing me of having been with another man. Leon admitted to himself that because he had had mumps as a teenager, he could not father a child.

Throughout this tumultuous time, Leon and I stayed together, living and working. I started writing in my spare time. I was homesick for the mountains, and the only way I found relief was to write about them. One of my first poems expressed that longing.

Mountains Fill Up the Night
I know the mountains covered with snow
And misty green of earth's awakening,
When they are drenched in summer storms,
Painted with master colors,
Softened with Indian Summer smoke.

Then dusky dark, its curtain silent;
The mountains grow starward
Around us, and over us and

Under. Even inside us.

Where do the mountains stop?

Leon was very unhappy with his job and wanted to move back to Kentucky. I thought it would be a good thing if I got away from Indianapolis and Andy. So we decided to leave Indianapolis.

I had started writing in earnest by then. *Mountain Life & Work,* a magazine published in Berea, Kentucky, had published a couple of my short stories even before I had left Stoney Fork. I had become acquainted with the editor, Bob Connor, and his wife, Phyllis, when he had come to the Red Bird Mission to help teach a two-week writers workshop that I participated in. Phyllis and I had corresponded since then. Now I wrote her to tell her that although Leon and I would be leaving Indianapolis, I didn't feel I could go back to Stoney Fork to live—at least not yet. Bob and Phyllis helped us to compromise on Berea. Leon and I bought a house sight unseen and moved to Berea in August 1962.

I was happy to come to Berea because it was the home of Berea College. Perhaps I could attend college classes, I thought.

I had a hard pregnancy with Bruce and almost lost him while still in Indianapolis. I kept having spells of bleeding; the doctor gave me a new medicine: Thalidomide. Later I learned how fortunate we were that Bruce was not born deformed, like so many other children whose mothers had taken the drug—born without an arm or leg, sometimes without both. The only way the drug seemed to have affected Bruce was in his baby teeth. The periodontist theorized that at the time when teeth are formed in the fetus, something stopped Bruce's development, and by the time it resumed, the stage for forming tooth enamel was passed. For whatever reason, Bruce's teeth started crumbling when he was two years old. The periodontist was able to preserve the spaces in Bruce's gums until his permanent teeth grew in.

I was six months pregnant when we moved to Berea. When I told the Berea doctor how tired I had been feeling, even early in the morning, he said impatiently, "Well, Mrs. Lawson, most pregnant women do get tired." They did not find out until I went into labor that my hemoglobin was very low. (Although my Indianapolis doctor had not tested my blood very often during my pregnancy, I thought they had done the usual blood tests when I was admitted.) By the time I was put into a hospital room after being admitted, I was told I needed a transfusion. This slowed my labor pains; it was thirty hours later when Bruce was finally born, on October 13, 1962, a little over two weeks before my thirtieth birthday.

I remember being on a table and hearing a baby crying. I heard the doctor say, "You've got a boy, Mrs. Lawson."

I thought, "Oh, no. I was hoping it would be a girl. A boy might look like his father." That was my first response. But when I held my baby for the first time and he nursed at my breast, I felt an overpowering love filling my mind and heart. It felt so right to hold him and nurse him. God had been good to me after all. He had given me a son who would come to mean so much to me.

Leon went on a hunting trip with his father and brothers early in the morning after I went into labor. A neighbor across the street drove me the short distance to the hospital. Miss Key, the British nurse-midwife in charge of the maternity floor, was upset that Leon was away. After all, they might need him to sign papers should a life-saving procedure be necessary.

Wayne was eleven when Bruce was born. Wayne had begun having what his dad called "spells." He would be doing fine, happy and playing, and then suddenly, just like the sun going behind a cloud, he would withdraw and you could not talk to him. He would not tell you what was wrong and wouldn't say if anything hurt; he would simply withdraw for a while. Then eventually he would be all right again. Spells like this became more frequent as he got into his teen years. I didn't understand what the trouble was; I could only see that Wayne was beginning to get into trouble more and more and it always seemed to have something to do with money.

Leon didn't understand Bruce any more than he had understood Wayne. He still threatened to send Wayne to reform school, and I was still sheltering Wayne, and later Bruce, from his rages. Leon loved Bruce, but he always felt deep in his heart that Bruce was not his son. He sought retribution by punishing me, sometimes in very subtle ways and other times openly, with physical abuse.

When Bruce was a toddler, I arranged to have individual counseling with the minister of Union Church in Berea. I had joined this historic interdenominational church before Bruce was born. The minister's name was Don Johnson, affectionately called "DJ" by the congregation.

By this time, Leon had bought a baby blue pickup truck. He would never let me even touch his truck, let alone learn to drive. He had convinced me that I was not capable of driving. I had very high blood pressure and suffered from the constant tension. I hoped, through counseling, to gain some self-assertiveness and independence.

After being in counseling for two or three years, when Bruce was five years old, I told Leon one morning at breakfast, "I am going to learn how to drive, and I will get my license. And there's not a thing you can do to stop me." Leon blustered and threatened. But I simply kept repeating what I planned to do.

Leon had a job as caretaker at Union Church at that time; he would walk to work and leave the truck parked at the house. One day I told him to not be surprised if he came in from work to find the truck gone. I would be out taking a driving lesson.

The next day Leon told me he was moving out. He said he had found somebody else. He had met a divorced woman at church who had a child. He said he loved her and intended to court her.

Of course he had no sooner moved out than he wanted to come back. But I was mindful of all that had passed between us and ultimately I would not agree to let him come home.

We had been together for eighteen years. Since I was fifteen, I had shared my life with this man, who had never learned how to love and to trust. He was always paranoid, and not just about me. He felt the world was out to get him and that he had to get them first. He did not have any close friends because he would turn people off with his sharp words. I'd given up a long time earlier the idea of entertaining or even having friends come to visit me at home because he would always somehow manage to insult them.

After Leon and I separated, however, I just withdrew even more, talking to almost no one except DJ.

DJ was a very liberal minister; he believed in individual freedom and said that no one owned another person. He impressed on me that I should never depend on other people for my happiness, that I either had it within me or I did not. Every word he said had the ring of truth about it. With DJ's help I was able to find the fortitude to hold firm when Leon wanted to reconcile. We filed for a divorce in 1967.

After the divorce was final, the judge gave Leon visiting rights. But he was never consistent about the times he would come and get Bruce or Wayne. Sometimes he would come on a Tuesday and sometimes on a Saturday. The boys never could count on any regular thing with their dad. The court ordered Leon to pay me $50 per week as child support until Wayne and Bruce became eighteen years old. He was never late with the payments, but he never hesitated to let me know he was having a hard time making them.

I was careful not to say anything negative about Leon to Wayne or Bruce. I knew that in time they would draw their own conclusions. I did not want to cause them to hate him. Bruce was angry with me for a long time; he would lash out if I were talking on the phone. "All you ever do is talk on the phone!" he'd say. "You won't talk to Dad or nobody else! You just stay on that old phone!" And he'd say things like, "Why don't you ever smile at Dad? You never smile at him." I figured Leon had said these things to him, influencing him.

Wayne never did finish high school. I could not keep him in school. I tried for a while. The two of us rode the bus once each week to a psychiatrist in Lexington, who I hoped could help Wayne, yet usually Wayne would just sit silent the whole hour and not talk to the doctor. He refused to talk about anything that bothered him. I despaired over my inability to reach him.

When he was fifteen, Wayne got the idea that he wanted to go into the Navy. He talked to a recruiting officer, who said that if I would sign for him when he was sixteen, he could join. Leon had been in the Navy, so that's what Wayne determined he wanted to do. Eventually I gave in.

Leon would not help me with Wayne; by then he was dating the woman whom he later married. Any spare time he had was spent with her. He did not have time for Wayne. After Wayne turned sixteen I signed the papers for the Navy, and he was inducted and sent to boot camp. Eventually, he was stationed in Puerto Rico; he loved that country and seemed to thrive there. But when his three years were up he decided not to sign up for another stint.

Wayne came home even more restless and discouraged than he had been before he left for the Navy. He was a very handsome young man, tall and slim, with brown hair and blue eyes. Girls swarmed around him wherever he went.

After Wayne had been home for a year he went to Indianapolis to look for a job. A few months later, he called to tell me he had gotten married and that he and his wife, Marilyn, were coming to see me. I wondered about their marriage and what his new wife was like.

By this time I had met Grant Farr and was planning to be married myself. Leon knew of my plans and said he would stop the child support payments if I married. Grant and I discussed it and agreed to let Leon stop the payments.

By this time Leon had married again. When he and his new wife wanted to see Bruce, or wanted Bruce to spend the night with them, I let Bruce go. I knew he loved Leon, but every time after he had spent time with Leon, he would come home angry with me. He would always push the limits until he had to be disciplined. It seemed as though Bruce had to reestablish his boundaries each time after he came back from a visit with Leon. I wondered what Bruce would think of Leon and me and his upbringing when he was older.

20

There Was Grant

It is not required of us that we succeed, only that
we be faithful to the highest good in us.

Leon and I were divorced in 1967. When school started at Berea College in September 1968, I met Grant Farr at a ballroom dance class being taught by a faculty member. I loved folk dances and went every time one was held on campus, but I joined the ballroom dance class because I wanted to learn about dances I had only seen on television.

Grant, who was certified to teach ballroom dancing, came to the class because, he said later, he "wanted to see how the faculty member taught." The teacher quickly realized that Grant was a skilled ballroom dancer. She asked him to be my partner and to help the other beginners. The first time Grant danced with me our belt buckles somehow became entangled. We had to stand still while everyone laughed as he patiently got us loose. Afterward members of the class stopped at Porter-Moore's Drugstore for Cokes. Porter-Moore had an antique soda fountain, and it was fun to sit at the counter and get acquainted.

I had joined Union Church shortly after Bruce was born in 1962. In addition to counseling me, the minister, Don Johnson, also did group counseling in which Grant (whom I did not then know) participated. As time passed, many in the congregation at Union Church were not satisfied with DJ's ministry. They thought he was far too liberal in his preaching and conduct, and in 1968 they asked him to leave. DJ was assigned to a Methodist church in Jenson Beach, Florida, and his family moved from Berea. We lost not only a pastor, but a friend and counselor as well.

When I joined Union Church, I began singing in the church choir. We had performed Handel's *Messiah* early each December for five years. That was an enriching and educational experience for me. I knew little about classical music and had never sung it.

Meeting Grant was also enriching. I saw him every week at the dance classes. I found out he had been born and reared in Black Mountain, North Carolina. At the time we met, Grant was a junior at Berea College. He told me he was twenty-three, a bit older than most of the other students. "Just a kid," I thought. I lived two blocks away from campus. I invited Grant to my house for a home-cooked meal (which was a rare treat to students who had to live on Food Service meals). After that, he came for dinner several times through that September and October.

I worked for the Council of the Southern Mountains. The Council had been formed in the early twentieth century to give various mission workers in Appalachia an annual gathering place. Eventually it was felt that a yearly conference was not enough, and a quarterly magazine was begun in 1925. I loved my job as associate editor of *Mountain Life & Work*. I often had the chance to attend workshops and conferences, and I made new friends. Feeling accepted and needed by those who knew all about me and liked me anyway, I was well off indeed!

Grant seemed so much older than he said he was, and I felt younger than I was. Early that December Grant told me that he loved me. And he kissed me. I was deeply moved. It felt like the first time I'd ever been really kissed. The depth of my feelings surprised me. He told me that he was bisexual. He said that for years he'd had relations only with men, but that after being in therapy for awhile he had learned to be intimate with women. I was so fascinated with him that I did not feel any concern about his history. The present was enough for me.

Grant went home to Black Mountain, North Carolina, for Christmas. On December 21, a Saturday, I brought Bruce with me while I had my hair done. While we were in the beauty shop, Santa Claus paid a surprise visit and gave us all a piece of candy. Bruce was delighted!

The next day, Sunday morning, I awoke with a sore throat and felt too ill to go to church. (I had a weakness in my bronchial area and often had bronchitis.) I lay on the couch and watched TV with Bruce. All day long the wind banged at the windows, snatched at half-opened doors, and fretted at the roof. I hate it when the wind blows like that. Intervals of dark rain were interspersed with the wind.

I wrote a special Christmas letter to Grant.

Words can be unpredictable. They can be weak and lazy, they can sing like naked willows in the wind, they can heal a wounded spirit . . .

I felt restless on Christmas Day. I sought tranquility by remembering the beauty of the silver wind, the spring violets, and the April greenery spread out in the hills. I remembered the warm black earth, sad with all its knowing sighs, which covers its face with dry and tender leaves.

I'm learning about love, I thought. Love, like words, is also unpredictable. Love is also a little plant that *will grow,* even if it has to push its way up through a cement walk, even if it has to live in a thimbleful of dirt in a rock crevice.

Grant called me on Christmas Eve and told me how much he loved my Christmas letter. He said he shared it with his mother, and she also liked it.

I wished Grant and I could be together when the New Year came in. We arranged to talk on New Year's Eve. He would not be back on campus until January 6.

Time passed slowly; I missed him so much. It frightened me to realize the depth of my feeling. What is it that makes a man and a woman turn to each other and feel instinctively, "This one I want to know better"? I felt that way about Grant from the beginning.

When Grant came back after Christmas vacation we saw each other often, always at my house. Our relationship became intimate and more and more intense. From early December to the middle of February we spent much time together. He'd come down for dinner on Friday and on Saturday and sometimes for an early supper on Sunday before chapel. We talked about how he was not doing enough studying.

One day in February I went to Richmond to look into the possibility of my attending Eastern Kentucky University. Grant offered to come to my house at five and cook dinner with Bruce. I got home at five-thirty; we had a wonderful time with Bruce before putting him to bed. That night Grant and I spent several hours together. For me, it was the apex of our relationship. Grant gave every indication that he felt the same way. It was Valentine's Day, and along with a beautiful card he gave me the book *Are You Running with Me, Jesus?* by Malcolm Boyd. I still have that book, and when I see it on my bookshelf a rush of memories floods in, bringing me the emotions of that evening once again.

Just one week later Grant told me he thought we were spending too much time together and that perhaps we should not see each other anymore. Sadness and a feeling of betrayal swept over me. I wanted to hold on tight to this person who had helped me feel like a teenager again!

That Saturday he seemed depressed. He said he couldn't come down to see me that night. I was very concerned about our relationship. Later he called and asked me to meet him at a local pizza place. Wayne happened to be home and agreed to babysit Bruce. Grant tried hard to be good company, but near the end of our meal he stood up, announced that he had to go, and left the restaurant.

The next afternoon he called and said he couldn't see me because he had to study. His voice was strained. I didn't see him until the following Friday night. Bruce was spending the night with his dad, and Wayne was out. Grant and I had the house to ourselves. We talked for a while, and we were intimate, but almost immediately afterward he left, saying he had a lot of studying to do. He added, "I won't be down this coming Friday because a friend of mine in the Air Force is coming to see me."

"Will he spend the weekend?"

"Yes," he said.

The Friday after that he called to say he couldn't come down that night. "I caught a terrible cold."

"What are you doing for it?"

"I went to College Health Service this morning," he replied in a tired voice. "I also talked with the school counselor a long time this afternoon."

The next day, Saturday, he came to see me, and we talked.

"Sidney, I don't know how I feel about us anymore."

"I love you, Grant."

"I still care for you, Sidney. You have gotten as close to me as anyone ever has. *I cannot allow to you to be that close.* I believed I was ready for an intimate relationship with a woman, but now I'm not so sure."

"But we have been so good for each other," I objected. "Can't we just slow down a little?"

"To go any further with you is not fair; you would only be hurt. Throughout our relationship I've not liked the fact that I have to come down to your house all the time. I hate it that I don't have enough money or time to take you out. It's not natural for us to spend so much time here."

"I have loved every moment we have spent here," I replied. "I know you're a student and don't have money to take me out to dinner in cities like Lexington. I understand all of that, and I don't care."

"Sidney, sex with you came to mean more than our relationship. I just can't ever let sex be that important to me in any relationship."

"I don't understand. Great sex is so important in a good relationship."

"But sex on a one-night-a-week basis is not good for either of us. I'd want to see you more often, and I'd be tempted to take time away from my studies and work. If I did that, I'd end up resenting you and hating myself."

"I will help you be aware of time and place. I promise to send you back to your dorm in time to study."

"But by taking up so much of your time, I feel I'm not being fair to you and the other men you might have a chance to meet. I want you to have the freedom to have other sexual partners, and I want the same freedom for myself. But the intense way we feel about each other would prevent us from exercising that freedom. I hope we can be friends and date casually, but the intimacy as it's been cannot continue. I'm not ready for that kind of relationship with anyone."

Grant and I talked a long time. When we said good-bye, we both cried. I stood on the sunporch and watched him walk up Center Street toward his dormitory. I stood there for a long time, hoping I'd see him come back. I couldn't believe he was gone for good. It started to rain. How appropriate, I thought. I felt desolate.

The next weekend the friend from the Air Force came again to see Grant and spent Saturday night with him. I couldn't help feeling that

Tony was part of the reason for Grant's break with me. I told myself I must not feel angry or hurt toward Grant. I had accepted him and learned to love him as he was. Life would go on for us both.

Around that time I found that I would be eligible for about $1,800 a year in grants and loans if I became a full-time student at Eastern Kentucky University. I'd have to sell my house and buy a car to commute to Richmond. If I sold the house, bought a car, and became a full-time student, I would be eligible to live in Berea's government-subsidized apartment housing in Dixie Park. The rent would be based on my income.

Selling the house would break my last tie with Leon. I was never happy in that house.

After pondering the difficulties of commuting to EKU, I realized it would be more sensible to try for Berea College, even though I would not be eligible for the grants and loans I would receive at EKU. Loyal Jones, my boss at the Council of the Southern Mountains, offered to help if I got in a financial bind. My friend Pam said I was a fool to think of EKU, but not because it was too far away. She said that if I was taking this step, why not let it be a long one, clear out of the state.

I went to talk with Alan Morriam, the admissions counselor at Berea College. He told me what I needed to do to enroll. First I had to take a two-day series of entrance exams. I took them and passed. I was rated in the 99th percentile for English/verbal skills and concepts—but only in the 35th percentile in math. I had to get a tutor that summer, they said, then be tested again before school started in September.

Meanwhile, I fought to hold back the hurt of losing Grant. I rationalized and analyzed until I was bone-weary. I reread all the letters he wrote me at Christmas, read the inscription in the books he gave me . . . and cried. I loved Grant, just as I had loved Edd Taylor. Was I to lose Grant, too?

Agnes Hart, a friend of mine, called and invited Grant and me to a party one Saturday night around this time. When I told her that Grant and I were no longer dating, she hinted that her guests were only couples, but said it would be all right if I came alone.

I did go to Agnes's party—with a friend from church named Martin. It was good for my morale. I wore a green sheath that made me look slim and brought out the highlights in my honey-blond hair. Martin introduced me to a man who looked at me and said to Martin, "I envy you, Martin. You have a lovely date."

During the next few weeks, Grant came to my house, sometimes for a meal, other times just to talk, but we no longer had an intimate relationship. One afternoon while he was visiting, he concocted a rum drink that we both loved: four jiggers of light rum, four jiggers of grenadine, and one small 7-Up. We named our new drink Red Devil. It inspired a poem I wrote and sent Grant that summer while he was home in Black Mountain.

Red Devil

I go to my room and try to sleep
    but I can't sleep
With the red devil singing in my blood.
It's gone to my head and I'm wild.
I hear music with every cell in my body
And feel the red devil with every nerve.
My room explodes in color
    and I run wild in the wind.
I run naked in the wild wind
And feel music in my feet.
I want to dance.
    I want to dance with my lover
    But he's not here.
I try to sleep but I cannot sleep
With this red devil in my blood.

Grant got a summer job working as a dance therapist at Duke University's psychiatric hospital in Asheville, North Carolina, that summer. I enrolled in Berea College as a degree candidate. I left my job as associate editor of *Mountain Life & Work* at the Council of the Southern Mountains, and was employed as a dormitory director at Fairchild Hall. I was paid $225 a month and lived in a dorm apartment. It was a big change for Bruce and me to move into an apartment on campus. I decided to rent my house for the time being; the rental income supplemented my salary as dorm director.

That summer I bought a 1963 Ford Fairlane, black with a red interior. Several of the male students, as well as my friends, gave me driving lessons.

On July 18, I watched the astronauts walk on the moon. What a thrill to see history being made by those first footsteps on the moon. Some of my people in the mountains didn't believe it was real. "If God wanted people on the moon," they said, "he would have created them there."

Bruce and I moved into Fairchild Hall near the end of August. There was a bedroom, a kitchen, and a bath in a suite on the second floor. The college gave me another adjoining room for Bruce. Bruce couldn't imagine living in a dorm with 103 girls. Neither could I. The girls moved in by Labor Day. When Bruce wanted to take a shower in the girls' shower area he had to call out "Man on the floor!" Also, when he'd come in from school and started up the stairs, he had to call out the same thing.

Grant came back to school in September.

"I missed you, Sidney," he said. "It's so good to see you again." We had supper together, and it was so easy to be with him.

"It is so good to see you and Bruce again," he repeated at the end of the meal.

After a few days of seeing each other, it seemed as though all the issues from the winter before had been settled in Grant's mind, but apparently he had decided not to talk about them. I avoided asking him because I was afraid of what I might hear.

The fact that I had so much going on in my life—adjusting to new living quarters, getting to know my girls in the dorm, attending classes—was another reason I didn't have the courage to bring up serious topics with Grant. I found myself doing what I had done in my life with Leon, retreating to somewhere inside and dreaming of life the way I wanted it to be. After a few weeks Grant and I became intimate again. Now, however, it was harder to find private time than it had been before.

I was enrolled in three classes: Psychology, General Science for non-science majors, and an advanced English course. They chose the ten students with the highest scores in English and put us in this special class. By the end of the semester my grades were a C in General Science and

Psychology, and an A+ in English. Grant decided to change his major again, this time from Civics to Philosophy and Religion.

The second or third day of my General Science class the professor started writing mathematical equations on the blackboard, and I was lost. The next day before class I talked with the teacher. I knew him well; we both sang in the choir at Union Church. He had read some short stories of mine when they were published. He said, "I understand, Sidney. If somebody assigned me to write a short story I would be lost, too." He arranged for a young woman in the class to tutor me. This worked out well enough for me to pass with a C. The professor made me feel better by the way he responded to my problem.

Bruce's seventh birthday was October 13. The girls in the dorm threw him a surprise birthday party. There was a mound of presents as big as a washtub in the middle of the parlor floor. He whispered to me, "I can't believe this, Mom."

When Halloween was near, the girls started planning an Open House. Bruce figured largely in their planning. Three or four of the girls had taken him under their wing. He spent a large amount of time in their rooms (I found out later that they had gleefully taught him how to play poker).

Almost everything that semester was an adventure for Bruce.

That fall, Wayne got a furlough from the Navy and spent several days with us. The Dean of Women at first refused permission for him to visit us at the dorm, but the girls all signed a petition demanding that Wayne be allowed to visit and presented it to her. She relented, but would not allow him to spend the night. Once he was there, it seemed all the girls developed crushes on him, handsome as he was in his blue-and-white uniform, before he flew back to Puerto Rico.

In November, Grant asked me to marry him. He was twenty-four; I was thirty-six. I knew I wanted to be with him for the rest of my life. I said yes, and we began making plans. We would finish the semester, sell my house, get married on January 24, and move to Asheville, North Carolina, where Grant would again work at Highland Hospital as a dance therapist.

We both wrote to DJ in Florida to tell him our plans. He wrote back, saying that he hoped he could come to our wedding, but it was not to be;

church and family activities prevented his coming. Before Christmas, at Grant's urging, I traded in my Ford for a newer car, a Chrysler.

During Christmas vacation, Bruce and I closed the dorm and with Grant we set out, in my Chrysler, for Black Mountain, North Carolina. Grant's mother had invited us to come with Grant to visit that Christmas when he told her we were going to get married. I was worried about what his parents would think about this older woman and their son.

We got caught in a huge traffic jam at Lake City, Tennessee. For three hours we moved forward only inches at a time. Grant had told his family we would be home in time for dinner. We arrived at 2:00 in the morning to find his parents still up, and they had kept food hot for us. We ate and stumbled into bed, almost too tired to talk.

The next morning they let us sleep late and fixed a hot breakfast when we got up. We sat around and talked, and I answered many questions about my background and life.

The second day I heard his mother on the phone with Grant's Aunt Kate, saying, "You know I've always felt like I didn't have a grandson. You know how little Mack's always preferred his grandfather's company?" She was talking about Grant's brother Jack's only son.

"Well, I'm here to tell you I have a grandson now!" and she proceeded to describe Bruce and some of the things they had done together that day.

Several days later Bruce announced, "I'm going to call her Gran." It was a name he had chosen by himself, I thought. But now I believe that Grant's mother may have influenced Bruce toward calling her by that name. She usually got her own way about things, I learned, especially where the family was concerned. I thought it was perfect for the two of them. Just before the wedding Bruce said, "I can't call Grant Dad, because I already have a dad. I will call him Pa."

The next day Grant took his mother Christmas shopping while Bruce and I stayed home. Grant's father was a quiet, dignified man with whom it was easy to establish rapport. We talked; he told me about Grant and his brother, Jack. He said he had taught a Sunday school class for years at their Baptist church. He told me how sad he and his wife were when Grant broke away from the church and started going to the Unitarian Church in Asheville.

The third day we were there, Grant and I drove to Asheville and did our own Christmas shopping. We also looked at apartments. That night we went to a Christmas party at the home of his friends Dick and Wayne. I had a really good time.

Mama Farr cooked a special supper on Christmas Eve; then we opened presents. Bruce was very excited to get so many presents at one time. The next day, Christmas Day, thirty people came for dinner!

Some family members had teased me earlier, saying, "Wait until Jeanette cooks a big meal, and see how you get along with her then!" All of them talked about how she used every pot and pan in the house. That morning I got up when she did and soon decided that the best way to help her was to keep washing pots and pans as she used them.

When the other family members arrived, the women hurried to the kitchen. They looked around with disbelief at the uncluttered kitchen. Mama Farr smiled and said, "I had a good helper today."

Dick and Wayne invited Grant and me to their New Year's Eve party, so we went, leaving Bruce with Gran. Several years later Bruce told us what happened that night.

"Gran decided to make a red devil's food cake and said I could help her. We got the ingredients together, and Gran started the mixer. Then she began telling me a story. Just when she got to the exciting part she forgot and lifted the beaters out of the dough. The red dough went everywhere!

"Gran was worried. She said the family always laughed at her when she accidentally did things like that.

"I helped her take down the white curtains and she washed and ironed them. After we got them back on the window, and all the splattered dough was cleaned up, Gran made another cake before you guys got back."

Gran got her first promise from Bruce that night not to tell anyone. She said the incident would just be their secret. What could a grandmother do to more endear herself to a boy? This was just the thing to bond the two of them.

After New Year's we returned to Berea and resumed our school activities as we planned our wedding. Just before our wedding day, the weather was bad for travel, and there were doubts that Grant's family could make it to Berea for the wedding. Finally Mama Farr declared that she intended to be there even if she had to fly (she had never flown before). Fortunately, the weather moderated somewhat, and Mama and Dad Farr, Grant's aunt and uncle, Kate and Haywood Farr, and his brother, Jack, arrived by car the day before. They stayed at a motel until our wedding, which began at 6:00 P.M. at Danforth Chapel on the Berea College campus.

I had bought a floor-length blue dress with silver trim for my wedding dress and a brown suit for Bruce. For years after that he called it his wedding suit. Grant and I had written our own wedding vows, which was unusual in 1970. In the following years it became much more common. A good friend, Barbara Shelton, who composed music and played guitar, provided special music for us. Grant gave her the poem I had written for him at Christmas the year before, and Barbara arranged the words and wrote music for it. She sang the song at our wedding; she also sang Judy Collins's hit song that year, "Both Sides Now," which Grant and I thought to be very appropriate for us.

After the reception and photographs, Bruce spent the night with Grant's parents in their motel, and then they took him home with them to stay for a week.

Grant and I chose not to take a honeymoon trip; we decided instead to drive to Asheville and get settled in our apartment before Bruce came home. We moved into the English Arms Apartments on the ground floor near the swimming pool.

Perhaps all the stress of selling my house, finishing the semester, packing to move, and having the wedding lowered our immune systems; in any case, both Grant and I came down with the flu. In addition, Grant had an abscess on his cheek for which he had to seek medical attention.

Fortunately, by the time Bruce came home at the end of the week, we were feeling better. Grant planned several things for them to do together. He told Bruce this was their "honeymoon time."

The three of us lived in Asheville, North Carolina, for a couple of years. Grant continued working at Duke University's Highland Hospital in Asheville as their dance therapist.

In his job at the hospital, Grant was responsible not only for private work with mentally ill patients of both sexes, but also for Saturday night parties. He wanted me to go with him to those parties. He told me to dance willingly with any of the male patients who asked me. I felt nervous about this, but I did go.

One Saturday night a tall, thin man asked me to dance. I had not seen him there before and was not even sure if he was a patient or one of the staff. We danced for a few moments before he started talking. I listened closely, ready to reply. He kept up his monologue, and I realized he was talking gibberish; I could not understand a word he said. I looked around for Grant to come to my rescue. The man kept on dancing and talking. I tried to follow his steps and act as though I understood what he was talking about. After what seemed like hours, the dance ended. The man bowed to me and escorted me off the floor. Grant later told me that the man was a new patient, one of the R. J. Reynolds Tobacco heirs.

Grant shared anecdotes about his coworkers and patients, and I began to feel as though I knew them. But if he talked often about one of the female staff, I would feel jealous and threatened. Obviously this was an unresolved issue for me, but I ignored it. I tried not to let it show.

Bruce took to this new life better than I could ever have hoped for. Grant had been so thoughtful in preparing Bruce for his first night in the apartment. He knew that Bruce would be alone in his new room after we went to bed, so he bought a teddy bear half as big as Bruce and left it in the bed as a surprise. Bruce was delighted to find the bear and I am sure whispered many secrets into Teddy's ear after he went to bed.

Grant drove Bruce to school on his way to work each morning. When school let out in the afternoon Bruce walked home with a group of students. He made friends. I was pleased for him.

For the first time in years I had time for myself. I wrote in my journal, tried out new recipes for dinner, and spent time relaxing.

Winter passed, and after the swimming pool opened Bruce was in the water every day. He quickly learned to swim and played with some of the other children at the complex. I tried to get in the pool each day for the exercise.

One young man in the complex came to the pool after work. He usually had two or three friends along. He loved to get on the diving board and jump or belly flop into the water, causing the waves to swamp the little kids who were at the shallow end and splashing anyone sitting poolside. This aggravated Grant, especially when it was repeated day after day. One time inside our apartment he called the man a "redneck." Bruce thought this was funny; he'd never heard that expression. Another evening, when it was very hot and the pool was crowded, Bruce walked over to the young man and looked closely at the back of his neck. Then he called across to Grant, "Pa, his neck's not red!" Some people laughed, but the young man flushed an angry red. Grant calmly but quickly left the pool.

While we lived at the English Arms, Wayne got out of the Navy and stayed with us for awhile. All the young girls at the complex flocked around him anytime he was outside. Wayne was a handsome young man, six feet tall, with dark hair and blue eyes. But he was restless and couldn't seem to settle down. He decided to go visit his dad in Kentucky, and from there went to relatives in Indianapolis. Eventually he got married.

That summer I began to have anxiety attacks. At first I did my best to ignore them, but eventually I told Grant. He wanted me to see someone at the Blue Ridge Comprehensive Health Center. I resisted at first, then promised to call the center. When I placed the call I felt intimidated, sure they would make light of someone who was just anxious about things. To my surprise they took it seriously and made an appointment for me to see a psychiatrist in a few days.

I liked the doctor and soon felt enough at ease to talk about my life. He suggested that part of the reason for the attacks had to do with my new lifestyle. He said that our lives can go on the same way for a long time and we get into a rut. Then change happens, the old rut is gone, and we are forced to make a new way, which causes us to feel anxious. That made sense to me. Life with Grant was so different—so much richer and more rewarding than my earlier life. Every day I felt like pinching myself to believe this happy life was real.

Grant was the only real father Bruce had while he was growing up. Up through his teen years, Grant was the one who disciplined Bruce and helped rear him.

Long after Grant and I were married, I still had a lot of anger toward Leon. When I married Grant, it felt as though I was living the "teen years" I never had. Grant and I grew together, played together, and had fun together. He encouraged me to write, in contrast to Leon, who was never interested in anything I wrote and would just grunt when I said something about a poem or short story. Leon never once read anything that I'd written. Grant did.

With Grant I got the tenderness, the romance, and the sensitivity that I never had with Leon. Grant was the opposite of Leon in every way. I'd had a rough, tough marriage with Leon, so it was natural that I'd pick someone who was the opposite of him.

Grant's parents were great; almost from the first I loved them as though they were my own. Mama Farr called me on the phone every day. So did her sister, Aunt Kate. Grant grumbled that one thing about having a big family was that they wanted to know everything that was going on, but I didn't mind talking to his family every day.

The summer and fall passed, and it was Christmastime again. Grant's job paid just enough for us to get by. We realized there would be no extras for decorating the apartment and putting up a Christmas tree. We talked about possibilities. We would, it was taken for granted, go to his parents' for Christmas dinner. They were coming to see us on Christmas Eve. Grant kept looking in the Christmas tree lots, hoping to find a tree on sale. Finally he bought a tall, skinny cedar that was on sale and brought it home. He helped set it up in one corner and turned to me.

"I won't get off work until ten o'clock Christmas Eve. Since Mama and Dad are coming for supper, you'll have to do the decorating and cooking on your own."

"I'm sure I can come up with something," I said. I bought some tissue paper in shades of lavender, purple, and pink. I started making paper flowers, dozens of them, attaching them to the cedar tree. When the tree was full of flowers, I strung icicles over the flowers and limbs of the tree. Grant had a blue floodlight, which we shone on the tree, and our first Christmas tree was beautiful!

When his parents arrived that evening they said the tree was lovely, though I did wonder if they really thought that using paper flowers and a blue floodlight was a strange way to decorate a tree. Grant came home from work, we had a late supper, and then we opened presents. Grant got

Bruce his first football; I remember how Bruce almost jumped into his arms, he was so pleased. (He has been a football fan ever since.)

On Christmas Day we all got up early and drove to Black Mountain. This Christmas was a repeat of the previous year. Mama Farr cooked, and I washed pots and pans as fast as I could. This year there were only twenty-five relatives and friends as guests.

During the next summer, Mama Farr and Aunt Kate went with Grant and me to Old Fort, across the mountain from Black Mountain. We shopped in several stores for fabric. I bought enough material for several dresses. Grant found some gray wool and hinted how much he would like to have a cape sewn for him. Mama Farr and Aunt Kate frowned at each other, but said nothing. After finding patterns, and buying red lining material and enough wool for a cape for each of us, we returned home. Aunt Kate assured me she would help with the sewing if I ran into difficulties.

The next few weeks my days were filled with sewing. I saved the capes for the last to cut out and sew. Aunt Kate kept advising me on certain aspects of sewing and lining a garment. At last they were done. Grant was delighted with his cape and began wearing it as soon as cool weather came. I have to admit that I cringed a little every time he wore it because I thought it made him look effeminate.

The year 1971 began with a New Year's dance at Highland Hospital. Grant planned all the activities, music, and refreshments. The night of the dance, the patients were excited. Grant danced with the patients, the women guests, and me. He had to make sure that all the patients got a chance to dance. This seemed to be no problem with the younger patients, but the older ones were shy. At Grant's suggestion, I asked several of the male patients to dance with me.

I was always so proud of Grant's charisma with people. Women and men alike were drawn to him. He was so gifted intellectually and musically and was also a certified ballroom dance instructor; I shouldn't have been surprised when people flocked to him.

All of my life, it seems, I have had an inner voice that puts me down, criticizes my efforts, and lowers my self-esteem no matter how hard I work at eradicating it. More and more often in my happy marriage with Grant I would hear this voice speak harshly to me.

"What would make a young man like Grant even look at an older woman like you?" it asked. "What makes you think you can compete with the young, beautiful men and women in his life?" I had no answer except to take comfort in knowing that he loved me. But that was never enough to stop the critical voice.

For our first anniversary on January 24, we wanted to do something special. Grant made reservations for us at the Sky Club on Beaucatcher Mountain. We had a wonderful time together, and, as we drove back home, I remember feeling utterly content and happy. This was the kind of life I'd dreamed about back in Stoney Fork.

We began talking about the need for Grant to finish his college work. I planned to take more courses, too, at whatever college we chose. We made inquiries at North Carolina colleges and universities and came to the conclusion that, for us, Berea College offered the most. Grant applied for readmission, and we planned to return in September. Through people I knew at the college, I got a job in the Development Office, sight unseen. We also rented a small house near the campus.

And so we moved back to Berea.

Our plans were that I would work full-time for the college until Grant graduated, then I would enter full-time and get my degree. I learned that full-time staff workers could take one class each semester, without a cut in their pay. I started taking one class at a time. Grant graduated and almost immediately enrolled in graduate study at EKU. I kept working and taking one class each semester.

Grant's father was diagnosed with bone cancer the year we moved back to Berea. We made many trips back and forth to Black Mountain during his illness.

I learned an important lesson about prayer at this time. Toward the end, Daddy Farr was in a coma, and as I sat by his bedside, I said the Lord's Prayer and read the Twenty-third Psalm. And I prayed. It would be so much better if you took him home while we were there, I reasoned with God. I prayed for him and Mama Farr, and for Grant and Jack, who were very close to their father.

Grant's father did not die until the next week, after Grant and I had returned to Berea. When we came back to Black Mountain, Mama Farr told us of his last days.

"He always loved it when I wore red clothing," she said. "He called me 'Red Bird.' The day before he died, I wore a red sweater to the hospital. When I got to his room he opened his eyes and smiled. 'Good morning, Red Bird,' he said. Those were the last words he ever spoke. I would not have missed that for the world," she told us.

If God had answered my prayer and taken her husband when I had asked, she would not have had this experience.

Some years later, in 1979, Grant's mother died from pancreatic cancer. I grieved with Grant over the loss of Mama Farr. I felt like I had lost my own mother.

The years passed. By doing independent studies, making special arrangements to take two classes at a time, and waiving as many classes as I could, I graduated from Berea College in 1980.

During the financially lean years, Grant and I were happy together. We acted in some of the plays produced at the college. Grant also organized and directed a singing and acting group he named "Encore." I was part of the group, and I loved every moment we were performing.

At the same time, through my writing and speaking about Appalachia to diverse groups at colleges and universities in the region and my published books, I was developing a reputation of my own. (Later, during our separation, Grant told me he got tired of being "Mr. Sidney Farr." I was shocked to hear this, as he had never mentioned this to me before, and I never once had an inkling that he felt this way.)

Grant gradually grew reluctant to go out socially. I was keenly disappointed, because in the isolated years of my first marriage I had daydreamed about going to parties and celebrations. I had put on weight, and I suspected that Grant was no longer as proud of the way I looked as he had been when we first got married.

Again I was repeating behavior from my first marriage. While I was married to Leon, sex was a chore, and my only comfort seemed to come from eating foods I loved. Now, with Grant and me having less sex than we'd had earlier in our marriage, I repeated the pattern. I sublimated my desire for sex into love of food. The more distant my husband became, the heavier I got.

We never talked about what was wrong. Grant said later that he didn't like to bring up unpleasant topics because he didn't want to hurt me. I did not bring them up because I was afraid of what he might tell me.

Before Grant and I were married we promised each other we would always be open and honest about everything that pertained to us as a couple. We promised to give each other freedom to be who we were and to express ourselves as we saw fit. Grant kept his promise all the way. He gave me freedom to be myself. He always encouraged me to be the best that I could be. He was never jealous or possessive in any way.

I could not give Grant the same freedom that he gave me. My heart implored, "Just let me be with you whatever you do, wherever you go."

Now I can see how I must have made Grant feel trapped. After the romance died in our marriage, I grew more afraid of losing him. I knew he was unhappy, but I could not seem to do anything about it. At this point we seldom did anything together just for fun. Grant was busy teaching piano and doing school counseling, and I worked full-time in the college library and wrote in my spare time.

While we still lived in Asheville, we began reading books about Edgar Cayce by Ruth Montgomery and Jane Roberts. For both Grant and me, the idea of reincarnation seemed to ring with truth. I knew Grant well enough by this time to believe that no one would ever choose to be homosexual. Perhaps, I thought, in many of his previous lifetimes he had been a woman.

When Grant and I moved back to Berea, we kept on reading all that we could find on the subject of past lives and other aspects of what was just beginning to be called the New Age genre. We met Phyllis Henson, who was also a seeker. With a friend of Phyllis's, Grant, Phyllis, and I began to have a meditation session once each week at our house. Our goal was to learn how to meditate and grow in spiritual truth. We felt that we were making progress, and the meditation sessions continued. Our small group grew to half a dozen people.

Then, in November 1984, Grant told me he wanted a separation. He told me he had met a man named Jack, who lived in Oregon. Jack owned an antiques shop and wanted to hire Grant to work in the shop. Grant informed me that he had plane reservations for December 4.

For the past three years Grant had been corresponding with several men he found on a "Brotherhood" listing—a network of gay men. I found this threatening—not just that he was in touch with people I didn't know, but that it was all gay men. Grant had met Jack through this network.

Grant and I had already made plans to spend Thanksgiving with Grant's Uncle Haywood and Aunt Kate in Swannanoa, North Carolina. The coming separation loomed over us during the drive to Swannanoa. Before we arrived, I developed a bronchial congestion and felt utterly miserable.

On Sunday morning of Thanksgiving weekend, while we were in North Carolina, a telephone call came for me. My sister Hazel, in Indianapolis, had suffered a massive stroke and was not expected to live. The family wanted me to come to Indianapolis as quickly as I could. Grant and I hurriedly took leave of the Farrs. We stopped at our house in Berea, packed some suitable clothes, and were on our way again. It was the saddest time for both of us. At the hospital we were told that Hazel had died an hour before we got there. We stayed with my sister Sharon Rose and her husband, Joe, until after Hazel's funeral.

At the funeral home, my son Wayne, who was by then divorced, came in with his three sons, Richard, Jason, and Justin. Wayne looked terrible. He had been working outside and his hands were raw in places from exposure to the cold. Grant told Wayne that he was leaving home and asked Wayne to come to Berea and stay with me for awhile. Wayne agreed. I was glad that Wayne was coming to be with me.

Bruce had graduated from Berea College in the spring of 1984 and had applied for and been accepted in a work-study program in London, England. He had left in September. He wrote occasionally, describing his job and London.

The first Saturday after Grant left was a bad day for me. The snow and ice kept me home. I thought I'd die being there alone, remembering other Saturdays and other weekends.

Wayne arrived from Indianapolis around 6:00 P.M. a week later. We spent Sunday at Pineville Hospital. Mama, who had been in intensive care for congestive heart failure, was now out of intensive care and in a private room.

We stayed with Mama until noon and then drove to Stoney Fork to have dinner with my sister Della. She was not yet home from church, but her daughter Linda was. She and I had dinner on the table when Della got home.

Then Wayne and I returned to Berea, and I immediately started the laundry. Six loads! It took me until eleven that night to get it done. I couldn't sit still anyway; I needed to keep busy.

On December 19, a letter came from Grant. "Mostly," he wrote, "I feel a sense of separation (not loss) from so much that I love—you, friends, Taylor [our pet dog]. I know this sounds terrible, but in a way Taylor is the most painful of all—for two reasons: (1) There was no way to explain my leaving to him. (2) I foolishly didn't allow myself to say good-bye to him; I couldn't handle it and saying good-bye to you, too."

Grant sent me an antique cobalt blue vase for Christmas. It is unsigned, so the maker and date are unknown, but its shape and pattern date it before 1940, he said. It was a very expensive piece. He wrote, "The vase has wonderful vibrations and I want you to have it."

He went on to write that he wanted to come home, but he had unresolved questions. "What did you do to me? What did I let you do to me? What did I do to you? Most of all, what *specifically* do I want to be different? What do you want to be different?"

I knew when I married Grant that he was bisexual, but I believed, albeit so naïvely, that our love for each other was so profound and true that he would never need/love/fear/require another man. From the start he encouraged me to make friends and have a life of my own apart from him. Grant said to me on more than one occasion, "If you see somebody that you find attractive, feel free to go to bed with him if you want. It won't bother me a bit." That hurt, of course. I wanted it to bother him.

After our relationship became strained, Grant turned more to friendship with other men in Berea, and began corresponding with still others. Every letter that came for him was a threat to me.

I believed that Grant was being unfaithful. As ardent as he had been when we first married, I knew his sexuality had not died. I raged at the thought that he could be satisfied sexually while leaving me to do without. But I never once considered someone else or was attracted to another man while I was married to Grant.

During those fifteen years of marriage, when Grant told me almost daily that he loved me, I believed him. I gained a lot of weight during those years. Not only did I use food as a substitute for sex; I rationalized my overeating by telling myself that if I were fat, I would be unattractive to other men. It was a coward's way of not facing facts. I got to eat what I craved and irrationally justified it as saving my marriage.

I decided to go to London and spend Christmas with Bruce. I asked Wayne what he thought of the idea; he said, "Go for it!" Brother Jeems, Della, and Linda also encouraged me to go. Even Mama didn't protest, as I thought she would. She did say she'd worry about me; I told her that I would probably be as safe in London with Bruce as in my own home, where I could fall down the stairs or suffer some other misfortune.

My first trip overseas! I am so glad that I had the courage to go, even having to borrow money to do it. The next chapter gives details of my trip to England that Christmas of 1984.

Berea in January 1985, when I returned, was filled with snow and ice. Wayne wanted to go to Indianapolis to see his boys. But we had to wait for the weather to moderate. Little Taylor, our dog, was so happy when I got home. I know he felt that Grant and I both had abandoned him.

Some days and evenings that winter I was fine; other times I felt as if the very core of my existence had been taken away. At those times I would take a tranquilizer and try to work hard at chores to keep busy, directing my frustrations toward the task I was doing. Or I would spend time on things I enjoyed, anything to keep busy and try to find meaning in my existence.

Wayne and I finally got to Indianapolis at the end of February, and then Wayne brought his boys back with us to Berea for a visit. I loved having my grandsons around. When it was time to take them back home, Richard begged to stay with his dad. Marilyn, his mother, agreed, so my grandson lived with me that winter, until Wayne got an apartment of his own.

On February 26, 1985, Grant wrote:

From November until now has been very difficult. So often I want to return home, and I only want to live with you—usually. Returning to live alone is sometimes appealing, but not usually . . . I can't really imagine living in Berea and not living with you. You are still such a vital part of my life. You are on my mind more often than you probably imagine.

Hopefully, if we do decide to try it again, we will be more appreciative of each other. I'm sure there were times when you would have liked for me to say I appreciated you and felt that I took you for granted. And I know I felt taken for granted often . . .

I . . . feel we are still married in the spiritual sense. I sometimes think we could never divorce spiritually because what we've shared and felt has indeed been very special.

During this time I recorded many reflections in my journal. In every human heart, I wrote, there is a book of truth, bound with worn-out strings and shredded ties. I think for me, the truth in my heart—my identity—is bound with strong fiber and tied with steel bands.

If I could make my body transparent and be able to gaze into an X-ray mirror, what would I see? Would I see an actress with her powdered face and rouged cheeks imitating beauty or ugliness, whichever the script calls for at that moment? Would I see an ugly form made of clay that is still malleable, still waiting for the master artist to complete his work? Or would I see a butterfly that has emerged from its cocoon only to find itself in a steel cage?

Other people tell me who I am, but after they leave their words fade and I still don't know. They praise the writing I do; but I look at it and know there are thousands in the world who could do it better than me. Somehow my mind and heart cannot hold the image of my reality.

Whether my time is long or short, and whether my being is broad or narrow, I must find my reality. I must take the chance of losing everything I now value in that search.

If I were a furnace, I wouldn't be afraid to melt fine gold or rough rocks or rusty iron. If I were a river, I wouldn't be concerned about the streamlets and muddy brooks that mingle here and there with me. I would only be concerned with my journey to the sea. So why should I be afraid to start this journey? Is it because I have to be so painstaking and conscientious about everything? (These may be virtues, but they certainly have not eased my mind or delighted my heart.) Why should these things stand in my way?

It's taken me a long time to find out what love for other people is all about. Now I've got to find some way to love myself.

This journey may bring death to many parts of the person that I am. I may have to be pulled, screaming, out of my shell. There may have to be fire and smoke and pain. It hurts to part with illusions, the old security of acting like a chameleon, taking on the virtues or the vices attributed to me by others.

One song the singers knew a long time ago was about valleys lifted up and hills made low—death at the heart of life and life in the midst of death. I may have to walk this valley, at least part of the way, to find what I must, and I have to walk it alone, because no one can go with me—not even Grant.

Who am I? I alone must decide this on the evidence I see and feel. Do I speak the truth? What is the truth? I've run the highways and the long corridors so long I've forgotten how to stop and look for truth about myself anymore.

So I speak of a journey—and yet part of it will be a journey standing still. I have read that only lonely people know freedom, that it's better to be on the outside in the dark and be free than to be in a gilded cage, looking beyond the bars.

But in the dark outside—if that is where I must go—where can I find the wind that blows and the new waves forming on sands of time I've never seen and don't know how to find? How can I hear a different drummer drumming somewhere—if that drummer exists? How can I find my true identity—if it's there? I believe it is there, behind that door or in the next room—but I have lost the key.

To find the key I may have to walk backward with bleeding feet and a troubled mind to the time in my childhood when in innocence I lost the key. Perhaps I just mislaid it. Perhaps if I go backward in faith even though it is a tortuous journey, a hand will guide me to the place where I left it. And I can unlock the door and be free! Oh, to know who I really am, to tread on the razor's edge for a while, to savor being free—the greatest gift God could give me.

GRANT DECIDED TO COME BACK in March. Bruce also came home from England and got a job at a motel in town. He did not think I should let Grant come back. There was tension between the two of them, but Bruce worked nights and weekends at the motel, and the three of us managed to live together.

My revived relationship with Grant was slow at first; I resented that he had gone away, resented all the pain and anguish his leaving had caused, lived with thoughts of his infidelities, wondering about the possibility that he would be unfaithful to me now, in Berea. Gradually we got to a place where we could make love again, but not very often.

At last 1985 drew to a close. Grant and I were invited to a New Year's Eve party at our neighbor's house. At that party we met a young man named Caleb. Little did I know how much meeting him would change our lives.

Grant had come back from Oregon with a real love for antiques. He decided to rent a booth in an antiques mall just down the road past a ceramics studio that Caleb owned. Grant began stopping often to chat with Caleb. Later in the spring Grant and I opened our own antiques shop on Short Street. During 1986, I began to notice how often Caleb's truck was parked on the street in front of our shop, and how often Grant's car was parked in front of Caleb's studio. If I said anything about it, Grant was immediately defensive, saying that I didn't want him to have any friends, that I was trying to control his life.

On December 12, 1986, I wrote in my journal:

> I keep looking for perspective and mostly find narrow frames of the here and the now.
>
> The wind is blowing . . .
>
> The winds pass, and something speaks to the souls of men. It is not required of us that we succeed, only that we be faithful to the highest goal in us.

The wind flows through the trees with the sound of water. I must
be the wind, listen to the message of the wind . . . fly with the wind.

I knew Grant would go on spending time with Caleb. But I was determined to trust his sense of fair play, to believe he'd spend some of his
quality time with me.

I decided to concentrate on change for myself. It was not too late to
change the way I looked and felt.

As I concentrated on me, I tried to release Grant. I decided not to
make any demands on him outside of the everyday, routine responsibili-
ties of day-to-day living. I knew I had to get on with my life. What I had
feared for the last ten years of our marriage had come to pass: Grant
had found that another component of his love needed fulfillment. And
he had found someone who could fulfill and satisfy him, someone who
made his life richer and fuller in every respect.

In December 1986, my mother died. She had been ill with congestive
heart failure for several years. Grant came down with a bad cold the weekend she died. He said he just did not feel like going with me to Stoney
Fork. I understood, but at the same time I could not help thinking of how
I had stood by him when each of his parents died. I did not admit it at the
time of Mama's death, but I was hurt and angry that Grant made no effort
to be with me. I imagined he would spend time with Caleb while I was at
the funeral.

Every day I prayed that God would take away the anger and bitterness
in my heart. Why should I seek to destroy every good memory and replace it with hate and bitterness? I asked the universe. If Grant were forced to
choose between Caleb and me, I knew that I would not be the chosen one.

On March 15, 1987, Grant moved into an apartment with Caleb—one
street over from where I lived. When I drove to work I passed the end of their
short street and always saw their two vehicles parked side by side. I would feel
such a wave of anger it would take an hour or so at work to cool down.

At the beginning of that year, I had joined a diet center, which required my going to the center every morning to be weighed. I believe that
daily routine saved my sanity.

In April of that year, the Berea Community Players cast a play entitled *The Octette Bridge Club,* about eight sisters. I auditioned and was cast as one of the sisters. Rehearsals and work kept me busy for weeks and I welcomed the activity.

On April 23, I drove to London, Kentucky, to speak at a district meeting of Girl Scout leaders at Sue Bennett College. A good friend, Mary Carnes, went along with me. I enjoyed her company, and we had a great day. When we got back to Berea, Mary spent the evening with me; we watched television and talked.

My friends Phyllis and Larry Henson had moved to Winston-Salem, North Carolina, and I missed them, especially Phyllis, who was a regular member of our meditation group. Phyllis and I talked on the phone a lot; she knew all about Grant's and my problems, and was a source of comfort.

Phyllis had begun going to meetings of the Spiritual Frontiers Fellowship and told the meditation group about them. I decided to register for the Spiritual Frontiers Fellowship Conference scheduled for that July. Phyllis invited me to fly to Winston-Salem (where she lived) and travel with her by car to Lynchburg, Virginia, where the conference was to be held. My experiences at this conference, and how life-changing it was for me, I describe in chapter 22.

That year—1987—proved to be both the best and the worst year of my life.

21

Going to London Town

Some of the older people in the mountains often
spoke of the "old country"—"that land across the
sea"—and told yarns about "London Town."

When I went to England in 1984, I kept a journal so I could recall the places, people, and events I experienced while traveling. With Grant having gone to Oregon, I was facing Christmas alone. Because Bruce and his friend Kimberly were already in London on work-scholarships, I decided to spend Christmas with them there. Bruce had invited me, although he believed it would be most unlikely that I would come. I had never been abroad, and the very thought of going frightened me. And yet my not wanting to be alone at Christmas was stronger than my apprehension of travel. So I firmed my resolve and decided to go.

Bob and Maxine Menefee drove me to the Cincinnati airport. We left Berea on December 21 in a cold, gray rain. It rained all the way to Cincinnati. The flight to New York went fairly smooth once we got above the gray clouds and rain.

It was completely dark by 4:00 P.M. when the plane arrived at JFK Airport. I walked about, looking at the shops and the people. I felt lonely and scared. I kept thinking what a comfort it would have been if Grant were with me.

While waiting for my connecting flight I sat at a table, drinking coffee and watching the travelers. Christmas music, familiar carols and songs, filled the air. I swear they played "I'll Be Home for Christmas" a dozen times as I sat there. It made me sad that Grant and I were separated and that neither of us would be home for Christmas.

Finally we boarded the plane. I was astounded by the Boeing 747. I never dreamed they were so big! Taking my seat and looking out the window, I thought the wing must stretch for a city block, at least.

My seatmate was an Italian woman who spoke very little English, so our communication was limited. Her husband was sitting in the seat directly in front of her. When she wanted to tell him something she leaned forward and hit him on his shoulder or his head. He jumped every time. They had been on holiday in Miami and were to spend three days in London before flying home to Florence.

I slept fitfully through the eight-hour flight.

As we neared London, at daybreak, I noticed first a tinge of cream color on the cloud floor. This widened and soon a narrow strip of red showed on the horizon. As we flew into the sunrise it was beautiful. I had to remind myself that back in Berea it was only 2:00 A.M.

Heathrow was crowded. Bruce had told me to meet him near the money-changing window. I got a porter to help with my bags and there I stood, not seeing Bruce anywhere. Thousands of people pushed by, mingled, hugged, kissed, and wept. I stood by a column and waited for what seemed a very long time for Bruce. Gradually I began to worry that he had been in an accident, although I knew Bruce was always late for everything. After I'd waited for forty-five minutes, he arrived. He had overslept, he said. I was so relieved and glad to see him and amazed at how much weight he had put on. When he had left the States in September he had weighed only about 150 pounds; now he weighed 170, he told me. I figured the food must be pretty good in England.

We rode a bus to his bed-sitter (which was basically one room), left my bags, and then walked about four blocks to a little restaurant located in West London at a row house, where Bruce took me for breakfast. I got my first taste of English bread and loved it. When we returned, Bruce showed me his and Kim's rooms and the bedroom he had rented for me from his landlady. I slept until 9:00 that night. Bruce and Kim had cooked a big kettle of chicken and rice soup. We ate, and I went back to bed and slept until late the next morning. Bruce had many things planned for us to do that day, but we slept late. I helped him fix a breakfast of bacon, eggs, and toast in the tiny kitchen that he shared with four other tenants. The floor was sticky in places. If I could have found a mop, I would have cleaned the floor first thing.

After breakfast we set out for the Victoria and Albert Museum. We walked four blocks to the subway station. There I had my picture taken and got a pass to ride the underground and the buses for a week. We changed trains twice and then walked through a long tunnel on our way to the exit.

At one point we heard Christmas carols being played on a strange instrument in the tunnel. A young man was sitting on the floor, leaning against the wall, playing an instrument that looked a little like a bagpipe. It was some kind of Middle Eastern instrument, I thought, and the musician looked Arabic. People dropped coins in his cap as they passed. He seemed to pay no attention; he just kept playing. He was really good.

Bruce had already been to the Victoria and Albert Museum, and I asked him to show me his favorite areas. One of his favorites was a clock exhibit. I fell in love with a copy of Michelangelo's *David*. Such perfection! I could have studied it the whole hour.

When we left the museum the streets were wet and the air was misty with rain. "I could be happy living here awhile," I thought. It was a magical sort of time, dark with lights glowing through the mist. Londoners do not decorate as lavishly for Christmas as we do. I noticed a few discreet door wreaths, candles in windows, and Christmas trees. The outside trees were strung with lights, which seemed to be larger than the lights we use in America. In the mist, the varicolored lights looked like big gumdrops.

When we got home I was exhausted. Kim fixed me a cup of tea, and never has tea tasted so good! After relaxing for a few minutes we were off again. We made a dash for the underground so as not to be late for the movie we planned to see in Piccadilly Circus: an adaptation of Dickens's *A Christmas Carol* with George C. Scott.

After returning from the cinema, we packed for our trip the next day. We left in the early morning to take a bus north to Windermere in the Lake District, where we would spend Christmas. The bus ride took eight hours.

We arrived a little after 4:00 in the afternoon and found we had to walk five blocks to the hotel. Bruce and Kim carried all the bags, and I still could not keep up. My legs hurt, and I hobbled along as best I could. I had something wrong with my left foot. It had begun to slowly turn in and made walking difficult. (Several years later I had to have surgery to correct the problem.) The weather was colder here than it was when we left London.

I must admit, I was a little disappointed with the Lake District when we arrived. The hillsides dotted with straggling pine trees that were frosted with a light snow looked familiar to me. It was like going to Stoney Fork for Christmas. I had hoped for something different!

On the way to Windermere were wide valleys and mountains, which reminded me of western North Carolina, though the mountains in the Lake District are not nearly as high. When we got to Windermere the hills had closed in and the valley was narrow; we could easily have been in eastern Kentucky. The Fir Garth Hotel rambled alongside the road, obviously having had several additions through the years. Behind the hotel was a little garden with a creek.

The rooms were comfortable, and the food was excellent. The son of the family that owned the place was a trained chef. Mrs. Mary McGrath, the owner, was a great talker, and sounded more Scottish than British. I anticipated some good conversations with her. She invited us to go with her later that night to a Christmas Eve service at a local church. Bruce and Kim declined, but I said I would go.

Mary said that dinner would be delayed until 8:30 because two incoming guests had been delayed en route. She added that there would be only three guests besides us. To her disappointment, a tour bus had canceled at the last moment that day; otherwise she would have had a full house.

We had time to unpack, rest awhile, shower, and get dressed for dinner. Then we went down to the bar area for a drink and visited with our hosts until dinner was served. I loved the fish course, Plaice St. Germain. The fish were small, a little bigger than finger-size, and fried crisp. Bruce and I had the roast duck, and we all had strawberry gâteau for dessert.

When it was time to go to the church service, I bundled up and Mary and I got into her small car. It was very foggy, misting rain and cold. Her car steamed up inside and I feared for our lives as she tore around corners and up side streets. It seemed to me she was driving by feel rather than sight. We arrived at the church early—it was a Church of England, Mary told me—and got a good parking place right in front.

Inside there were candles everywhere and banks of purple iris and white chrysanthemums. There were holly and poinsettias also, but I was more aware of the purple and white flowers. The ritual of the service reminded me of an Eastern Orthodox service Grant and I had attended at Easter the previous spring with our friends, Walter and Sally Odum. There was no incense, but the readings, responses, kneeling, and bowing were just as frequent.

The main part of the service was over by midnight, and then communion was served. This took a long time. People lined up and, led by altar boys, came forward one by one to be served. All drank from the same cup; the priest put the bread on each person's tongue. This was my first Church of England service.

After the service Mary said, "that was too high church for me. I don't think I'll go there anymore." I gathered that she only went to church at Christmas and Easter.

We arrived safely back at the hotel after another steamed-up tear through the small streets.

The next morning, I awoke to Christmas Day in England.

This was the first Christmas I had spent apart from Grant since we were married. I felt grief; it did not at all seem like Christmas, but I knew I would have felt worse had I stayed home.

We went down to breakfast about 9:00. When we got to the dining room, the stereo was playing ballroom dance music, and Mary and her husband were dancing. They were really quite good. We enjoyed a feast of bacon, eggs, grilled mushrooms, tomatoes, and lots of toast with jam. Bread in England is wonderful, more like our homemade bread, solid, with no holes like commercial yeast bread in the States. It makes delicious toast. I could see why Bruce had gained weight with that kind of bread and real butter. In England, butter was much less expensive than margarine. We watched the queen on TV, then went back upstairs; Kim and Bruce went back to bed and slept until around 2:00.

There was nothing to do within walking distance and no bus service until two days after Christmas. The day after Christmas was Boxing Day, a legal holiday.

William Wordsworth's home was nine miles from Windermere. Beatrix Potter and John Ruskin had also lived near there. Scotland is just fifty miles from Windermere, Mary said, and Edinburgh one hundred fifty. If I had had access to a car, I would have gone to Scotland for sure.

Bruce and Kim invited me to their room to watch *Mary Poppins;* it cost 50P to watch TV for several hours. At 4:00 we heard a knock at the door, and there was Mr. McGrath with a tray on which were three mincemeat tarts. Each of our rooms was equipped with a teakettle, sugar and cream, instant coffee packets, and, of course, tea bags. We had tea and ate the excellent tarts while we watched the rest of the movie. I never liked mincemeat pies the way they are done at home, but these were delicious.

Dinner that night was at 7:30—a scrumptious Christmas dinner. The tables were decorated with flowers and candles and at each place there was a Christmas cracker, a colorful tube of paper tied at each end with ribbon. You take an end in each hand and pull sharply, and there is a loud explosion, like a firecracker, with pieces of confetti bursting out. The ladies had fun with ours, but the men did not touch theirs.

We stayed in the lounge for awhile. We watched television with the other guests—a variety show, then a murder mystery, *Home for the Holidays.* Kim went up to read, Bruce went to play pool with Tim, the chef, and I stayed near the pay phone in the hall, trying to call Grant.

I had tried all day to get an international operator so I could place a call to Grant, but there had been no answer. I also had tried to get a call through the night before, but with no luck.

At 2:00 A.M. I finally succeeded in getting a call through, thanks to a helpful operator. He explained to me about British telephone queues. There are queues for everything here, he said. If you get a busy signal and hang up, you go to the end of the queue every time. He let the phone ring about ten minutes before an operator finally answered it. You let it ring until it is answered. The operator and I had a friendly talk while the phone was ringing. He told me of some local history. I finally got through to Grant and we had a tearful conversation. We recalled Christmas the previous year, when our friends, Phyllis and Larry Henson, came to spend the night with us in Berea. Our house was decorated beautifully, the prettiest it had been in many years. We had cooked a simple, but elegant, dinner that night.

The next morning Bruce and Kim did not feel like getting up for breakfast, saying they preferred to sleep late, take a walk later in the day, and get something to eat then. The breakfast menu varied only in a choice of sausage or bacon. I did not like English sausage at all. Mary sat down and kept me company while I ate breakfast, and she talked every second. I learned much about her family, her childhood, and her philosophy of life.

She offered to provide transportation if I wanted to get out in the afternoon. The nearest little town, Ambleside, fronts on the lake, she said, but it was too far for me to walk. At 2:00 I got my coat and went down. Tim drove me to Ambleside and said he would return for me at 4:00.

I walked to the lake; it was cold, and there was snow on the mountains beyond the lake, making them crystal white. I watched people queuing up for a boat ride. A large, grayish swan was in the water near the boat dock, but it paid no attention to the people. Seagulls were flying overhead. We must not have been too far from the ocean. Quite a few tourists were walking up and down the streets, as I was, looking in the windows, taking boat rides, and buying things in the only two shops that were open. Except for some gift shops and tearooms, all the stores were closed; it was Boxing Day.

At 3:00 I went into a tearoom and had tea. I felt so elegant and proper, sitting there sipping tea and eating scones. I loved it. There were dozens of hotels and lodges in this small town, and in Windermere there are dozens more. One section of Ambleside is named after famous writers. There I saw Wordsworth Court, Potter Guest Cottage, and other such places.

Mary told me that when she bought her hotel it was the only one in the district. Then the Lake District was developed and hotels, inns, and various kinds of lodgings sprang up like weeds. She said she was feeling the pinch of competition.

The landscape in England's Lake District is as varied as southeastern Kentucky or western North Carolina. There was also a great diversity of colors: greens, browns, purples, all blending perfectly. The hills wore bands of mist, like frothy lace. I recalled certain periods in my past, the history of this place, and the people who had lived in these hills and valleys so long ago and who had, in a fierce desire for religious freedom, migrated to the United States and thence into the hills and valleys of Appalachia, perhaps because it so resembled these highlands in northern England and Scotland.

Tim picked me up and took me back to Fir Garth. I was in my room when Bruce and Kim got back. They had enjoyed their walk. Kim said later that the walk made the whole trip worthwhile to her. We dressed for dinner and hurried down, eager to see what gourmet delights would be waiting for us. We were not disappointed—it was another good meal and, overall, a Christmas I would never forget.

The bus ride back to London was tiring. The road was covered with black ice in parts. The bus was twenty minutes late; we waited in the cold. Then we had a few panicky moments when the driver said he did not have room for us. He finally agreed to let us stand in the aisle until we reached Kendal, where we would be able to get another bus. After we had left Kendal on the second bus, Bruce realized he had left his backpack, which contained his passport and other important items, on the first bus. The bus that took us from Kendal to London was very cold. My feet got so cold I thought I would not be able to stand it.

Since the bus was late, the driver was not inclined to make rest stops. There was supposed to be a twenty-five-minute stop at Birmingham, but traffic was bumper-to-bumper and he decided to keep going. Finally he pulled into a little place for a ten-minute rest stop. Kim and I flew to the bathroom, and then bought drinks to go with the chicken sandwiches I'd had the foresight to ask Mary to pack for us.

Then it started getting dark, even though it was only 3:30! It kept getting darker and darker, and then suddenly we passed through one spot where the sun was shining dimly into darkness again. I realized we had been driving into a London fog—our first. The bus had to slow down in the fog. Bruce was fretting by now, knowing he was gong to be even later for work than he had anticipated. He was supposed to have been there at 3:00.

We finally pulled into Victoria Station at 5:30. It was a madhouse. I thought Heathrow was bad, but it was nothing compared to the dozens of buses pulling in and unloading passengers here. The driver told Bruce that the bus we had originally been on was just behind us, and the best way to retrieve his backpack was to wait for that bus. So we stood there, bumped, jostled, jabbed, and cursed at by a throng of people of all nationalities and colors, all getting off buses, trying to get their bags, and lining up for taxis. I told Bruce to go to the other side and watch for the bus, while Kim and I stayed with our luggage and watched from our side. Soon Bruce returned, smiling, with his backpack. Then he said he needed to run because he was already so late for work. Kim started crying. "Bruce, how in the world do you think your mom and I can carry all the luggage to the underground station?"

"I will gladly pay for a taxi," I said.

"That will take a long time. Just look at those long queues!" she said.

Bruce rushed off; Kim and I struggled with the bags, eventually reaching one of several long taxi queues. Kim kept crying, saying it would take us an hour to get one. I began affirming Divine Order, saying a prayer acknowledging God's will and letting go. In twenty minutes we were on our way home.

Alone in my room that night, I experienced new depths of depression and despair. I missed Grant; I missed my dog, Taylor; Bruce was working; Kim was resting; there was no radio and no television; and the damn lights were too dim for me to read. I took a pill and tried to rest awhile. It was a very low evening for me—the worst.

Bruce and I both slept late the next day. Kim had to go to work at 10:00. We ate toast and jelly with instant coffee, then got dressed and headed downtown. Bruce wanted to take me to Harrods, and from there I was going to sightsee on my own.

We went to Harrods, found a lunchroom, and ate first, then we shopped. It is truly a magnificent store. You can buy anything there— trips, airplane tickets, even a chalet—anything you can imagine they can get for you, for a price.

After Harrods I went with Bruce to the Marriott Hotel, where he worked. I called the hotel where Ethel Capps, a friend from Berea, had told me she'd be staying. Ethel invited me to go with her tour group to the National Theatre that night to see Chekhov's *Wild Honey*. Unfortunately, I couldn't get a ticket—they were sold out for the whole weekend. I agreed to meet Ethel at her hotel at 10:00 the next morning. She and I would spend the day sightseeing with Wayne and Marybelle Allen, two former Berea Country Dancers who had moved to England.

Later that day, after I got home, I took a walk to High Street–Kensington to do some browsing. At a department store that was having a sale on kitchen utensils, I bought some things for Bruce and Kim—a dish drainer, a dishtowel, and a soup ladle (Bruce ate so much soup and had to use a teacup to dip it out), all the same color: deep cherry red. Kim was delighted with my purchases. She said that they made their place finally begin to look like a kitchen.

The next morning I got up at eight o'clock, quickly ate breakfast, then walked down to High Street to catch Bus 73, which would take me straight to Oxford Street near Ethel's hotel, Stratford Court, where I was to meet Ethel at ten. I was leery of riding the underground by myself, though Bruce insisted it was safe. I preferred being above ground at all times, even back home.

The bus stop was at Selfridges department store and, since I had a few minutes to spare, I went inside to see this famous store. At a quarter to ten I went outside and asked a policeman where the Stratford Court Hotel was located. He told me, but I misunderstood part of his instructions. I walked down Oxford Street, block after block, until finally I was way down in Oxford Circus and knew I had gone too far. I asked a number of people but no one knew the hotel. At last I found a security officer who told me where to find the hotel. To my chagrin, it was only three blocks from Selfridges! He very kindly let me use his phone to call Ethel. She did not answer; I wondered if she had already gone.

So here I go, walking fast as I can, through the dense crowd of shoppers downtown for the after-Christmas sales. Finally I found Ethel's hotel and called her again from the lobby. This time she answered, and told me that of course she would not have left before I arrived. The Allens hadn't arrived yet, either, so Ethel and I chatted in her room. Wayne and Marybelle and their two kids arrived sometime after 11:00; we all visited a bit and then set out. Ethel had thought Wayne would bring his car and take us sightseeing, but he had parked on the outskirts of London in order to avoid the traffic, he said. We took a bus to the British Museum first, to see a special exhibit on the Anglo-Saxon Golden Age (960–1060). Ethel insisted on paying my way into the exhibit, which was great; I am so glad I got to see it.

The children got tired and hungry, and their parents decided we should all go to the lunchroom and eat. We went through the cafeteria line, and Wayne paid for everybody's lunch. He and Marybelle had graduated from Berea College in the mid-1960s; Wayne's career in the Navy was what had brought them to England. Ethel and the Allens decided that if we were to have any chance of seeing the Tate Museum, Westminster Abbey, and St. Margaret's Church, we needed to leave the British Museum after lunch. So we did. We only had to walk a few blocks to see Big Ben and Westminster Abbey. Part of Westminster was closed because of a choir rehearsal. It was nice to look around, though, as we listened to the choir sing. When we left Westminster Abbey, we went next door to St. Margaret's, a very old church dedicated to women. I was even more impressed with St. Margaret's than I was with the Abbey, which was wonderful.

After that we took a bus to the Tate Museum. In the Tate we saw hundreds of paintings. I fell in love with the works of John Constable and J. M. W. Turner.

At the end of the day we were tired but happy. Wayne and the children took a bus back to Ethel's hotel, but we women got a taxi in front of the museum, splitting the fare.

After a brief rest in Ethel's room, the Allens left. "What are we going to do now?" Ethel said to me. "We can't stop now," she said. "The day's not over yet!"

After looking through newspapers for a movie or play, to our surprise and delight we found that there was to be a preview of Dickens's *Great Expectations* at the Old Vic. We reserved tickets, grabbed a taxi, and took off.

As we rode the taxi across the Thames, we marveled at the lovely sight. Christmas lights shone on both sides of the river, down near the water, with the rows of lights outlining the curves of the river. Beautiful! It cost us £9.50 for each ticket and we spent £6.00 on taxis, but the experience was worth every bit.

I had asked Bruce to come to Ethel's hotel when he got off work at 11:00 (it was only a short distance between the two hotels) and wait for me, because I knew it would be too late for me to catch a bus and I was scared to ride the underground alone, especially at night. By the time Ethel and I got back, Bruce was impatiently waiting. He and I had a twenty-minute wait for the tube, and then while we were in the train somebody pulled the emergency stop. We had to sit and wait another twenty minutes while the officials went from car to car, trying to determine what was wrong. I began to get a suffocating feeling, sitting there in the dark tunnel. Finally we were on our way again, and got home around 1:00.

The next day, Sunday, December 30, Bruce and I went downtown because he wanted me to see the famous Portobello Road Flea Market. The weather was cold and misty. Again, as was the case everywhere I went in London, we had a long walk to the flea market. When we finally got there, no one was in sight. It turned out that the flea market was held on Saturdays, not Sundays, as Bruce had thought. We were very disappointed.

Bruce and I ate lunch in — of all places — a Pizza Hut (it was his choice). The pizza was good, but it tasted different than what we were used to in the States. After we ate, Bruce left for work and I took a taxi to the Victoria and Albert Museum. I spent a delightful afternoon seeing things at my own pace. That is the way to visit museums, I decided. I saw exhibits we had not had time for when Bruce and Kim had brought me to the museum a week earlier.

I went to the china and pottery floor and saw dishes from the earliest days up through modern times. I went to the rug and tapestry room and saw a large exhibit on the Lake District and an exhibit on William Wordsworth. I saw great paintings in oil done by British artists of the past two hundred years; then I went back to the Italian rooms and spent much time looking at the larger-than-life works of Michelangelo. I browsed in the card shop the last ten minutes before the museum closed, then took a taxi home. I waited up to share a bite of supper with Bruce and then went to bed. I was restless all night because I was sore from all the walking.

Monday, December 31, was to be my last day in London. I wanted to cram in as much as possible. Bruce had the day off from work. We first went to the British Museum. We ate breakfast at the coffee shop before we saw any exhibits. I had a meat pasty. I had read about meat pasties in British mysteries and always wanted to taste one. The pasty was so-so, meat and vegetables mixed in a sauce and baked in a small pie.

We spent a long time in the museum library. I enjoyed looking at some of the first-edition books and the manuscripts. The music manuscripts in particular awed me. To see Beethoven's, Bach's, and Liszt's original scores in their own handwriting was awesome. Beethoven wrote his scores in incredibly small handwriting, and so did Liszt and some of the others. Bach, however wrote in large, bold script.

Then we went to the Egyptian room and saw all kinds of artifacts, including mummies. I did not care for that room at all, and could not wait to get out of there. I was getting very bad vibrations there, whether from the mummies or the living people, I did not know, but I did not like that place. From the Egyptian room we went to see the clock exhibit. I was astounded at how many varieties of clocks had been manufactured over the centuries, and the intricacies of the models from two and three hundred years ago. I had trouble dragging Bruce away from the clocks, because he was so fascinated with them.

We went to other exhibits also, where we saw china, furniture, textiles, ancient writing on stone, a special exhibit on Germany, and a room full of Japanese artifacts and paintings. I know Grant would have loved the Japanese room.

I had promised Bruce that I would buy him a pair of pants as my Christmas present to him. Reluctantly we left the British Museum in order to get downtown before the stores closed, and before we were due at Ann Colcord's for tea at 4:00. (I had gotten to know Ann the previous year, at a writer's workshop in Hindman, Kentucky. Ann lived most of the year with her family in London, and she had invited Bruce and Kim to stay a night or two with her when they first arrived in the city, until they could get settled in their jobs and find a place to live.)

What a madhouse downtown was! The shoppers were all pushing and shoving to get at the after-Christmas bargains. Bruce lectured me about not fighting the crowds; he said I should just flow with the stream. He had learned to do that, he said, and it made walking so much easier. So I tried to flow. It was all right as long as we were all going the same way, I said to him, but what if you crash headfirst into people "flowing" in the opposite direction?

He laughed and said, "Come on, Mom, we're almost there!"

Selfridges was even more crowded, if that were possible. I knew I could not get through a crowd like that to find pants for Bruce, so we caught a bus and went back to High Street, near his lodgings, and went into a men's shop there. He found a pair of jeans he liked, and I bought them. I also bought him two pair of woolen socks at a store nearby.

We had a pleasant visit with Ann and her mother, eating mincemeat tarts and drinking delicious tea. (Tea in England is so much better than what we get in the States.)

Kim had made reservations for the three of us to eat New Year's Eve dinner at a Chinese restaurant in Covent Gardens, but Kim was delayed more than an hour getting home from work. We dressed and took the subway, having to change twice before we got to our destination. Already crowds of young people were on the subway, passing around bottles and cans of drink, talking loudly, and pushing each other playfully. In Covent Gardens hundreds of young people were drinking and milling around in the streets. We speculated the pubs were all filled to overflowing, and would-be patrons had spilled out into the streets.

The restaurant was a gem. We were taken to a small, empty dining room downstairs and soon the other table, a round one, was filled with three Italian couples. I felt truly cosmopolitan, to be sitting there as one of three Americans in the same room with six Italians and a Chinese manager and waitresses to serve us. I ate the best Chinese food I had ever tasted. We had seaweed sautéed until it was crisp, barbecued ribs, sweet corn soup, sweet-and-sour prawns, a chicken dish, and a plate of stir-fried vegetables over rice. Dessert was toffee apples.

By the time we finished dinner, it was late. Kim urged us to hurry so we could get home before the drunken crowds poured in from the big celebration that took place at Trafalgar Square. Bruce said that Trafalgar was like Times Square in New York on New Year's Eve. When we got home, we listened to the radio together until 1985 was born. Then I went to my room, did some packing, and went to bed.

I got up early and finished packing, and Bruce and I took the subway all the way to Heathrow, a thirty-five-minute ride. Part of the trip was underground and part was above ground. Bruce helped me get checked in, and then we went to find some breakfast. After breakfast, Bruce and I said our good-byes.

The plane took off on time. I had asked for a window seat in the non-smoking section and was told no window seat was available in that section, but an aisle seat was. I took the aisle, thinking that it would be better than sitting in the middle seat. I was disappointed about not getting a window seat because I had hoped to be able to see the ocean. (As it turned out, no one saw the ocean; it was cloudy and we flew high above the clouds all the way.) My ticket said 25G, so I went to what I thought was my seat, sat down, and got settled in. A few moments later a young man came and said I had his seat. I looked and, sure enough, I was in 25C; 25G was an aisle seat in the middle row of seats. The young man said that was okay, he would just take my seat. I thanked him warmly, and settled back to enjoy the ride.

My seatmates were a middle-aged man and an Asian woman, who had the window seat. After awhile I noticed the book the man was reading, an autobiography of a yogi. I spoke to him, and we talked a bit about his book. Soon we were talking about meditation, past lives, spiritual growth, Zen Buddhism, and other related topics.

His name was Dennis Carney, and he was a clinical psychologist from Connecticut. He was reared a Catholic, but never found spiritual satisfaction in that church. Dennis told me that he had begun his spiritual quest after a Zen Buddhist leader came to his hometown. Dennis had attended study groups, conferences, and meditations in California, Puerto Rico, Honolulu, and other places. He had read a lot of books on spirituality I had not yet read. He gave me a list of books I might be interested in. We had a fantastic conversation.

When we left the plane Dennis walked with me to the baggage claim area. Once we were there, we shook hands. I told him I was glad I'd made a mistake in seats and got to sit with him. He looked into my eyes. "It was no mistake," he said. "We'll see each other again."

I had no trouble finding my bags and then going to the customs counter. The customs man looked surprised when I said I was bringing back less than ten pounds in merchandise. "What did you go for, then?" he asked. "To spend Christmas with my son," I replied. "Didn't he give you any gifts?" he asked. "The trip was the gift," I said. He just waved his arm for me to go on through. I suppose I looked trustworthy. I felt a little bit like the fictional Mrs. Pollifax, who traveled to exotic places and worked for the CIA.

It was now 3:15 P.M. New York time (8:15 in London), and I was sitting in a coffee shop in the Pan Am Building, looking out across the landing field as I waited for my flight home. It felt good to be on American soil again, and closer to Grant.

22

Tom Sawyer

*I often wished that just once a person could come
back from the dead and tell everyone what God
was really like.*

As a little girl I needed to know what God was really like, and I kept
asking the adults around me. I heard many answers: "God is love."
"God is this really old man with a long white beard." "God is everywhere
and sees everything you do. If you are a bad girl you will make God cry."
"God will be angry if you are not good and then he will let Satan take you
to hell."

I had a hard time trying to understand why, if God loved me "like a
father," he would be willing to let the devil take me away. I grew up wanting to be shown the reality of God's love. I believed in it; I knew there
was something like grace that could show us God if we had enough faith.
I prayed; I read; and I searched for the reality that I knew must be there
in the mist, or beyond glorious sunsets or thunderstorms that lashed the
trees on the hillsides and brought rain to flood the creeks and streams.

I often wished that just once a person could come back from the dead
and tell everyone what God was really like. I believed that Jesus rose from
the dead, but in my heart I did not believe it was possible for an ordinary
human being to come back from the dead; otherwise someone would
have come back to tell people about it long ago.

My parents belonged to a religious group that believed if you did not
serve God the same way they did you were bound for hell. Even as a child,
untutored in spiritual matters, I felt there must be more to God than that.

My good friend Phyllis Henson knew of my search, and in 1987 she
invited me to join her in attending the Southeastern Conference of the

Spiritual Frontiers Fellowship in Lynchburg, Virginia. That conference—and a man I met there named Tom Sawyer—would change my life.

I flew to Phyllis's house in Winston-Salem, North Carolina, on July 18, 1987. Phyllis's house was old and big, with lots of trees in both the front yard and the backyard. After a restful night, we left for Lynchburg late the next morning, arriving around 3:30. There was much confusion as the teachers, consultants, and other staff worked to get organized before the week-long conference began. Phyllis, one of the staff, was scheduled to attend a banquet that night.

I awoke the next morning to the smell of coffee from Phyllis's room next door. Her roommate Roberta, Phyllis, and I went to breakfast together. Phyllis was scheduled to work at the registration desk, and I went with her. As Phyllis worked, I looked through some brochures and announcements. One flyer announced that a man named Tom Sawyer was to arrive on Wednesday of that week. He would talk about his near-death experience. I wondered what in the world that would be like!

The conference opened with dinner that evening. The rest of the week was packed with activities. I attended several workshops and healing sessions.

The first workshop session was spellbinding. Dan Chesbro talked about Tom Sawyer. He told how they had met and described some of the work they had done together, and he spoke of the Order of Melchizedek. As Dan described this group, it felt familiar to me. Over the years, whenever I was reading the Bible and reached the part about Melchizedek calling the priests, I would feel excited and somewhat homesick. Dan said the priests have been called many times when the world faces changes and transitions. He compared the priests to midwives. I was sure that I'd been part of that group before.

My first healing session was with a young man named Jake. It was very intense. He could tell that before physical healing could take place for me, there had to be work done on the emotional level. He asked me one or two questions, and I burst into tears. I told him I'd been going through a time of intense grief because I'd lost my husband, who had chosen to live with someone else instead of me. Jake asked enough questions to learn my story. I cried as he worked primarily in the solar plexus and heart regions. Jake talked harshly about homosexuality. He said he believed it was a curse against humanity. He said I was lucky to have escaped.

By the end of the session, Jake told me that he had released part of the burden from my heart and solar plexus, but it felt as though my lower abdomen was tied in knots. He said I was expressing rejection in the female organs and that even though I might have come to terms with it intellectually, emotionally I was feeling rejection as a woman in those areas. His remarks about homosexuality made me extremely angry. I knew about homosexuality from fifteen years of firsthand experience. I knew it couldn't just be dismissed as a "curse against humanity."

At the workshop the next morning, Dan talked some more about Tom Sawyer and Melchizedek. His teachings about Melchizedek were profound. Dan said he had been commissioned by seven archangels to "call the priests according to the order of Melchizedek" and "teach them how to fly." He had been ordaining priests all over the country and said that within two years the order would be global.

Dan announced ordination services for Wednesday night that week. I felt a strange yearning to become part of this group. Dan said he was not permitted to invite people to join, they must come of their own free will, answering the call within their own hearts. He also said that at the next day's workshop we would experience "flying"!

The next morning Dan instructed us to lie down on the floor in groups of three. It was important to form triads for this meditation, he said. He counted us off; the other two members of my group were a woman from Boston and one from Sedona, Arizona.

Each triad lay on the floor on blankets with feet and hands outspread so that we were each like a five-pointed star. Because I had meditated for more than ten years, thus honing my imagination, I had no trouble "steering my ship" by feeling in my right and left fingertips and right and left toes to get the ship to move. We seemed to rise up from the floor and then through the ceiling and over the building. Then, in formations of three ships we rose into space, guided by music and Dan's voice. He told us to stop when we could see the moon. "This is your point of departure," Dan said, "and you will come back to this spot when you hear my voice. You are to go off alone to a point you have picked out, or you can ask your higher self to guide you to a place you need to be."

I asked for guidance and went off. I flew over mountains and cities, and slowed down at a place I knew to be Scotland. I was offered an opportunity to visit there, but thought it was my mind playing tricks and it was not real. I moved on and flew alongside an ocean for awhile. I could see blue water and incredibly golden sand. I went over some strange-looking mountains and came down in a city of light.

Two beings—a beautiful woman dressed in a spun silver gown with a silver and diamond tiara on her head, and a tall, handsome man with piercing blue eyes—met me. They called me daughter and said they'd been waiting for me for a long time. The woman's name was Libra and the man's Maxwell. I somehow knew that this was a future life for me and that these two would be my parents. They showed me lovely art treasures in high buildings—paintings that seemed to be made of living color, statues, and all kinds of objects. To travel, they instructed me to step on two round disks that moved; these took us wherever we thought to go. We moved inside and outside buildings at a smooth, even pace.

Libra and Maxwell had both been born on a different planet but had come here to live. Maxwell asked if I'd like to see my grandfather and grandmother, and I said yes.

We went through a kind of tunnel, perhaps a time warp machine, still traveling on our disks. Then we got off and walked into a green grove of trees. To my amazement, my grandfather and grandmother were apes! They welcomed us, hugged and kissed me, and talked to me, but I couldn't understand them. Libra and Maxwell translated. We ate some strange fruit with them. Then it was time to go.

As we returned to the city of light, I heard Dan's voice calling all the ships back to the departure point. Libra and Maxwell hugged and kissed me good-bye.

It was thrilling to see all the little ships converging near the moon. Dan told us to form a circle and called for two tardy ships to hurry and come on in, it was time to go. Again we formed our triads and flew home.

To this day that meditation is vivid in my mind, especially Libra and Maxwell. I feel homesick for them sometimes, and believe they are waiting for me in my future.

After the session, I knew for sure that I wanted to be ordained into the Priesthood of Melchizedek that evening.

In the afternoon I went to the Healing Center for a session with a woman named Doris. Her method of healing was through music therapy. She had me lie on a bed, and she played several selections of music while she sat nearby. She spoke about a telephone call she had received the night before, that one of her sons had been badly burned. After giving details of his accident, she started talking about another son, who had tried to commit suicide several times, and how hard she and her husband had worked to save him each time. Finally, she said, she knew they had to release him to whatever would be. She spent one last week with him and left, she said. Three days went by with no word, and then he called. He'd made all the preparations, gone into the woods to kill himself, and somehow could not. He made the decision to live, turned his life completely around, and now enjoys every moment he lives.

I cried profusely during the session with Doris. At the end of the session, she hugged me and told me I was loved by many people and was called to do a special kind of spiritual work. I left her feeling tired and sad.

That night at 9:30 I made my way to room 24 of the Hopwood Building for my ordination service. It was the same time as Tom Sawyer's scheduled appearance in the ballroom, and I wished I could hear him speak, but I knew I was meant to be ordained into the Order of Melchizedek.

How can I ever find words for that incredible experience? I felt like a different person—I was a different person from the one who entered that room. There were fourteen to be ordained, and it took a long time. The ordinations lasted until 12:20 A.M.

I felt so drawn to see and hear Tom Sawyer that I stopped by the ballroom after the ordination service was over. Tom was sitting on the stage, and people in the audience were sitting in chairs and lying on blankets. I stayed, spellbound, until after 2:00 A.M. I was glad to know that he would be at the conference for the rest of the week.

Dan's workshop the next morning was spent mostly in answering questions about things Tom Sawyer had said the previous night.

That evening the healing service was for the whole congregation. After the service, I hurried to Hopwood to hear Tom. I sat in a chair from 9:30 that night until 4:30 the next morning, spellbound. (I didn't even need to go the bathroom!) Tom talked about his near-death experience. At times he'd choke up and have to rest a few minutes. Here is Tom's story as he told it that night.

It was a perfect spring day in Rochester, New York, where Tom lived with his wife, Elaine, and their two sons, Todd (nine and a half years old) and Tim (four years old). Tom was working on his truck. He intended to replace a tie rod end and repair or rebuild the transmission linkage. Just as he began working on the transmission linkage, the truck started to move. It seemed, he said, to fall in extreme slow motion. The frame of the truck fell across the center of his chest between his bottom rib and his breastbone. When it came down, Tom heard no sound; he only experienced the pressure. His neighbors later told him they heard the truck crash down.

Tom fell unconscious and saw colors, opalescence, phosphorescence, fluorescence, infrared, ultraviolet—millions of hues.

His heart stopped; all went black; he experienced clinical death. Then, Tom said, he had a feeling of becoming wide awake. All the pain and pressure were gone. The blackness took on the shape of a tunnel, and he felt increasing speed.

Tom sensed himself fumbling with the jack. A neighbor reached under the truck and took it out of Tom's hands. For some reason Tom knew the man didn't know how to operate a hydraulic jack.

The next thing Tom was aware of was a speck of light he could see in the distance. It was extremely bright, and very intense. The appearance of this light brought Tom a sense of great love and a feeling of camaraderie, greater than any he'd experienced in his thirty-three years of life. He realized that the light was coming from outside the tunnel.

Tom felt eager to get closer to the light. The light meant the same thing as God to Tom. It was in fact the Light of Jesus Christ, he said.

There came a feeling of warmth and love from the light. Then Tom received a communication, not in words. "Tom, before you is the Light. Any question that you can conceive of will be absolutely answered."

One of the questions Tom asked (which he later thought was rather arrogant) was "What about the Jesus stuff? Was there this dude, Jesus of Nazareth? Was he real—was he a live person? And was it historical truth? Was he the Son of God? Is he divine? Is he at the right hand of the Father? What about the Jesus stuff?" Tom said that at one point it felt as if he were a speck of light on Jesus' shoulder, and he was able to experience full knowledge of all of Jesus Christ's incarnations from the beginning of time.

At the time this happened, Tom was an agnostic. He had a Catholic background, but at that point in his life, religion was to him meaningless. He felt he didn't need any "hocus-pocus" stuff from the church.

The communication continued. "Tom, you have a choice. You have the opportunity to choose on your own decision to return to normal life. If you have that desire, it will be facilitated instantaneously, with no strings attached. If you decide to become totally homogeneous with the Light, that's okay. But if you choose to stay, you will never again be able to choose, on your own decision, to return to normal life."

Tom remembers taking a step and leaning forward, indicating he wanted to stay. Immediately he was engulfed by the light and was told and experienced much. He was given specific instructions about things he must do back on earth. Then he felt himself going backward through the tunnel and "slamming" into his body again. "I am the only human I know who was kicked out of Heaven!" he joked.

Since Tom's recovery he has traveled the world, healing, teaching, and being a witness to the fact that there is a God, that He is totally love and light. Thousands of people have met Tom in workshops and conferences, through television interviews, and individually. They love the God they feel in him, and they long to be in Tom's presence.

I am convinced that Tom is telling the truth about his experience. I have worked with him on many levels in the ensuing years and know him to be completely truthful. I doubt that he could tell a lie. Many times I've heard him interrupt himself or another person in order to get the details exactly right.

After hearing Tom's story, and being in his presence in the ballroom that night, I knew I would love him through eternity.

The birds on campus were whistling for daylight as we walked back to our rooms. But I knew that Dan's workshop that Friday morning was meant for me. First Dan led us in a meditation to help us overcome a fear or phobia. I knew I had to deal with my fear of snakes.

As we meditated I found myself able to look at a big snake lovingly, and I willingly talked to it. It told me that in a past life I had been an African woman who was captured, tortured, and thrown into a pit of snakes. The snakes in the pit were not attacking me maliciously, the snake told me—they were just following their nature to protect themselves, and they were sorry I died. I felt compassion for the snake as it spoke to me. Dan told us to ask for a gift to bring away with us. The snake gave me three gold rattles and said to take them and use them as a blessing to my people.

"The next meditation will help you release a person, place, or thing that you need to release," Dan said. My heart constricted; I knew that this was what I'd come for. He told us what he'd ask us to do and said we must be sure we wanted to do it before we entered the meditation.

I found myself standing on a hillside under a tree. I was holding a beautiful pink helium balloon by a string. Inside the balloon was Grant. Dan said, "Now let yourself climb inside and say good-bye to the person, place, or thing." I did. I could see Grant's beloved face so clearly. We talked. I told him what I must do, and he said he knew it was right for both of us. He said he loved me, would always love me, and that he knew I loved him. I felt he'd been waiting a long time for me to give him his freedom. I started crying. He held me, tenderly, lovingly, and we communicated without words.

"Now say good-bye and let yourself climb back outside and see yourself holding the string of the balloon," Dan instructed.

Grant and I said good-bye and I was again standing on the hillside.

"Now, if you are a hundred percent sure you are ready, let go of the string when I tell you to, but only if you're absolutely sure."

I held tight to the string, tears streaming down my face.

Dan called, *"Now let go."*

I couldn't for a moment, but then I released the string. The balloon started rising and floating out across the river.

"Good-bye, Grant," I called. "I release you to go to your highest good. No longer will you be tied to me on any level."

Then I was aware that Christ and I were sitting on a bench at the top of the hill under a large tree. He put his arm around my shoulders. We watched the pink balloon move out over the river and disappear.

In the weeks and months after that meditation, this image stayed strong in my mind. I had released Grant. Some of my pain went away. But it took three years for me to experience a final release.

When Dan called us back to the room and our chairs, I could hear people sobbing all over the room. A woman came, sat down beside me, and put her arms around me. She held me for awhile as I cried. It was a time of intense grief. If Grant had been dead and this was his funeral, I don't believe my grief would have been any deeper.

After the class ended, Dan told us good-bye and thanked us for allowing him to do what he loved best.

I decided to ask Tom privately if he would lead a meditation for the group. Dan had said that if we ever had a chance to be in a meditation with Tom, do so, because powerful things happened with him. I wrote Tom a note:

> Dear Tom,
>
> I want to ask if there's any possibility of your having a meditation with some of us. I would so appreciate such an opportunity. I came to this conference for two specific reasons, (1) to receive physical healing and (2) to release a beloved husband who has chosen to live with someone else. This morning in Dan's workshop we had a meditation on release. I feel so privileged to be able to be in your presence and listen to you talk.
>
> Sidney Farr

I'd made an appointment for a healing that afternoon, but decided it would be more beneficial to go listen to Tom. When I went to the healing center to cancel, a woman named Helen King was standing there. I heard her tell the woman at the desk that she was available if anyone needed a healing. I asked if she could work with me right then. She said yes. We went to her healing room. She used the laying on of hands and psychic powers. I felt powerful currents surging through my body. Afterward she looked directly into my eyes and said, "You have passed the test. You chose a very hard life this time around, but you have done well in meeting every phase of this life. You are now coming into your most specific and valuable work. Your power is in your hands." She blessed me and let me go. I thought she meant I would be using my hands to heal people; only later did I realize I was to use my hands in writing.

When I got to Hopwood, Tom was sitting in his usual seat. He had put my note in his bag. I began to feel that whether he mediated with us or not, his love and compassion were already working on my behalf. I listened to him until 5:00, at which time a woman interrupted and reminded him she'd promised to see that he had time for a shower before dinner and the evening lecture. The others left, and he gathered up his things.

Some of us walked to the dorm with him. He showed us pictures of his truck, the spot where the truck fell on him, his wife, his sons, and other photos.

A butterfly suddenly flew in front of us. I was delighted, because I've always loved butterflies.

"Did I tell you what happened at the airport?" Tom said. "I came outside with the young man who met me and suddenly a cloud of butterflies flew all around us and settled on me—even on my duffel bag." He laughed and said how surprised the young man had been.

After the evening service, Phyllis and I went to a meeting of all the ordained priests. Dan talked with us about our ordination and what we could expect to have happen to us in the following weeks, now that we were newly ordained members of the Order of Melchizedek.

When we got back to the registration area, someone said, "Tom's there around the corner." It was now past midnight. Tom was leaning against the wall by the elevator, holding a yellow rose in his hand. He looked straight at me. "The answer is yes!"

I was confused because I didn't understand. (Several years later Tom told me what he meant. Months before the conference, God had told him he would be meeting a woman who would write his book. Tom said that when I walked down the hall, he knew I was the one.)

Then he smiled and held out the rose to me. He said someone had just given it to him. "Can you imagine me with a rose?" he smiled. "A few years ago, if someone had offered me a rose, I'd've hit him."

Tom talked to our little group for a while, answering questions. He told of being at Virginia Beach and that, while he was swimming, dolphins surrounded him. He said he communicated with them.

Finally Tom said he was going to turn in. He was going to lead a meditation early in the morning, he told us, and he needed to see Dan. I offered to take him to Dan's room upstairs. The group left, and Tom and I walked up one flight of stairs and down the hall. I told him Dan had ordained me earlier in the week. His face lit up. He put his arm around my waist. "Already I can feel so much change within," I said, and he smiled.

Dan was not in his room, so I walked with Tom to his room. I offered to take a note to Dan if Tom wanted to write him about needing to do an early meditation. Tom laughed, "You worry about details too much. It will be all right." He hugged me. I said, "See you in the morning," and he said, "Yes, and if not here, then in the other place."

I woke up early the next morning. Phyllis and I went into the chapel to listen to Laraaji, a musician who was playing at the conference. At the end, Tom walked to the front of the chapel, spoke quietly to Laraaji, and then turned to us. "When I was lying on my couch those three days after my accident, I discovered I liked all kinds of music on the radio. As soon as I was able to go, my wife took me to a concert. I loved it. Then a New Age school invited me to speak at one of their sessions. A young man played wonderful, strange music beforehand, and that man was Laraaji."

Then Tom directed us to go outside and form a circle in front of the chapel. We did so, and I noticed that Laraaji positioned himself directly across from Tom in the circle. Two large men were beside Tom, one on either side. Dan had said Tom seldom permitted himself to be in a circle of any kind. I felt privileged to be in the circle.

Tom had us close our eyes, and he prayed. Then he asked us to send love to the person on our right. After a few seconds he said send it on to the next person on our right, and so on around the circle. Before my thoughts of love got past three people, I began to receive what was coming to me from my left. I've never felt such power. It felt like a strong, thick rope around us at waist level. At that instant the sun came out.

I began to "see" things, strange city skyscrapers, sunsets, a city where everything was some shade of red. I saw Tom walking beside me up the steps into a building. We entered a large room filled with books. Tom led me to a particular shelf and motioned for me to look at the books. A shelf or two contained books that all had my name on them as author. Somehow I knew this was to be in my future. Tom talked to the people in the circle lovingly, and then blessed us.

As our circle broke up, I noticed that a young mother with a child, perhaps a year old, who had been standing about three removed on Tom's right (my left), was lying flat on her back, unconscious. The child was lying face down on her chest. Tom quickly approached the pair and touched the child first, then started working with the mother. Her young husband kneeled beside them.

Tom told me later what had happened during that morning meditation. The two men on each side of Tom in the circle were testing Tom, determined to prove he was a fake. Tom had asked Laraaji to stand opposite him in the circle as a balance in the "struggle." The young woman near Tom felt the crosscurrent of power and passed out. Neither she nor the baby was hurt. The two men did not succeed in their plans to discredit Tom and quietly left the circle.

After breakfast that day, I walked over to Hopwood alone. People were standing outside, bewildered to hear that Tom had already done the meditation. They thought it was going to be done there, outside Hopwood, at 9:15. I felt sorry for all those people who'd missed his meditation. Then I realized that exactly the people who were meant to meditate with Tom had done so. There are no accidents, Phyllis likes to say.

A young musician at the conference played her harp in the auditorium and sang a couple of songs at the last meeting of the conference, then announced that her last number was going to be "Amazing Grace" and that she wanted to dedicate it to Tom Sawyer and for all he stood for. Then she started crying. We cried with her a moment or two. Finally she gained control and did a beautiful rendition of that old hymn. Afterward, hugging, tears, and laughter filled that room and all along our path back to the dining room for lunch, as people said their good-byes.

Phyllis and I loaded the car and headed toward Winston-Salem. We got there about 6:00 that evening. I spent the night at Phyllis's, visiting with her and later, in my room, thinking over all that had happened during the week.

The next day I boarded a plane for home. The ride to Atlanta was smooth and quiet. From Atlanta to Lexington, my seatmate, an engineer at the space center in Florida, helped pass the time by talking about his world travels. He was from Ireland, and his extended family still lived there.

Near Lexington we ran into a thunderstorm. As the plane detoured and circled to find another approach to the landing field, I looked out my window and gloried in the storm. It was impressive to fly through the dark clouds, and I felt like I was up with the gods. At one point we flew through some serious turbulence, and I said over and over, "Holy, Holy, Lord God Almighty, who was, and is, and ever shall be. Amen." It felt good to say that up there in the clouds.

Grant called me on Wednesday of that week. He asked on the phone if it would be all right for Caleb to come with him to the airport to pick me up. They wanted to take me to dinner. I had looked forward to having that time alone with Grant, to share parts of my week with him, to talk about the future, to talk about whatever. After my experience of releasing Grant on Friday morning, though, it was all right for Caleb to come with him.

They were waiting at the airport when I arrived. Grant gave me a chaste little kiss on the cheek and half hugged me. I knew he didn't want to do more than that in front of Caleb. I understood. I turned to Caleb and held out my arms. He gave me a big hug. We got in the car and headed for Berea, having dinner on the way.

Being there with Grant and Caleb, I was surprised to find that I did not feel the kind of the pain I'd felt before when I saw them together. There had been times since Grant moved in with Caleb that I felt my heart had broken and was lying in shards like splintered glass somewhere in my chest cavity. But now it felt okay to see them together. Thank God for showing me the way to release the hurt and pain.

I will carry only good memories of all Grant and I shared together for fifteen years. We raised a son; we got college degrees; we shared the deaths of his father and mother and my mother; we shared in learning about spiritual things through reading, talking, listening, and meditating. We also experienced tremendous growth periods together, giving each other encouragement and patience, and working through our frustrations. No one can take those years away.

I am grateful to Grant for many things. He taught me how to feel young again; he shared his gift of laughter with me, especially in the early years. And threading through all that, like a gold thread in a rich tapestry, were his piano music and songs—"Help Me Make It Through the Night," "The First Time Ever I Saw Your Face," Floyd Cramer arrangements, spiritual and gospel songs, and other kinds of music. It became so much a part of my daily life at home that I took it for granted, like one takes running water or electricity for granted. I missed Grant's songs and music.

In August, I decided to write to Tom. I asked if there was any possibility that he could come to Berea to speak on campus. A little over a year later, in October 1988, Tom did come to Berea. This was the first of what became many trips after I began working on a book about him. The accounts of some of those visits are in the two books on which we collaborated (*What Tom Sawyer Learned from Dying*, 1993; and *Tom Sawyer and the Spiritual Whirlwind*, 2000).

SEPTEMBER IS A SAD TIME OF YEAR for me because my grandson, Richard Lawson, was killed in an automobile accident on September 21, 1990. He had lived with me for four years, so I got to watch him grow into a teenager before his death at fifteen. He had just started his sophomore year at Berea Community High School.

Richard's family life was a troubled one. His parents were divorced, and Richard desperately wanted to keep his family together. His father, Wayne, remarried. Richard's mother, who lived in Indianapolis, decided to move to Berea so Richard could live with her. She rented an apartment, found a job, and things seemed to be going well. Then suddenly she took off back to Indianapolis, leaving Richard with me. Richard would tell me how sad he felt that his mother had not stayed. He said he was just beginning to feel at home with her again.

Richard was in a car with friends when the accident happened. None of the other teenagers was hurt, but Richard was killed.

After Richard's death I was astounded to hear from people all over Berea, expressing their grief and telling me stories of how Richard had helped them, how he had made their days more cheerful. Over five hundred people came to his funeral at Union Church.

The following school year one of his teachers sent me an essay that a boy in Richard's class had written and turned in as a class assignment. The boy told how Richard had befriended him, a newcomer, to the school that year. He expressed regret that he did not have a longer time to be with Richard. I treasure that essay, and all the other stories about Richard I've been told by people who had grown to know and love him.

Richard never had the family security and the love he ardently craved, so the people of Berea became his new family. Richard was one of those rare individuals with spiritual charisma, and this drew people to him. His light stopped shining in 1990, but the afterglow lingers in our hearts and minds.

I was grateful that Tom Sawyer had been in my home and got to know Richard before he was killed. In fact, Richard helped me transcribe some tapes about Tom for our first book. He knew of Tom's near-death experience and asked a lot of questions about it.

Tom was a comfort to both my son Bruce and me as we grieved for Richard. Tom told us he knew that Richard went straight to God, and that his existence is glorious.

Tom's greatest gift is his teaching that God is love and that He loves us unconditionally. We can overcome. Tom teaches that our fear that death is the end of all life is false, that life in the next world is paradise, and the light in paradise is God.

Tom Sawyer has changed my life. I am not the same person I was before I met him in 1987. I am more confident.

Tom began that change by telling me I was a worthy person. "God don't make garbage," he said. Bless his heart, he didn't give up on me. "If you only knew who you are," he often said. When I told him about the loving response I received from the women in Ginny Carney's class in Alaska, he said, "Of course they loved you because they sensed who you are." I drank in Tom's teaching about God's love and other things of the spirit, and the hole in my psyche is now filled.

Tom set out to prove to me that I was worth something, that I mattered. It took many years, but I now believe that I am worthy, that I do have talent, that people do like to read the stories and poems I write. Tom has helped me accept the fact of God's love for each one of us. Because of what he's taught me about God and myself, I am contented and whole.

23
The Art of Writing

As a child I craved to put words together in fresh
and enlightening ways. I wrote poems that were
like square soldiers on a page. Then I wrote verses
like high clouds before it begins to rain . . .

While still married to Leon and living at Stoney Fork, I received a scholarship to attend a Bob Laubach "Each One Teach One" Writing Workshop. At that time different groups of people were teaching illiterate adults how to read. Soon there was a demand for books and other literature to be written at about the fourth-grade level for these newly literate adults. The purpose of the "Each One Teach One" writing workshops was to have the participants rewrite such things as government pamphlets, drivers' manuals, and the like so that a person who had very little education could read and understand the material. Each workshop participant chose what he or she would write as the class project. I chose to rewrite Kentucky's Home Demonstration Manual on how to prepare fruits and vegetables for the freezer.

Several people from different parts of the country were lecturers and teachers for the workshop I attended. After a week of rewriting material and hearing lectures on how other classes did it, I was bored. That weekend I wrote my first short story. I shared it with our minister's wife, who was also in the workshop. She asked permission to show it to some of the instructors.

On that Monday, in the afternoon session, one of the instructors discussed a manuscript submitted by a workshop participant that was intended to retell the Book of Ruth in the Bible. The instructor pointed out how miserably the author of this piece had failed and why. He said that she didn't understand what the story was about, that she did not have the soul to attempt that kind of rewrite. Then he said, "At noon today, a short story was passed around, and I read it. I don't know who the author is, but I can tell you she is a good writer. She has the soul to rewrite the Book of Ruth." I sat there stunned, thinking, "He said I am a good writer." I felt as though I had just been born again. His statement authenticated me as a writer.

One of the instructors, Robert Connor, was editor of *Mountain Life & Work,* a publication of the Council of the Southern Mountains (CSM) in Berea. He invited me to submit some of my work to be considered for publication in *Mountain Life & Work.*

I sent Bob a story that fall entitled "The Worry Mouse." He published it, and the story, retitled "Hill Country Christmas," was later reprinted in *Teen* magazine. For the reprint I was paid $75. This was the first time I was paid for my writing. That same year a publication called *Cycloflame,* in Texas, bought one of my poems. They sent me a check for $2.

I corresponded with Bob Connor and his wife, Phyllis, for a couple of years after the workshop. Bob published another short story of mine after Leon and I moved to Indianapolis in 1960. After living there for two years, we moved to Berea in 1962. My son Bruce was born in October of that year.

A year later, around the time I was looking to return to work, I heard that the Council of the Southern Mountains needed a person for the staff of *Mountain Life & Work.* The CSM was founded in 1913 as a meeting place/clearinghouse for missionaries, teachers, and health-care workers in Appalachia. In 1925 the Council began publishing a quarterly journal that became *Mountain Life & Work.*

In the early 1960s President Johnson's War on Poverty was going strong. The Council was invited to join in the effort and provide training for workers who would be coming into the area. The first group to be organized was the Appalachian Volunteers. Ann Pollard, associate editor of *Mountain Life & Work,* joined that group.

I applied and was hired as associate editor of *Mountain Life & Work,* replacing Ann. Thus began a new phase of my life. During my first year of work, I met writers James Still, Jesse Stuart, Harriet Arnow, and Wilma

Dykeman. Later I encouraged Gurney Norman, a fairly new writer, to submit fiction to the magazine. Gurney credits me for having his first short stories published.

Before I was a college student, I had already been published several times. I entered the *Writer's Digest* contest for short fiction one year, and placed thirty-seventh among 10,000 entries. I was awarded a deed to one square foot of Gettysburg Battlefield. Over a number of years I attended writers' workshops at Hindman Settlement School in Knott County, Kentucky, and other places, hoping to learn how to write in a way that would please the outside world. The workshops instead gave me the courage to write about what I already knew—people, places, social events, and nature.

When I enrolled in Berea College in 1972, a woman named June and I were the oldest students in the college classes. The freshmen were young enough to be our children. I was amazed at how well they accepted us. While our classmates knew about things through reading, June and I had lived them. They asked us questions and told us about themselves.

After I graduated from college, I continued working as an assistant in the Archives and Special Collections Department of the Berea College Library. When the decision was made to move *Appalachian Heritage* from the Hindman Settlement School to Berea College in 1985, John Stephenson, the college president, appointed me as that publication's editor. Thus another new phase opened in my life.

I would not have missed being the editor of *Appalachian Heritage* for anything. It was a tough job because I could only work half-time on the magazine while continuing my duties to the department. But I met writers from all over the region in person, by telephone, through correspondence, and through their submissions. I also kept up on what was happening in Appalachia by reading seven or eight daily newspapers from different Appalachian states. I marked articles, features, comments, and scholarly works that were in the papers. Students clipped the articles I'd marked, which were then categorized and put into the large collection of books and files on Appalachia. The Berea College Library made this resource available to scholars, authors, and students researching the region.

My greatest pleasure during my years as editor was to introduce new writers to the reading public. Having their pieces in *Appalachian Heritage* was the first time many of them had been published. Among that number, Silas House, Anne Shelby, Mary Hodges, Carolyn Bertram, and many others went on to gain greater recognition and win awards for their writing.

When I retired from the library in 1999, I looked forward to having more time for my own writing. But after a year I realized that something was lacking. I missed meeting and working with fellow writers. I needed the fulfillment of contributing to the world of writing, not just creating my own.

I decided that teaching writing in my home might help fill the void. I sent out a word-of-mouth announcement, and six women joined my class. Instead of giving lectures, I simply allowed the students to pick my brain for what I know about writing. I taught them how to edit both their own and their colleagues' work. I asked each new student to select a subject she wanted to work on—essays, poems, a memoir, a play, or a novel. I promised to help them reach the place where we considered the work ready to be sent out.

I have known the joy of seeing my students become better writers, some getting their work published. In the years when I worked as associate editor of *Mountain Life & Work* and, especially, as editor of *Appalachian Heritage,* what I most enjoyed was getting acquainted with new writers and helping them to get published.

It is gratifying to attend conferences and workshops and have people seek me out and thank me for their first publications. Some of them have gone on to become well-known writers. Several have won prizes for their work. In return, over the years I have gleaned words of wisdom and advice from good writers that have become my own guidelines.

To prepare for my first at-home class, I brought together materials about writing. I told my new students that there are three key activities to remember when writing:

Feel—Clarity, sentence flow, pace, rhythm, movement.
Tighten—Less is best.
Polish—Reword, rephrase, and repicture.

I also advise students to avoid using more than fifteen words in any sentence—unless it really "swings" with more! To help them craft their sentences, I tell them the following:

- Do not use the same word twice in a sentence, or even a paragraph, unless you do so deliberately for emphasis.
- Avoid using the word "that" more than once in a sentence.
- Never use more than one adjective at a time. If you use two or more you have not found the right one.

I tell students to work with the *sound* of words (rolling thunder, soothing rain, sharp winds, silence of the snow, the crack of ice, crystal clarity, snap, crackle, pop), and the *color* of words (silver on the poplar leaf, gold on the willow stem, morning-glory blue, black night, gray fog, dusky dark). I also tell them to pay attention to the *portent* of words, both their meaning and their connotation.

I try to write the way little children talk. Children express themselves with absolute clarity before adults make them lose self-confidence and cause them to become afraid of expressing themselves simply and directly. There is no artifice in children. They are honest and bold when they express their true feelings.

Given my love of words and the joy that I feel when I write, it was inevitable that I would write a poem about words.

The Living Word
 Is sought by poets and writers.
 It often comes at just the right time
 To turn a phrase, make a perfect rhyme.
 Then come the ecstasy and the pain
 As hard and gentle as falling rain
 On April fields plowed for planting.
The Living Word
 Comes in unexpected places:
 An autumn leaf floating to the ground,
 A winter bell calling, the sound

Ringing clear across the miles. The pain
Of a good-bye in summer. Thunder followed by rain
Falling on the sleeping fields.
The Living Word
Comes in various shapes and sizes:
Icicles hanging from the eaves,
Wind blowing among ice-laden trees,
And all white flowers in May. A silver brook,
A loaf of bread, a well-read book,
June roses for a bridal bouquet.
The Living Word
Is found in many places:
In a red apple on a backyard tree,
In a blueberry pie baked for me
By Granny Reed. In red clover
And sunset when the day turns over
To sink and rest in the cool black night.
The Living Word
Will come to poets and writers
Who eat and drink living words.

I used to think of poetry as water, and not just because water is essential to life. When it rained long enough for little springs to gush out from the hillsides, out of crawdad holes, out from underneath rocks, and run down little gullies, I spent some of my happiest hours outside. I played in the tiny streams, channeling one into another until I had larger ones running together until they reached level ground. Playing in water and looking for new streams became symbolic of poetry to me.

My great-grandmother, Granny Brock, and other mountain women worked hard, cooking, cleaning, spinning, and caring for home and family from daylight to dark. They made all of their family's clothes and warm quilts for their beds. They found creative satisfaction in their quilts and embroidered pieces.

Today there is not so much need for quilts and warm clothing. Mountain women no longer have the opportunity to satisfy their creative talent as they work. Instead, they write stories and poems, weave tapestries, and paint pictures to satisfy their creative urge. I needed an outlet for my creative urge, and I found it especially satisfying to write poetry.

Over the years people have tried to define poetry. Some say it is like trying to paint the wind. Others call it "the language of amazement." It has been said that "science is for people who learn; poetry is for people who know." John Donne says poetry is counterfeit creation. Robert Frost says that poetry is a way of taking life by the throat. Samuel Taylor Coleridge says that if prose is the right word in the right order, poetry must be the best word in the best order.

I took a poetry class one semester while I was a student at Berea College. One Friday assignment was to write ten haiku and bring them to class on the following Monday.

Up to that time I had never read a haiku, let alone knew what kind of poem it was. The professor explained the form and suggested we read a collection or two before we began our assignment. I doubted I would be able to write even one decent haiku, let alone ten of them.

That weekend I began both reading and trying to write that form of poetry. Here are the ten I turned in the following Monday:

Death
Facing east he lies.
Morning sun touches his grave
My heart is still dark.

Fear
Verbena blossoms,
Darkness gallops up the hill,
Quick! Hide your children.

Reality
Battered old woman
Selling flowers in the street.
Ah, look, my mother!

Blackbirds
Thirty-three blackbirds
Stripping the tender green corn.
Scarecrow meditates.

Faith
Homemade grave basket
Adorning our piano.
Music does not die!

Revelation
Raindrops falling, break
And wet the silver lichen
Look! A burning bush.

Lost Love
Ah, shattered dewdrops—
Crystal pieces of a broken dream.
It ended today.

Curiosity
A snowball bloomed out
In July instead of May
Wonder what it means?

Grace
Angry waves dash high
Noise is wasted energy
Manna falls at dawn.

Experience
Sad with her knowing
Earth sighs and covers her face
With old and tender leaves.

Dr. Sears, the teacher of that course, gave us many assignments throughout the semester, but none was more challenging than writing haiku.

I fell in love with the discipline required for this form. Most of my poems in my first book of poetry, *Headwaters,* are in free verse, but a few are written to form. I like to think of poetry as freedom within discipline. First you learn the techniques and forms, and only after learning those do you take wing and fly.

MY FIRST BOOK, *Appalachian Women: An Annotated Bibliography,* was published in 1981. It grew out of the first independent study I did at Berea. Loyal Jones, one of my sponsors, suggested that I see if the University Press of Kentucky might like to publish it. An editor came to Berea each spring to talk with prospective authors on campus. Berea College was part of a consortium with the state university system. This meant that a committee on campus first had to agree the manuscript was worth publishing. If the committee agreed to publish, Berea College would pay 50 percent of the publication costs. Revenue from sales of the book would then go to Berea College until the college was reimbursed.

Putting all the annotations into manuscript form was a big job for me. At the end I had 1,800 index cards. A very good friend of the College Library, Alfred Perrin, offered to pay a typist to get it ready to show a publisher. The University Press of Kentucky accepted it for publication, and the book came out in the spring of 1981. It garnered good reviews in both print and on radio broadcasts and was used by students, classes, authors, researchers, and others.

My next book also began as an independent study, after a suggestion made by James Still. I first met this well-known Appalachian writer when I was associate editor of *Mountain Life & Work,* and he became my mentor and my friend for more than thirty years. One day, on a visit to Berea, he invited me to lunch. In the restaurant he talked about mountain food and how it was cooked before the advent of electricity and microwave cooking. "You know, the old ways are fading out," he said. "Someone should write a book about mountain food. I can't do a book like that, but you can." I was amazed when he offered to tell his agent about it.

Thus inspired to collect recipes of Appalachian cooks, I found a sponsor for the project in Berea's Home Economics Department. On the advice of my sponsors and friends, I submitted the manuscript to the University of Pittsburgh Press, which at that time was interested in publishing regional works. After some rewriting and editing, the manuscript was accepted. *More than Moonshine: Appalachian Recipes and Recollections* was published in 1983. It was widely reviewed in this country and in England. Reprinted six times, it has earned more royalties than all my other books combined.

My next book was another cookbook. *Table Talk* came out in 1995. For it, I received a grant to help with expenses as I traveled to different states, interviewing a variety of Appalachian residents about their history with food. I started each chapter with a brief introduction, then deleted my questions from the interviews so as to allow the rest of each chapter to be in the interviewees' own voices, with their favorite recipes printed at the end of each chapter. I am proud that my two cookbooks, *More than Moonshine* and *Table Talk,* have preserved the history of mountain people and mountain cooks.

My first book about Tom Sawyer, *What Tom Sawyer Learned from Dying,* was published in 1993. It described Tom's early years, his near-death experience at the age of thirty-three, and how that experience changed his life.

When friends and coworkers heard about my plans to write a book about Tom, several implored me not to do it. In essence, they said I had established a good reputation for myself as an Appalachian writer. To do a book that was so different—so "New Age"—would hurt that reputation. When people told me this, I felt some of the same feelings I'd had when Dad came to my house and cried because I wouldn't agree to join the Holiness Church. Was I right in believing God had chosen me to write Tom's story? Intuitively I felt I must do the book. The idea haunted me—it would not go away.

Tom Sawyer and the Spiritual Whirlwind, published in 2000, was about Tom's trips to Tibet and his meeting and assisting the Dalai Lama in Canada. The book includes a chapter about a tornado in Berea in 1996, when Tom was at my home.

Getting to know Tom, witness his work, and hear his teachings has answered many of my questions about God and church. The two books I have published about Tom Sawyer and his near-death experience have sold widely. I have received many letters and telephone calls from appreciative readers.

Headwaters, my first book of poetry, was nominated for the Pulitzer Prize in 1995. This book is a collection of poems written from my early years until when I met Tom Sawyer. I am so grateful that Mary Holliman at Virginia Technical College in Blacksburg, Virginia, who owned Pocahontas Press, took a chance on publishing my first poetry book. I am currently working on a second collection.

The Spoonbread Cookbook I published myself in 1996. It was compiled at the request of the Berea Chamber of Commerce when they were planning the first Spoonbread Festival in Berea. It has sold well.

Like many writers, I have had my share of rejection letters. I know all too well what getting such a letter feels like. While I was editor of *Appalachian Heritage,* the hardest task I had was rejecting submissions. If I could not use a writer's work, I wrote a personal letter explaining why. Sometimes I gave advice about how I thought the piece could be improved.

I always love to attend the writers' workshops at Hindman, Kentucky. In August, participants come from North and South Carolina, Tennessee, Virginia, West Virginia, Ohio, New Jersey, New York, and a number of other states across the country to the lovely settlement town of Hindman, which sits in a small valley completely surrounded by hills. At the time of the writers' workshops, everything is lush and green from spring rains, and flowers are blooming everywhere you look. In this neat, well-groomed pocket of civilization, you can sit in a rocking chair on the porch and look into the spaces between trees in the uncut forest, which come down the hill just a few yards from the porch. No matter how hot it gets during the day, at night it cools off, and the next morning dawns cool and damp from heavy dew. Many of the workshop participants, including me, rise early. After getting a cup of coffee in the dining room, we sit in the rocking chairs on the porch and read, meditate, write, or chat with others while waiting for the bell to ring for breakfast.

The workshops feature classes on the writing of novels, poetry, children's books, and nonfiction. A number of participants find success with regional and national publishers. Some return to teach classes at the workshop.

In July 2004, the Appalachian Writers Association named me the Appalachian writer who contributed most to the region and its people.

And in December 2005 I was named Writing Sister of the Year by the New Opportunity School for Women Writers. I was given a scrapbook containing letters of appreciation for my books, my teaching, and my mentoring. The letter from Linda Caldwell, an internationally published writer, sums up what most of the letters and comments say.

> Sidney,
>
> You have been a mentor to Appalachian writers and especially to Appalachian women writers. For this we admire you.
>
> You have been a rock for the NOSW Writers over these past five years. You have gently encouraged writing, revising, and submitting. You have been a quiet cheerleader and wise woman. For this we love you.
>
> Your excellent example in writing and life has given a pattern to follow. For this we admire you.
>
> You are a model woman that all would like to be. You "walk in beauty."
>
> I am ever so privileged to know you.
>
> With love and respect,
> Linda Caldwell

Writing has been an essential part of my life for as long as I can remember. It has brought me recognition, some money, and a sense of fulfillment that nothing else brings. My books go out into the world and make new friends for me. They serve as teaching tools for those I cannot reach.

I am glad I am a writer. I am privileged to have worked with well-established authors, and especially with brand-new ones, sharing their elation in being published for the first time.

24

As the Sun Goes Down

*The last lingering rays of sun paint the Pilot
Knob hills in pale gold, and highlight a distant
tree. Smudges of charcoal-colored clouds drift in
the pale pink sky that the sunset left behind. It is
time to go inside to the big warm kitchen for the
evening meal.*

Berea, Kentucky, is situated directly on the old Wilderness Road,
which brought the first settlers into Kentucky. Daniel Boone came
through Cumberland Gap for the first time on a hunting trip, and later
a band of thirty men with axes cut the Wilderness Road into Kentucky.
This opened the great west for one of the mightiest migrations in human
history. From 1775 to 1796, more than 200,000 men, women, and children traveled over the Wilderness Road on horseback and on foot, seeking
homes in mid-America and the northwest.

The town of Berea grew up around Berea College, which was founded
in 1855. The college was founded to promote the ideal of Christian brotherhood and equality on a nonsectarian and interracial basis. Berea College
experienced some turbulent days and nights both before and after the
Civil War.

Berea is an area as varied as Kentucky itself; and it has been my home
since 1962.

AT FIRST I FOUND LIVING IN BEREA so different than where I'd grown
up. I missed the presence of tall mountains. I liked the convenience of city
life, but I longed to wade in creeks again, to hear whippoorwills calling

in the evenings, to hear cowbells ringing as cows were driven home for milking.

My older son, Dennis Wayne, was eleven years old when we moved to Berea from Indianapolis; my son Bruce Alan was born in Berea. I feel that in a way I grew up in Berea along with my boys.

Being on the *Mountain Life & Work* staff in the mid-1960s, I was privileged to meet some of the workers engaged in the War on Poverty. I met both established and emerging writers. I learned more about Appalachia and my people by viewing them through the eyes of newcomers.

In 1984, before Dr. John Stephenson was inaugurated president of Berea College, I was initiated into the honor society of Phi Kappa Phi and was named by the national office to represent Phi Kappa Phi at the inauguration. This was astounding to me—that I, from the hills of southeastern Kentucky, a new college graduate, would be able to don a cap and gown and participate in the activities.

Grant and I invited the Stephensons to our house for dinner in November 1984. At the table, John told us that *Appalachian Heritage* was being moved from Alice Lloyd College to Berea, sponsored under the college umbrella. He said he was looking for just the right person to be the editor.

My heart jumped into my throat and I could hardly get out the words: "I'd give my eyeteeth to have that job."

"You're the perfect person!" John exclaimed. "I've read your books. You know Appalachia better than most people I could think of for the job."

Just like that the decision was made (and it gave me something to live for after Grant left for Oregon).

I MET TOM SAWYER IN THE SUMMER OF 1987. That meeting, and my working with him on two books, changed my life for the better. Moving to Berea was also a positive development in my life and the lives of my sons. My son Bruce was born in the Berea College Hospital. I got a job with the Council of the Southern Mountains as associate editor of *Mountain Life & Work*. I was accepted as a degree candidate at Berea College. On my first visit to the college library, I was too scared even to think about checking out a book; later, I was employed as a full-time staff member at that same library and worked in the Special Collections and Archives Department for twenty-four years. My first book, *Appalachian Women,* was published as a result of my work at Berea. I successfully bridged the psychological gap between the mountain community of Stoney Fork and the academic town of Berea.

As I end this memoir, it is with good feelings about ongoing projects. I continue with the writing class in my home. A book study group also meets at my house each Tuesday evening. The New Opportunity School for Women has a writers' group that meets monthly. I have served as mentor to the group and have witnessed exciting growth and opportunities for those women.

Looking back on my life has shined a spotlight on my naïveté, hidden motives, deep anger, remorse, repentance, and revelation. Telling my story has brought me pain, tears, dreams, and remembered grief. It has also enhanced the gratitude I feel for my heritage. I believe that my life has been unique, and that I have had rare opportunities and gifts.

There are many good books still to be read, and more for me to write.